JULIA RILEY

LIVING *The* POSSIBLE DREAM

THE SINGLE PARENT'S

★ G ★ U ★ I ★ D ★ E ★

TO COLLEGE SUCCESS

Johnson Books: Boulder

This book is dedicated to the late Professor Kenneth E. Eble (1923–1988), Department of English, University of Utah—the most extraordinary and humane teacher I've ever known.

ISBN 1-55566-086-X
LCCCN 91-75687

Printed in the United States of America by
Johnson Printing
A Division of Johnson Publishing Company
1880 South 57th Court
Boulder, Colorado 80301

CONTENTS

INTRODUCTION

If you are a single parent who wants to embark on the challenging but infinitely worthwhile journey of attending a college or university and earning a certificate or degree, but you're not sure just how to get started, you're wondering if you could make it, or you're afraid to try, this guidebook is for you. If you're already on your way in school but need some good ideas to help you along, *Living the Possible Dream* will assist you, too.

You'll learn how to keep your family, health, and sanity intact during your trek through school. You'll find practical suggestions, concrete advice, and tips for solving and preventing all kinds of problems you will face while you're raising your children alone and traveling toward graduation. This guidebook will point you in useful directions, answer many questions, teach you how to overcome obstacles, and refer you to people, organizations, and books for further help.

Throughout the chapters you'll find comments from single parent students in colleges and universities all over the United States and Canada. They talk about their lives as students, problems they've encountered and solved, and offer you some advice. Not all the comments are cheerful or uplifting, and you or I may not even agree with all of them — but they are all certainly *real.*

Special features such as "Spotlights on Success" and "Spotlights on College Programs" will give you even more inspiration and encouragement.

Be sure to see Appendix A for specific information that comes straight from state social services administration departments. Here you'll discover what types and amounts of social services aid are (or are not) available to single parents in college in your state. Appendix B contains information about child care resource and referral agencies. Be sure to consult the Bibliography to find other sources of great information and encouragement. Find some of the more interesting titles in your library to help you to plan and carry out a successful journey through college.

ACKNOWLEDGMENTS

First of all, I owe my parents, Philip and Belle Marie, a debt I can't possibly repay for teaching me that education is *the* answer, and for their unwavering support, encouragement, guidance, and love, particularly during my time in college as a single parent. And thank you to my children, Bryan, Maria, and Jenny, for being such good troopers and just plain wonderful kids. Last, but not least, a special thank you to my husband, Eric, for his courage in taking on an instant family and for his look-at-the-world-upside-down sense of humor, for helping pay my bills while I wrote this book, and for being the best partner and friend I could imagine.

Next, a heartfelt thank you to all the single parent students who answered my questionnaire, talked with me, and let me have a glimpse of their lives and dreams. Special thanks to Joan Otting and Elaine Viens.

I sincerely appreciate all the folks at Johnson Books, for believing this book should be published, and for doing such a good job.

I would also like to sincerely thank Inez Peterson, former director of the Early Childhood Education Center at the University of Utah. She and her staff provided an excellent child care setting for my children while I was a student, and worked so hard to try to create additional child care services at the University. Thanks to Beverly Purrington, formerly of the Women's Resource Center at the University, for her interest in and support of single parent students. And unending thanks to Irene Fisher, former director of *Utah Issues*, and the whole *Utah Issues* staff who stood up for us and battled our state legislature time and time again for enough child care and other funding so we could make it through school. Thanks to the Utah Department of Social Services, and especially the Office of Recovery Services, for going after the child support due my family, and for providing social services support through four-year college programs here in Utah. Thanks also to the Wasatch Chapter of the American Business Women's Association, and the Psychology Department at the University, for their vote of confidence and support in the form of tuition scholarships.

A special thanks to Bruce Spector and Doug North, for their help and encouragement, and their hard work in getting the Consortium for Single Parent Scholarship going.

Thanks to Steve Szykula, Ph.D., psychologist, who was my employer and colleague for several years. Much of the parenting advice in this guidebook comes from what I learned while working with him.

Thank you to all the professors, graduate instructors, and staff at the University of Utah who were flexible, supportive, and caring — and hats off to the folks in the Financial Aid Office for creating reasonable financial aid packages for us single parent students, and for going the extra mile to assist us.

Thanks to all my single parent student friends that I traded child care with, traded shoulders to cry on, and who were just good companions through my journey. I hope that you and your kids are all doing great!

Finally, I owe sincere thanks to many individuals and organizations for providing generous assistance, advice, and information during the preparation of this guidebook. If I've forgotten about anybody or misplaced anyone's name in my files, I hope you'll holler at me and demand to be added to the next edition! They are, in alphabetical order:

Ruth Lugo-Alvarez, Dean of Student Affairs, Lehman College, the City University of New York; Orlo Austin, Financial Aid Director, University of Illinois at Urbana-Champaign; C. Patrick Babcock, Director, Michigan Department of Social Services; Marilyn Ballance, Director of Financial Aid, University of California Riverside; G. Barnes, Utah Arts Council; Brenda Bartellotti, Carleton Association of Mature and Part-Time Students; Polly Basore, Editor, *The Daily O'Collegian*, Oklahoma State University; Linda Beauvais, Director, Planning and Policy Formulation, Louisiana Dept. of Social Services; Judy Kasten Bell, *Utah Issues*; Gina Bertolini, University of Wisconsin; Oscar R. Best, Jr., Director, Bureau of Employment Programs, New York State Dept. of Social Services; Ray Boldreghini, Associate Director Financial Aid, University of Texas at Arlington; Nancy Boldt, Single Parents Program, Champlain College; Florence L. Borton, Manager, Financial Aid Services, Antioch University; F. Melia Bosworth, Student Parent Project Coordinator, University of California, Berkeley; Charles Boulton, Office Manager, National Coalition for Campus Child Care; Shirley Bradshaw, Ypsilanti Free Methodist Church, Ypsilanti, Michigan; Nancy Brandt, North Carolina State Division of Social Services; Dot Brauer, student intern, Single Parents Program, Champlain College; Michael Buckley, Manager, Income Maintenance Section, Oregon Dept. of Human Resources; Sabra Burdick, Director, Bureau of Income Maintenance, Maine Dept. of Human Services; Tom Burke, Chief, GAIN Program, California Dept. of Social Services; Marianna Bury, Executive Aide, Arkansas Dept. of

Human Services; James D. Butts, Administrator, Income Maintenance Administration, District of Columbia Department of Human Services; Linda L. Caballero, Administrator, Idaho Dept. of Health and Welfare; Joe Campbell, News and Publications Director, University of Saskatchewan, Canada; Reinaldo Cardona, Director, Bureau of Employment Programs, New York State Dept. of Social Services; Karen E. Carter, Director Career Planning, Ashland University; Steve Carter, Chief, Analysis Section, Pell Grant Branch, U. S. Dept. of Education; Veronica H. Celani, Commissioner, Vermont Department of Social Welfare; The Center for Law and Education, Cambridge, Massachusetts; (Mr.) Carol L. Chapman, Social Welfare Specialist, North Dakota Department of Human Services; Margaret Charles, Displaced Homemakers Network; Deanna Chitayat, Dean, University College for Continuing Education, Hofstra University; Katherine Coles, Utah Arts Council; Connie Cowley, Program Specialist, Utah Department of Social Services; JoAnn Cummings, Counselor and Coordinator, Counseling Program for Adults, The University of Northern Iowa; Daphne Dalley, Director Single Parents/Displaced Homemaker Program, Southern Utah State College; Dan Davenport, Director of Financial Aid, Gonzaga University; Lois Deily, Supervisor of Teacher Placement, University of Nebraska at Omaha; Delaware Health and Social Services; Sue DeMartini, Financial Aid Officer, Brigham Young University; Mary De Mouy, Program Associate, Project on the Status and Education of Women; Mary K. Deyampert, North Carolina Dept. of Human Resources, Division of Social Services; Lynda di Caro, Financial Aid Administrative Analyst, University of California Irvine; Maureen Duane, Child Care Resources, Arizona State University; William A. Dunbar, Acting Director, New Mexico Human Services Department; Dorothy H. Duncan, Financial Aid Office, Southern Arkansas University — Main Magnolia; Jerry Evans, Program Development and Support, Arkansas Dept. of Human Services; Mary V. Fallen, Acting Deputy Director for Income Maintenance, Missouri Dept. of Social Services; Jennie Farley, Associate Professor, Cornell University; Ronald Feinstein, Community College of Philadelphia, Pennsylvania; Financial Aid Director, Concordia University; Carol Fleck, Director of Student Awards, Ottawa, Ontario, Canada; John Fransway, Administrator, Employment Support Services, New Hampshire Dept. of Health and Human Services; Beth E. Fraser, Communications Officer, Connecticut Dept. of Income Maintenance; Jerry W. Friedman, Deputy Secretary for Income Maintenance, Pennsylvania Dept. of Public Welfare; Georgia Dept. of Social Services; Matthew R. Gould, Program Administrator, Family Assistance Administration, Arizona Dept. of Economic Security; Joseph E. Graves, Jr., Deputy Director, Michigan Dept. of Social Services; Gail Gray, Director, Montana Dept. of Social and Rehabilitation Services; G. H. Green, Awards Officer, University of Saskatchewan, Canada; Mark Greenberg, Center for

Law and Soicial Policy; Cindy Haag, Director, Office of Family Support, Utah Dept. of Social Services; Barbara Hales, Utah State Office of Education; Donna Hall, Office of Conferences and Institutes, University of Kentucky; Desiree Ham-Ying, Andrews University, Berrien Springs, Michigan; Leila Hardaway, Chief, Bureau of Work and Training, Ohio Dept. of Human Services; Karen Heikel, Counseling, Career Development & Placement, University of Minnesota Duluth; Judy Hersey, Assistant to the Dean, Wellesley College; Sandra Hillman, Administrative Clerk, Student Awards Office, University of Alberta, Canada; Jeanette Hills, Acting Chief, Eligibility and Payments, Nevada Dept. of Human Resources; Matthew Hoffman, the *Daily Lobo*, New Mexico Public Interest Research Group, University of New Mexico; W. W. Hogue, Division Administrator, Family Support Services, Oklahoma Dept. of Human Services; J. F. Houwing, Senior Research Officer, Association of Universities and Colleges of Canada; Mabel A. Huber, Adolescent Parent Programs, Minnesota Department of Human Services; Larry R. Humes, Assistant Director, Information and Publications Services, University of Florida; JoAnn Hunt, Director Student Financial Aid, University of Missouri, Kansas City; Indiana Dept. of Social Services; Larry D. Jackson, Commissioner, Virginia Department of Social Services; Donald K. Johnson, Director of Family Support, North Dakota Department of Human Services; Ronald W. Johnson, Financial Aid Director, University of California Davis; Elizabeth Keeler, H.O.M.E., Spokane, Washington; Carol R. Keyes, Past Chairperson, National Coalition for Campus Child Care, Inc.; Christiane Jacox Kyle, Program Manager, Women's Program, Co-Director of the Single Parent Project, Eastern Washington University; John Lanigan, Director of Research, Massachusetts Dept. of Public Welfare; Judy LeCheminant, Assistant Director of Financial Aid, Utah State University; Bob Lipman, Iowa Dept. of Human Services; Stefanie Madak, Information and Media Relations Officer, The University of Manitoba, Canada; Dimna Marrero, Program Director, Services to Families with Children, Puerto Rico Dept. of Social Services; Sara Martin, Assistant Director, The Student Assistance Center, University of Kansas; Massachusetts Dept. of Social Services; John J. McCarthy, Director, Division of Training and Dissemination, United States Department of Education; Patricia McConnel, writer; Carney M. McCullough, Chief Policy Section, Pell Grant Branch, U. S. Dept. of Education; Marj McEwen, Staff Assistant, Women's Resources and Research Center, University of California, Davis; Sandy McIntyre, Community Relations Coordinator, Oregon Dept. of Human Resources; Kermit R. McMurry, Director, Nebraska Dept. of Social Services; Ronald G. Merrill, Chief, AFDC & Food Stamp Policy Implementation Bureau, California Dept. of Social Services; Mississippi Department of Human Services; Montana Dept. of Social Services; Wanda Moore, Director, Program Services, Tennessee Dept. of Human Services; Bernice Morehead, Director, Division of Income Assistance, Washington Dept. of Social and Health Services; Stephanie Mueller, University of Tennessee, Home Economics; Myra Munson, Commissioner, Alaska Dept. of Health and Social Services; Nancy Murphy-Chadwick, Director of University Housing, Texas Women's University; Arnold Neiderbach, Fiscal Officer and Policy Analyst, University of California Berkeley; Andrew T. Nilsson, Associate Professor, Eastern Connecticut State University; Douglas North, President, Prescott College, Prescott, Arizona, and Director of the Consortium of Single Parent Educators; Judith Ooka, Public Welfare Administrator, Hawaii Dept. of Human Services; Janet L. Osborne, Director, Women's Center for Lifelong Learning, Utah State University; Mary Frances Payton, Director, Work Support Services, South Carolina Dept. of Social Services; Sister Margaret Petty, Coordinator of the Single Parent Program, St. Mary College; Deanna Phelps, Director, Office of Project Independence Management, Maryland Department of Human Resources; Gloria Phipps, Director, Public Assistance Division, Indiana Dept. of Public Welfare; Lisa Pottie, Editorial Assistant, *Women & Environments*; Robert V. Pliskin, Director, New Hampshire Dept. of Health and Human Services; James E. Randall, Director, Division of Management and Development, Kentucky Cabinet for Human Resources; Marion E. Reitz, Director, New Jersey Department of Human Services; Mike Richardson, Director of Financial Aid, Western Montana College; Celestene Robb, ACCESS Program Coordinator, Ohio State University; F. Alexis H. Roberson, Director, Department of Employment Services, DC; Mike Robinson, Commissioner, Kentucky Cabinet for Human Resources; Mike Rauseo, South Carolina Dept. of Social Services; Winona E. Rubin, Director, Family and Adult Services Division, Hawaii Dept. of Human Services; Joseph A. Russo, Director of Financial Aid, University of Notre Dame; Linda A. Ryan, Administrator, Nevada Dept. of Human Resources; Jo Sanders, Women's Action Alliance, Inc.; Joel Sanders, Work Programs Supervisor, Alabama Dept. of Human Resources; Dr. Bernice Sandler, Executive Director, Project on the Status and Education of Women; Karen Saum, AFDC Advisory Council of Maine and H.O.M.E., Inc.; Ben Schlesinger, Professor of Social Work, University of Toronto, Canada; Jaque Schmidt, Emporia State University, Emporia, Kansas; Steven Sesit, Associate Director Admissions/Financial Aid, American University; Glenda Brock Simmons, Vice President for Student Life, Texas Women's University; By Sims, Editor, Public Relations Department, University of Utah; Dorothy G. Singer, Department of Psychology, University of Bridgeport; Ellen Skinner, Director of Policy and Program Design, Texas Department of Human Services; Shirley Smith, Financial Aid Officer, Northern Arizona University; Dorothy Solomon, writer; South Dakota Dept. of Social Services; Bruce Spector, Director, Single Parent Scholars Program, Trinity College, Vermont, and The Consortium for Single Parent Scholarship; Thomas G. Sticht, Applied Behavioral & Cognitive Sciences, Inc.; Karel Swift, Director of Student Awards, University of Toronto, Canada; Jeannette Tamayo, Illinois Department of Public Aid; Susan K. Tellier, Vice President & Treasurer, Wells College; Jane Ann Thomas, President, National Coalition for Campus Child Care; Paul Timm-Brock, Director, Assistance Payments Division, Minnesota Dept. of Social Services; Sue Tuffin, Self-Sufficiency Coordinator, Colorado Dept. of Social Services; Marjorie J. Turner, Director, Job Preparation Programs/ KanWork, Kansas Dept. of Social and Rehabilitation Services; Sara M. Turner, Department of Sociology, Anthropology, and Social Work, Humboldt State University; Gregory A. Vadner, Deputy Director, Income Maintenance, Missouri Dept. of Social Services; Barbara Van Burgel, ASPIRE Coordinator, Bureau of Income Maintenance, Maine Dept. of Human Services; Carol Vines, Program Assistant, Women's Center, Eastern Washington University; Dr. Jacqueline Wade, Director, ACCESS Program, Ohio State University; Diane Waller, Director, Office of Welfare Reform, Wisconsin Dept. of Health and Social Services; Donna Walsh, Coordinator of Services for Nontraditional Students, The University of Georgia; Phil Watson, Director, Oklahoma Dept. of Human Services; Gary Weaver, Assistant Director Financial Aid Office, Ohio State University at Lima; Marvin A. Weidner, Administrator, Division of Economic Assistance, Iowa Department of Human Services; Nick Whelihan, Financial Aid Director, University of Minnesota Duluth; Don Winstead, Assistant Secretary for Economic Services, Florida Dept. of Health and Rehabilitative Services; Steve Withorne, Coordinator of Financial Aid & Academic Advisor for American Indian Students, University of South Dakota; Vince Wood, Program Administrator, Family Assistance Administration, Arizona Dept. of Economic Security; W. G. Wyckoff, Director of Financial Aid, Mississippi University for Women; Wyoming Dept. of Health and Social Services; and Susan Young, Program Coordinator, Child Care Connection, Salt Lake City.

1

MAKING MOLEHILLS
OUT OF MOUNTAINS

If I told you that you have the opportunity to go on an incredibly interesting journey that will greatly benefit yourself and your children, would you go? If I told you that there will be many professional people along the way who are there just to help you, would you go? If I told you that you and your family would have enough food, shelter, and other resources throughout your journey, would you go? If I told you that you would have to walk the entire distance with your children, but that people would be alongside the path to help you when you stumble or feel lost, would you go? If I told you that the journey would take more hard work than you've probably ever done, that you'll be exhausted some of the time, and that you'll often wonder if it is worth it, would you go? If I told you that many other people just like yourself will be traveling along your path and similar paths, but that every traveler must carry her or his own load, would you go? If I told you that the way would be very steep at times, and that you would have to somehow get around or over many obstacles in your way, would you go? If I told you that this journey would be one of the best you'll ever undertake, and that the skills and insight you'll gain will help you with all other journeys in the future, would you go?

Some single parents believe that someone might as well suggest that they climb Mount Everest (with children in tow) as go to college. Are you one of them? Do you think it would be just too hard, that you don't have what it takes, or that it's really not worth the effort? One main goal of this guidebook for your college journey is to convince you that you can do it, that it won't be too difficult, and that it will, indeed, be absolutely worth all your hard work and effort.

Journeying through a college or university for a degree is an exciting, stimulating, maturing, growing, developing, challenging, mind-opening, career-preparing experience. You can eagerly look forward to the kinds of positive experiences that can only be gained as a student in post-secondary (beyond high school) education. You may be someone, however, who has to get through or past some negative thoughts and feelings about entering or getting through school before you can experience those positives. This chapter focuses on some fears you may have surrounding going to college. (If you're not afraid of anything and are simply bursting with self-confidence and positive thinking, just skip this part and start with Chapter Two!)

You probably have several questions about this journey. What is college like? How do I get in? Can I make it through? Am I smart enough? Will I be the only single parent on campus? Can I afford it? What will my kids think about it? Can I do it all? How can I raise my kids while I go to school? All these unknowns can create some anxiety when you're thinking about going to college.

The unknown is always a little scary, and every new journey has many unknowns. Even if you don't particularly like your life right now, it's probably comfortable—if only in the sense that it is familiar. You know the paths you regularly take, you know which trails are safe and which aren't; there aren't many surprises. Your first goal, then, is to make the unfamiliar more familiar. The more information you can get before you begin college, the better able you will be to cut your fears down to size. Then they won't become roadblocks in your way, and you can jump right over them. With some fact-finding now and a little experience later, most of your concerns about going to school will disappear or diminish considerably with time. Simply reading this book is a great beginning.

If you were going on a long walking journey with your children through unfamiliar territory, what would you do? You would probably study maps, try to get financial and other kinds of support from various people, ask others who have already taken the journey what it is like, find friends to help you along the way, and try to get yourself and your children in the best physical shape possible. You'll need to do similar things before you begin college. You'll also need to talk to the experts (financial aid counselors, admissions personnel, social services caseworkers, librarians, college career counselors, and so on) for help in planning your journey. But more about all that in Chapter Two.

> *Talk to other single parents to get an accurate idea of what life as a single college student who is also a parent can be like. That way, problems encountered won't be a surprise—it's quite an undertaking, and none should try it without knowing what they face or might face. Money, day care, time to yourself, etc., they take a toll!*

You may decide you want to go to college, but you might be afraid of something. When Dorothy traveled down the yellow brick road, she and her companions were afraid of "lions and tigers and bears, *oh my!*"—and one or two witches, too. While college doesn't at all resemble the Emerald City (though you may find an ivory tower or two), and a yellow brick road won't be there for you to follow, you may feel just as spooky about your journey as Dorothy felt about hers. You might have big fears and small fears. What are your own personal "lions and tigers and bears?"

When you think about journeying through college, are you afraid of being the only single parent on campus? Failing? Looking stupid? Problems with your children? Not being able to cope? Not having any time for yourself? Making mistakes and bad choices? Not having enough money? Health problems? Being isolated? Getting into debt? Conflicts with an ex-spouse or your family about your decision to attend college? Do any of those sound familiar to you?

These and other fears are very real, and they can keep us from doing what we want and need to do. Let's take a look at each fear, one by one, and look at what it might mean to you. Then we can figure out some ways for you to cut any Mount Everest-type fears down to molehill (or at least foothill) size, so you can get over them, get around them, or get through them and into school.

But I'll Be the Only Single Parent on Campus!

No, you won't. My informal survey of several colleges and universities across the country in 1988 revealed the following numbers:

American University, Washington, D.C.	750 single parent students, 15% of total
Gonzaga University, Spokane, Washington	250, about 3% of total
Mississippi University for Women, Columbus, Mississippi	147, 7.3% of total
Ohio State University, Lima, Ohio	200, 8% of total
Southern Arkansas University, Magnolia, Arkansas	160, 8% of total
Southern Utah State College, Cedar City, Utah	195, 7% of total
University of California, Davis, California	2000, 10% of total
University of California, Berkeley, California	344, 3.7% of total
University of South Dakota, Vermillion, South Dakota	825, 15% of total
University of Texas, Arlington, Texas	200, 1% of total
University of Utah, Salt Lake City, Utah	1,000, 3% of total
Utah State University, Logan, Utah	500-600, 5+% of total
Western Montana College, Dillon, Montana	35, 4% of total

You can bet that any college campus will have a substantial number of single parents, and you won't be alone. The numbers get larger every year.

More and more single parents are realizing that the only way they can support their families alone is to get more education and a better-paying career.

I'm Afraid I'll Fail

The fear of failing academically is a major fear for the majority of new students, not just single parent students. It can be overwhelmingly strong at the beginning of your journey. You may see yourself as having "failed" in some major endeavors in the past (perhaps a marriage or a job) and you might doubt your abilities. You may find yourself feeling anxious about your basic competence to be in college. You may feel like you're just not smart enough to make it.

If you don't have any idea what college or university life will be like, you may even think that you will be required to pass tests like this fourteen-question exam (I found this gem on the office door of a professor with a sense of humor):

Graduate Qualifying Examination

Instructions: Read each question thoroughly. Answer all questions. Time limit: four hours. Begin immediately.

1. History. Describe the history of the papacy from its origins to the present day, concentrate specially but not exclusively on the social, political, economic, religious, and philosophical impact on Europe, Asia, America, and Africa. Be brief, concise, and specific.

2. Medicine. You have been provided with a razor blade, a piece of gauze, and a bottle of Scotch. Remove your own appendix. Do not suture until your work has been inspected. You have fifteen minutes.

3. Public Speaking. 2,500 riot-crazed aborigines are storming the classroom. Calm them. You may use any ancient language except Latin or Greek.

4. Biology. Create life. Estimate the differences in subsequent human culture if this form of life had developed 500 million years earlier, with special attention to the probable effects on the English Parliamentary system. Prove your thesis.

5. Music. Write a piano concerto. Orchestrate it and perform it with flute and drum. You will find a piano under your seat.

6. Psychology. Based on your knowledge of their works, evaluate the emotional stability, degree of adjustment, and repressed frustrations of each of the following: Alexander of Aphrodisias, Ramses II, Gregory of Nicoa, Hammurabi. Support your evaluation with quotations from each man's work, making appropriate references. It is not necessary to translate.

7. Sociology. Estimate the sociological problems that might accompany the end of the world. Construct an experiment to test your theory.

8. Management Science. Define management. Define science. How do they relate? Why? Create a generalized algorithm to optimize all managerial decisions. Assuming an 1130 CPU supporting 50 terminals, each terminal to activate your algorithm, design the communications interface and all the necessary control programs.

9. Economics. Develop a realistic plan for refinancing the national debt. Trace the possible effects of your plan in the following areas: Cubism, the Donatist controversy, the wave theory of light. Outline a method from all points of view. Point out the deficiencies in your point of view, as demonstrated in your answer to the last question.

10. Political Science. There is a red telephone on the desk beside you. Start World War III. Report at length on its socio-political effects, if any.

11. Epistemology. Take a position for or against the truth. Prove the validity of your position.

12. Physics. Explain the nature of matter. Include in your answer an evaluation of the impact of the development of mathematics on science.

13. Philosophy. Sketch the development of human thought; estimate its significance. Compare with the development of any other kind of thought.

14. General knowledge. Describe in detail. Be objective and specific.

Funny as this satirical "test" is in daylight hours, it's what some potential or beginning students' nightmares are made of. To counteract their fear of such horrible imaginary monsters and their inability to vanquish them, they might study like crazy and really go overboard with what they need to do. They might treat every word the instructor speaks as gospel, and take volumes of notes as if their very lives depended on the number of notebook pages filled. They might try to memorize their textbooks. Well, if you do all that, you'll soon end up exhausted, your children won't know you anymore, and you'll wonder if getting through school is worth it.

If you work reasonably hard at paying attention in class and studying, you won't fail. College is worth a lot of hard work, but you don't need to make it harder than it really is. If your study skills, math skills, or writing skills are rusty, take some remedial or brush-up courses before you take harder or more demanding ones. Most colleges offer these courses especially for nontraditional students who haven't studied for a while, or can at least refer you to community education or adult education courses that will help you prepare for college work.

After a while, when you get through a few classes with reasonable grades, pass some tests, learn a little, and realize that you can DO IT, your fear of failing will mostly go away. It might never leave you entirely, though, and it may come back full force when you are faced with a particularly difficult class or assignment. However, your self-confidence will grow and grow, and by the time you have earned your degree you'll believe you can do just about anything! And you'll be able to!

> *I would say that it's not easy, but returning to college has been the best and most rewarding experience of my life. I had become a non-person in my own life and coming to school has renewed my faith in life generally, and myself specifically. When it seems tough, just stick it out. It's well worth it.*

I'm Afraid I'll Look Stupid

This fear comes from a genuine lack of self-confidence—or perhaps from being treated as if you were stupid way back in your childhood by a parent, or maybe more recently by a spouse. Have you ever been called "dummy," "stupid," "ignoramus," or other such name by someone close to you? Have you been treated by people in the world as if you were incompetent, unintelligent, and otherwise just plain no good? If this has happened a lot, you may have come to believe it. You may not believe it intellectually, but the emotional fear may be there. You try to believe that you're smart and capable, but the nagging doubt seems always to be present.

If you've ever been to college before and did pretty well you'll have less of this fear, of course. Or if you did well in high school, that experience will help, too. But if you've never set foot on a college campus before, and you've been out of school for a while, you might be full of fear and trepidation about your ability to convince both yourself and others that you are an intelligent person who is quite capable of earning a college degree. You may have such a low opinion of your intellectual abilities that you make all kinds of excuses why you shouldn't even try to go to college. One of the goals of this book is to convince you that you can indeed attend college, do well, enjoy learning, help your children learn to value education, and go on to the kind of career you want and need.

After you enter college, you still may hesitate to make comments or ask questions in class because of this fear of looking stupid. Guess what? All of the other students in your classes have this same fear to one degree or another, and are so busy worrying about themselves that they won't pay much attention to whether or not your utterances are up-to-snuff. Would you snicker or laugh at someone who was trying to phrase a question just right and who wasn't quite sure of the right words? Of course not, and your classmates won't, either. Neither will your professor. Would you think less of someone who asked the professor a question if you knew the answer? Everybody is there to learn, and since you are there to learn also, it naturally follows that you may not know a great deal about the subjects you are studying. Ask questions.

College is for reasonably smart people who are willing to work hard. That's you! It takes neither an I.Q. of 140 nor incredible ability to successfully complete college and earn a degree. It takes your willingness to learn how to learn, plus organization, hard work, dedication, and perseverance—qualities you probably have in abundance.

While you are in college, you will also be teaching your children the value of higher education. They will watch you, learn from you, and will be much more likely to go to college themselves someday, if they see you do it now. So, if you want your children to finish high school and go on to college, give them your example to follow. They'll believe that if their mom or dad was smart enough to go, they certainly will be.

I'm Afraid It Will Be Hard On My Children

Single parents worry about how their college attendance will affect their children. It's hard to be a single parent in college; I won't try to convince you that it isn't. Actually, it's awfully hard to be a single parent doing anything! And our children seem to be bottomless pits when it comes to their needs and wants—and often ungrateful bottomless pits, at that!

I'm convinced, though, that the few years you will spend in college will bring tremendous long-term benefits to your children, even if things are tough on your family in many ways while you are in school. You can enlist the aid of your children to help you through, and can help them feel like they are very important to your success (they are). You can take them to class with you sometimes. You can encourage them to check out books from the library, and "study" with you. You can take your children to special activities on campus. You can expose them to new ideas and ways of thinking about the world. You will give them hope of a better future.

Some single parent students are afraid that their children won't get what they need and that the kids will run away (this mostly haunts parents of teens). Others are afraid that their ex-spouses will think that children shouldn't live in a student parent household and will steal them away. Most fear losing touch with their children because they are so busy and have so little time to devote solely to their offspring.

Even those major fears are manageable, especially if you spend some special time with your children regularly (see Chapter Five). You'll also need to force yourself to treat your ex-spouse or your child's other parent in a positive, friendly manner, always—even if he or she doesn't always treat you the same. Avoid saying anything bad about your children's other parent to your children. Believe they are smart enough to form their own opinions. Allow your children to spend as much time as is possible with their other parent. The more you can encourage contact between your children and their other parent (if he or she is at least a minimally "okay" parent and treats the children well), the less likely that person will be to feel out of control and to do something drastic.

> *My ex-husband and I have good rapport because we work at it!*

I'm Afraid I Won't Be Able to Cope

You and I know that life is hard being a single parent. You think it might be too hard if you try to be a student, too. There is a big difference, though, between feeling stressed as a single parent just trying to tread water, or feeling stressed as a student parent. In the first case, you know you probably aren't going anywhere or making life better. You're just trying to cope with life and trying to support your children in the best way you can, and circumstances just don't seem to be getting any better.

When you enter college, though, you'll be working toward a great goal. You'll be improving yourself and making it much more possible for you and your family to have the kind of life you want in a few years. When you feel like you're making progress and moving ahead, the stresses of life and of being in school will seem much more bearable. It will be hard, but it will be a *good* kind of hard.

Once you're in college, though, you may sometimes get very depressed, or anxious, or feel like you're the only one who's working so hard to get through. You may feel very alone. Your level of stress will be held at a pretty constant high, so you'll need to give yourself and your children stress-free breaks that can last anywhere from minutes to hours to days. As a single parent student, you will be using all your internal and external resources to cope with the pressure, problems, and demands on your time. When you're in school, though, you'll learn your own special ways of managing those demands. You won't go crazy, but you will strengthen your mind and make it better—especially if you don't isolate yourself. Constant isolation from others can cause additional problems for you. How?

There is a thing called "reality checking." This simply means you check your version of reality against that of other people. Reality checking automatically happens when you communicate with other well-hooked-together people outside your immediate sphere and spend a little time with them. One of the most dangerous things about isolation (and single parents are often isolated) is that you can more easily get a kooky idea or an irrational thought in your head. If you remain mostly alone and let such an idea run around in your mind, it can persist or get all blown out of proportion. This can happen if you don't talk to other folks and realize that you have just a nutty idea that came at a stressful time.

Some examples of nutty ideas (I've had most of these): "I'll never get through school." "I'd be better off staying home on welfare." "I'll always be a failure in everything I try to do." "My kids would be better off without me." "No one will ever really care about me." "I'm not smart enough to go to college." Do you ever find yourself thinking those things?

Whole families can get really kooky, too, if they never spend any time with other people and just hang around each other all the time. Family members can reinforce each other's crazy ideas, and keep them going. We all get weird ideas in our heads from time to time. But, if you talk with some other reasonably rational person, it will help you get rid of your nutty idea. College is chock-full of other intelligent people to talk and interact with. Take advantage of their support, good will, and ideas.

So, when you think you'll lose your mind and your ability to cope, realize that the feeling and any kooky ideas that go along with it are transitory. When you're in school, sometimes it will be your exhaustion that makes you feel mentally and emotionally off balance; sometimes it will be because because you'll feel so overwhelmed from time to time. Maybe you haven't been eating right, or maybe you're fighting off an illness. So get some sleep; eat a good meal. Take a little time off. Call a mental health professional if you're extremely bothered about something, or at least call a friend or trusted family member. Talk about it.

Counseling service on a sliding fee scale has been helpful for divorce issues and building self esteem. Families help when they can, but no one understands what divorce and single parenting and poverty are like. My family is pleased I'm "handling everything so well" and finishing school, but they are very critical of my hopes to move away and attend graduate school. A support group for newly single people is helpful when I can afford a sitter.

I'm Afraid I Won't Have Any Time to Myself

How much time do you have to yourself now? Not much? How much time do you think you'll have for yourself in college? Even less? Maybe, but then again maybe not.

As a single parent student, you'll need to structure your time and your life. Everybody needs some time and space alone to do something they like to do—make sure you do this at least once a week when you're in school. (See Chapter Six and Chapter Eleven.)

While you're in school, the more organized and streamlined you can make your life, the more time you'll have for some relaxation and recreation. Being a college student will force you to become a creative time manager and an organized person, if you are going to successfully make it through. The practice you'll get in college doing all that will help you through your whole life.

I'm Afraid I Won't Make the Right Decisions

The fear of making mistakes and bad choices comes from just living. You've made lots of mistakes and bad choices, and so have I. So has everybody. You will continue to do so from time to time; so will everybody who is human. One good thing about life, though, is that most things we decide about are not written in stone and can be changed.

So, if you find yourself in a bad class, perhaps with a foreign graduate student instructor whose English you can't understand, withdraw soon before it will negatively affect your grade. If you are spending too much time with someone you don't really like, stop. If, after investigation, you find out that college isn't for you and you'd rather be a gardener or carpenter or plumber or singer, switch gears, plan carefully, then go for it. People are sometimes so afraid of change, and see the world as making choices for them, that they get stuck in the mire and can't see their way out. You might feel like you're stuck right now, but nobody can get you unstuck but you.

I believe that we actually have a lot more choice about things than we sometimes think we do. We're often just afraid to accept the consequences of our choices. It can be much more comfortable to blame our circumstances on other people or things. I am the first to admit, though, that our possible choices are most definitely constrained and limited by factors out of our control—genetics, the economy, the government, our health or lack of it, the fact that we have children, and so on. But, it's your life; grab hold of the reins, use your spurs if you have to, and work at getting a little control within your own particular set of constraints. You must also work at taking most of the responsibility for your choices, a sometimes unpleasant thing.

> *I charged my ex-husband with incest. I obtained sole custody of my girls. I am the sole supporter of them. I felt I needed to better our financial situation so I chose to finish my B.A.—that was my goal. However, returning to school has caused many personal changes for me. I now feel I am capable of a great deal more. I love what I am doing! Because I am happy and successful, I provide a good role model for my daughters.*

But I Can't Afford to Go to College

Thousands of single parents are going to colleges and universities, right now. Most get help from social services, but some don't. Some work, too; some just go to school. Some get help from extended family, some are completely on their own. The great majority get all the financial aid they can. If they can manage it financially, so can you. You just need to learn how. But if you fear not having enough money, you're in good company.

The best way to counteract this fear is to work as hard as you can at getting information about financial aid and assistance, and not be too proud to take it when it's available to you. None of us are independent of others for sustenance, at any time. Use temporary forms of help and then pay it back when you're out of school by working in a career that pays a good wage and also provides the government with ample taxes. Then you'll be helping the next single parent who's going through the same financial crises that you have gone through.

> *It's a lot of work, some days very frustrating, and most of all it's worth all the effort you put into getting and being there. Find other single parents to talk to, and use whatever is offered you. Someday in the near future you will be a productive member of the career world, and your example will give hope to others who follow.*

Money problems always plague single parent students, and you and your children will go without lots of things you'd like to have. You will long for the day when you can afford to have a lifestyle that isn't just survival mode. But if you go to college, receive school financial aid and maybe social services aid, and perhaps even work part-time, you'll do okay. You and your children won't starve, you won't be sleeping on the street, and you won't go bare.

Remember, the concept of poverty is always relative to what people around you have. While you are in the company of other students and single parents, you won't feel so down—they all worry about money, none of their children have fancy clothes or toys, and they don't live in fancy places. Stick out the poverty for a while, and know that things will be better when you're out of school and working full time in your chosen career.

I'm Afraid I'll Become Physically Worn Out and Get Sick

The best way to conquer fears about health problems for you and your children is to really pay attention to taking care of yourself and them. Start now, even before you begin school. Get lots of sleep, eat good food, exercise some every day, try to relax as much as possible, stay away from drugs and other garbage, and you know the rest. Do you put all this into practice? You'll need to, and soon.

While you're in school it is essential for you to treat your body with the utmost respect. You'll need to pace yourself, and find the best way to get everything done. Are you a "long-distance runner" or a "sprinter" in life? Or are you a "fast walker?" Different combinations of these strategies will be necessary on your journey through college, reflecting your changing stamina levels.

Any time there is a high concentration of people in a relatively small space, such as on a college campus, germs have movable parties. Stress-related illnesses are common among college students, and you'll need to take every precautionary step you can to keep yourself well. When you work on developing and maintaining good health, you can do just about anything, and you'll be able to make it through.

> *When I started this course, I didn't really think I was all that much older than I had been twenty years earlier—I felt not much older than my fellow students (some over twenty years younger than me). These two years have taught me clearly that I am older—because of stamina problems.*

I'm Afraid I'll Be Too Busy to Have a Social Life

You may fear being alone and lonely and isolated while you're a student. Your feelings may become even more acute when you are surrounded by lots of people at school. You may fear never having time to meet and get to know another partner to spend some, most, or all of your life with. You may fear that you will always be a single parent (unless, of course, you want to be) and that no one will want to get involved with an instant family. There are several ways to battle these fears (see Chapter Nine).

One most welcome by-product of going to school is that it will, gradually, increase your feelings of self-esteem and self-confidence. This happens a little at a time, not all at once. But it will happen. This alone will help you be able to interact with other people in ways that will enable you form the kinds of relationships that you want.

I'm Afraid I'll End Up Owing the Moon to Somebody

You probably fear going into debt. College costs money, more and more all the time. You've probably seen magazine covers or newspapers with headlines like, "College Costs Skyrocket," "Can You Afford to Send Your Kids to College?", and "Higher Education Costs Going Out of Sight." Don't let these headlines scare you away—you *can* get enough financial aid to go to college. The financial aid office, however, will likely offer you a lot of loan money as part of your yearly financial aid "packages," perhaps 50 percent of your total financial aid or more. Don't take a lot of loan money if you don't want it and can manage to get by without it. Stand firm, and find other sources of help (see Chapter Three).

You may be better off working part time and attending school part time. You might need to take longer to get through. Explore every alternative with school financial aid counselors; consider even ideas which may not seem reasonable at the moment. They may trigger other creative ideas that will help. Ask if you can work a minimum number of hours a week instead of taking out loans. Ask other single parent students what they do to survive. Taking a little bit of loan money can help motivate you to stay in college (since you have to start paying it back when you stop taking classes), but taking too much loan money can put more pressure on you than you need to bear.

I'm Afraid of What Other People Will Think or Do

You may fear conflicts with family members or an ex-spouse over your decision to go to school. Such conflicts are emotionally difficult and can be a continual source of stress unless you deal with them right away. Other people in your life may feel that you will look down on them if you become more highly educated. They may fear that you will change your value system to be less compatible with theirs. They may feel that your decision isn't very good for your children.

I suggest, first, that you be as firm, steadfast, and calm when confronted with unsupportive people as you can. (See Chapter Sixteen.) You may just need to state your goals and desires over and over for a while. You may need to talk about all the positive things about going to school as you can, and simply not bring up the negative ones (in case others jump on them as being the most important). Other people may simply be jealous of your fortitude and resolve, and you'll need to accept and then ignore this—it's their problem, not yours. If an ex-spouse threatens you or otherwise makes you feel that you are doing the wrong thing, get some professional counseling on how to deal with that particular person and your relationship.

If you have extremely supportive family and friends, you're very lucky. They will make your journey a lot easier. If your family and others are unsupportive at best and hostile and angry at worst, you'll need to create your own support system of folks who both care about you and will help you along the road emotionally and otherwise.

My extended family members think I am too old to return to school.

Confronting Your Fears

You may have many more fears and concerns about going to college than were discussed in this chapter. Confront them now, and figure out ways to deal with them using the instructions in Chapter Eleven. It might help you right now to consult that chapter, list each of your specific fears on a piece of paper, and then practice some creative problem solving alone or with a companion. You can write down some possible solutions and ideas that will help you make molehills out of your mountains.

If you still find that your fears are stopping you from trying, or are hurting you once you're enrolled, talk to a counselor to help you overcome them or reduce them to a level you can live with. Remember, isolation increases fears and anxiety; talking with someone who can give you good suggestions will help immensely. It's entirely appropriate for you to get some professional counseling before you even begin school, or soon after you enter to help you deal with your special set of problems and fears. You can call the on-campus student counseling center and ask if there is someone on staff who is familiar with the special needs of single parent students. You can also call and ask the nontraditional student center or women's center if they know of a single parent student who would be happy to tell you about college life and how he or she resolved conflicts and fears. If you can't find anyone on campus, call your local community mental health organization and ask for someone who could be of assistance. Even talking with an empathetic family member or friend will help you clarify your goals and come to terms with some of the compromises you will need to make. Be advised, however, that sometimes a person outside your family or circle of friends, someone with a different "world view," can offer different ways of looking at fears and conflicts and help you discover some alternative ways of coping.

Above all, please don't let your fears, whether you feel that they are reasonable or not, keep you from going to school if that's what you want, need, and expect of yourself.

SPOTLIGHT ON SUCCESS
From the University of Florida at Gainesville

When M. decided to come back to school, she was well aware of the difficult task that lay ahead. After a nine-year absence, she wondered if she could once again become disciplined to study like a good student and take care of her home and five children. But M., 32, did succeed. She came back to the University of Florida as a single parent, and took eighteen hours of classes in her final semester, making the Dean's list with a 3.0 cumulative grade point average. Last May, she was awarded a Bachelor of Arts degree in elementary education.

M. said coming back to school was in the best interests of her children. She felt that obtaining an education was important in order to properly provide for them. "I knew I would be a single parent, and I have five kids to raise," said M.

A junior majoring in education, she left UF in 1976 because of marital problems and ultimately filed for a divorce. She left both her job and her home in Gainesville to seek protection and counseling at the Refuge House for Battered Women in Tallahassee. She stayed at the Sexual and Physical

Abuse Resource Center (SPARC) Shelter for Battered Women in Gainesville four months later when she returned to complete the divorce proceedings.

During her divorce proceedings, M. said she lacked direction and was anxious to find any kind of job in order to survive. She also said the counselors at the Tallahassee shelter and at SPARC encouraged her to finish school. She became convinced that starting a career might be more profitable than going from one menial job to another. And the counselors told her it was quite obvious to them that teaching was something she wanted to do.

Most important to M. was being able to spend adequate time with her children. She knew that if she went back to school and got her degree, she could work full time and be home evenings.

"Most divorced women are forced to take a second job and are not able to spend sufficient time with their kids," said M. "I needed a job that would allow me to spend time with my kids. My kids are the most important thing to me."

M. returned to school in the fall semester of 1985 to get the degree in education she had wanted for so long. She knew it would take careful money and time management, especially since she was a recipient of state and federal financial aid. But she earned her degree last May.

"There were some very trying times," said M. "Many times it was very frustrating without a steady flow of income."

She said that when her financial aid didn't arrive on time, it only added to her frustrations. "I have a very long list of people I owe," said M.

M. said getting a degree in education is like a dream come true. "It's something I always wanted to do," she said. "I love education."

U.S. Senator Bob Graham, who met M. at the commencement ceremonies, wrote her a letter congratulating her for her outstanding achievement. He also invited her to come visit him whenever she is in Washington, DC. M. said receiving the letter from Graham was truly rewarding. "Senator Graham is a man who stresses excellence in education," said M. "He also strongly supports the public school system."

M. is taking some post-graduate courses at UF and plans to pursue her Master's degree in the near future. She said she wants to teach full time and get established financially, then work slowly toward her master's. This way she can enjoy the kind of family life she insists on.

Craig Young
Reprinted with permission from Information Services,
University of Florida.

2

PLANNING FOR YOUR JOURNEY NOW

Now let's leave Dorothy behind on the yellow brick road and concentrate entirely on you. Even if you are just thinking about going to college, you can start gathering specific information today. You can get most of the information you need by telephone or mail. At the end of this chapter you'll find a list of particular questions to ask staff people in offices you should contact, if you can't find the information in written material such as college catalogs or social services literature.

Also, go to your local public library soon for general information on careers, schools in your area, financial aid, study skills, child care. Use some of the resources listed in the bibliography. Start reading; you might as well practice now!

Which School?

Before you inquire about a particular college's or university's programs, financial aid availability, housing, child care centers, and so on, make sure that each school that interests you is accredited and professionally recognized as being of high quality. Look for the following qualifications:

- Highly experienced accredited faculty members.
- Respected programs and courses in varied fields.
- Availability of support programs for students.
- Distinguishing excellence in teaching or research or both.
- A respected undergraduate and/or graduate degree program.

Just remember that no matter which school you choose, make very sure that you check it out thoroughly before you enter. Make sure it offers courses of high quality. How can you tell? Your state's office of higher education would have this information. Contact them; the phone number is in the phone book under state government, or call "information" to obtain the number.

It also wouldn't hurt to call the personnel offices of several large businesses and industries in your area, and ask the personnel or human resources director if their firm respects an associate, bachelor, or graduate degree from the institution, or if a degree from the college you're considering is believed to be inferior to degrees from other schools in your area.

A College or a University?

Now, in some states there are places called colleges and places called universities, and sometimes there are no clear qualitative distinctions between the two titles. Quantitative distinctions do often exist, however: universities are often larger than colleges, and offer more areas for study, particularly graduate study (master's and doctoral work). The size of the institution does not necessarily correlate with its quality, however. A small college may have a far better undergraduate (bachelor degree) program than does a large university. Or a medium-sized university may have a better research faculty than a large college. You must judge each institution on its own merits.

When you're trying to decide which institution to enter, ask each admissions office exactly what their institution has to offer you. Get the yearly catalog which lists the areas of study, faculty members, and classes offered. Remember, you can also call your state's higher education office and ask relevant questions about each institution of higher learning that you need information about.

Whatever you do, don't get fooled by one of those "fly-by-night" colleges that offers easy diplomas in questionably useful fields. Make absolutely sure, before you plunk down any tuition money anywhere or sign your name on any dotted line, that you thoroughly check out any college. If the name of the school includes "The University of XYZ," "Something State College," or "Community College of ABC," you're probably safe.

Throughout this book I will refer to all institutions of higher education as colleges. Just remember that the term "college" is used here and elsewhere as a generic term indicating either a college or a university.

Should You Move?

As you make your preliminary investigations and decisions regarding which school to attend, you might consider moving to another city in your state if it offers a better school than one which is closer to you now. You want to get the very best education you can for your time and money. I don't recommend you move out-of-state, though, unless you plan to live there long enough to gain resident status before you begin school. Nonresident tuition is much higher than for residents, and you may have difficulty obtaining social services aid unless you have lived in a state a certain length of time before you apply for help.

If you are truly stuck in one location, and have only one or at most two schools from which to choose, simply get the best education you can at the one you pick. A highly motivated, independent student at a "second-rate," smallish college can learn much more than a less motivated student at a first-rate large university! If the school you must attend because of its location is not particularly distinguished by its faculty or programs, and is merely average in most areas, make sure you distinguish yourself above most of the other students who attend it. Then you'll do fine during school and also later on in the job market.

You can distinguish yourself in many ways, not just by getting good grades. You can work hard in someone's lab, you can become involved in single parent issues on campus, you can organize your peers for political action. You can and should do any number of things during your time in school that will distinguish you as a person of intelligence, creativity, motivation, insight, and action—qualities important to employers.

On-Campus Housing

Even if you don't need to move to another city to attend a good school, I do highly recommend that you move to an on-campus family housing facility or complex if one is available. These housing units are generally safe, well kept up, and you will cut down on your travel time to and from school. In addition, you'll be surrounded by other students and their families, and everyone typically helps each other out. Your children will play with other students' children, and the entire atmosphere is one of learning, cooperation, and striving for reachable goals. It's an upbeat place to be.

If your college doesn't have family housing, I recommend that you find the safest, best place as close to campus as you can. And I recommend that you find a good enough place that you will plan to stay there throughout your entire college education. It's very, very hard to move once you become a student—it's disrupting to you, your children, and your studies. You might want to start looking around now for good housing for your time in school. Certainly call the college you plan to attend and ask about housing availability.

Obtaining Information About Financial Aid and Child Care Services

While you're deciding which institution to try to enter, what must you know how to get before you can actually go to school? That's right, *money!* Call the financial aid office at the college or university you might attend. When you get through to someone, explain your desires and family financial circumstances briefly. Then request every scrap of information that they can mail to you. Call the college admissions office and do the same things. (You'll need to be admitted to the school before the financial aid office will consider your formal financial aid application, but the financial aid office will send you basic information about financial aid even before you are admitted.) The very best time to do your phoning and requesting is on a Monday morning, when the clerks and secretaries are rested and ready to go. Always avoid calling late in the day or week, no matter whom you're trying to contact.

Call or write to your local social services office and ask for information about what will happen to various benefits when you go to college if you depend on them now for any manner of assistance. (See also Chapter Three.) If you don't get social services help now, ask them how you can get some assistance like AFDC or ADC, food stamps, medical help, and child care subsidy aid if you enter college. (Be sure to consult Appendix A for specifics about your state's social services level of assistance to single parent college students.)

You can also contact, by phone or mail, the student services center, nontraditional students' center, women's center, or their equivalents on campus. Ask the people in these offices if the school has any special programs for single parent students. Some campuses have established organizations to help newcomers. Call the student resource center, if one exists, and ask for any and all help and information they can give you.

Investigate child care centers close to home or the campus if your children will need one and don't already attend. (See Chapter Five.) You can do most of this investigating by phone, although you will want to drop in, unannounced, on a few centers to find out how they operate. Find out about after-school programs for school-age youngsters, and other programs for teenagers, to help them keep safe and busy while you are in school and/or working.

Who will have child care information? The college you plan to attend might have an on-campus child care center. Local YWCA and YMCA centers may have school-age child care programs, as might local schools, Boys' and Girls' Clubs, local churches, and so on. Your local social services office will have a listing of child care centers which are licensed (a licensed center is probably necessary if you will request assistance from social services to help pay for it), and they may also have information about other kinds of care for older children. There may be a "Child Care Connection" organization in your area—look in the phone book under "child care" or "day care." A women's or nontraditional students' center at your college or university may also have information on child care services. You can also look for an "Information and Referral" phone number in the phone book—the staff of this organization has information about and addresses and phone numbers of all sorts of helping organizations, agencies, groups, and individuals. In addition, Appendix B lists organizations in your state that can help.

> *Be prepared fully before you start. Find good day care and always have a backup. On campus is normally the best idea. Check with the financial aid office on grants, scholarships, and so on.*

Get the Information You Need—Right Now

Even though you can get most of the information you need by phone or mail, you'll need to get started on information-gathering right away. Most of the information will need to be received by you from three months to even a year or more before you start school—especially financial aid and child care information. Obtaining most government financial aid through your college requires that you fill out forms and applications a good nine months to a year before you even start classes. There may also be a waiting list you'll need to get your child(ren)'s name(s) on for space in a child care center. There may be a long waiting list of people wanting to receive government subsidized financial help for child care. In short, you can't decide this week that you want to attend college, and start next month. It doesn't work that way, unless you're rich.

If you have gone through your social services system for any kind of assistance, or have experience with any other major bureaucracy, you know that people seldom volunteer information. Ask, ask, ask! Be a pest, but be a polite pest. If you're applying to a small college or university, they are likely to have only one or two places that will have all the information you'll need. Large campuses have more student centers and offer more specialized personnel to help you with concerns. The same applies to large or small social services offices—some may be more specialized than others, and you'll need to talk with from one to several people to get the help you need.

Do be aware of the fact that the budgets of financial aid offices and social service offices are increasingly tight, and one of the first things to be affected is personnel. That is, you can bet that each office probably doesn't have enough staff people to help you at the very moment you desire help (you'll probably have a wait), and for as long as you'd like to receive the assistance during each interaction. Just keep that in mind, and it will save you frustration. Be patient; staff people these days have more and more people to help, often with less and less resources and time to do so.

> *The first few months are always tough. Don't work, get as much money as possible from student services and government, and focus on your child and your schoolwork. If you do a good job in both, your self-esteem rises, and that helps you cope with everything else.*

Now Just Whom Did You Talk With, and About What?

Each time you phone or visit any office, always get the names of the persons you speak with. Get their titles, like "financial aid counselor" or "social services caseworker, Team B." Note the date and time you talk with anyone as a matter of course. Then write down what each person tells you. This will save you endless hours later, when you're trying to remember just whom you contacted and what they told you. It helps to have a notebook or legal pad set aside just to keep track of information received, telephone conversations, and other contacts with people in offices when you're finding out about school and child care. Keep a running log of communications with these folks. Document everything by keeping all material sent to you; get a box or large envelope to store information you get in the mail.

Dealing With Problems in Obtaining Information

When you speak to members of any organization when you want information, the more professional and polite you can be the better they will respond, and the more useful information you will obtain. Sometimes, though, you will talk to someone who seems absolutely incompetent and totally unable to help you. Or, you may feel like you're getting the runaround. People who yell, get annoyed (out loud or in their body language), use bad language or sarcasm, or do anything else that alienates the person who is on the other end of the telephone line or on the other side of the desk do themselves a great disservice.

Always keep your cool if you find yourself in a stressful situation with someone you need help from. Demonstrate that you have brains, not just feelings. Other people will listen to you and help you more if you do.

There are some things you can do if you're not getting the information you need. If you're on the phone, you may politely end the conversation, and call back, hoping to get someone else from that office on the line. You may ask to see or speak to another person in that department. Or, you may certainly ask to speak to the person's department supervisor if the person is being really unhelpful (the supervisor might be busy—you might not get to talk to her or him right away.) You may also ask if you can be referred to someone else or another agency that might better be able to assist you.

Patience, persistence, and calmness will pay off in your search for information, now and during all your years in school. If you sound or look annoyed or frustrated, that will only put up brick walls between you and the information you so dearly need. If you lose your temper, the person you're talking to might tell you then that there isn't anyone else who could help you (when of course there is). Remember, too, when you're under a lot of stress, that it is not the caseworker's or secretary's fault that your ex did not pay the child support this month, or that the legislature just cut the day-care subsidy budget, or that the whole world just seems to be beating you up in general and not making your path nice and smooth. How you respond to such situations will determine, in large part, how well people help you.

Sometimes trying to get valid, correct, and useful information from some people and departments over the phone or even in person can be incredibly frustrating and maddening. If you express frustration or anger, the people you're talking will tune you out fast. Unfortunately, human service workers must deal with angry, unprofessional clients all the time and don't like it. Burn-out (a fancy term for "enough is enough and I'm quitting!") happens all too frequently to workers who deal with people all day, especially in social services offices. So, when you're having a hard time, be smart and remember to keep your frustration, anger, or exasperation to yourself (at least at that particular point in time) and try again after you are fairly calm, or contact someone else. If you don't get the help or response that you want when you first try, remember that the other person may just be having a lousy day, may be new at the job, or may simply just not know what you need to know.

There is a good rule to remember here: "Never put down to malice what can be explained by ignorance or incompetence." Always try again with someone else, or try at a different time. Above all, *do not give up* when it seems like you aren't getting anywhere with people. If you can't continue because of mounting frustration or anger, try again in an hour after having something good to eat, or tomorrow after a good night's rest. Try another person or another office.

Conversation Examples

Here are two examples of hypothetical telephone conversations between a single parent (SP) and a social services caseworker/case manager (C). In the first example, the single parent is not using the best strategy to get help. In the second example, the single parent uses a more effective strategy. Look for subtle differences in the way the single parent handles the conversation. Compare the amount of information the single parent receives in each example, and how the caseworker reacts in each example.

Example 1

C: Hello. Social services department. May I help you?

SP: Hello, um, I just got divorced, I have two kids, I want to go to college, and I need some help.

C: Just one moment please. I'll connect you with one of our JOBS program caseworkers.

C: Hello, this is Mary. How can I help you?

SP: I read that I can get help from social services to go to college.

C: Give me your name please, and tell me a little about yourself.

SP: My name is Cynthia Weston, and I have two children. I just got divorced and I can't find a decent job. I want to go to school.

C: I see. What are your children's ages?

SP: Matthew is five, and Sarah is two.

C: And you want to go to college?

SP: Yes. I'd like to start at the community college right away.

C: I don't know if that is possible, but we'll try to help you as much as we can. I recommend that you come in to the office and talk with me or another caseworker in person as soon as possible.

SP: Can't you help me on the phone? I don't have a car, and it's really hard for me to drag the kids around on the bus.

C: I'm sorry, but I can only give you general information over the phone. You'll need to see a caseworker in person to discuss your goals and develop an employability plan.

SP: What do you mean, an employability plan? I want to go to college, not work! I can't make a decent living on minimum wage! I've already looked in the paper for a job, but I know I can't make enough to support my family. And my lousy ex sure isn't helping any.

C: Well, our new JOBS program has been developed to assist people who are otherwise dependent on social services to become self-supporting. Education and training are two components of this program. One of our caseworkers will help you develop the best plan for you and your family.

SP: Look, I already know what the best plan for me is. Just tell me if I can get some help from you or not.

C: I can only tell you what you're eligible for after you come in and fill out an application and talk with a caseworker.

SP: Okay, okay. I didn't know it would be this much trouble.

C: Our office is open from 8 A.M. to 5 P.M., Monday through Friday. Our address is 110 Rosemont Avenue.

SP: How long will this all take?

C: Probably an hour or so for your initial consultation.

SP: Okay, I guess I'll try to come in this week.

C: I hope you can make it in soon. Goodbye.

SP: Bye.

Example 2

C: Hello. Social services department. May I help you?

SP: Hello, my name is Cynthia Weston. I just got divorced, I have two kids, and I want to go to college. I think I need some help to do it, though.

C: Just one moment please. I'll connect you with one of our JOBS program caseworkers.

C: This is Mary. How can I help you, Ms. Weston?

SP: I read that I can get help from social services to go to college, but I need some more information. Can you help me?

C: Yes. Tell me a little about yourself.

SP: Well, I'm 25, and I have two children. I just got divorced. I'm not working, and I'm broke. My ex-husband hasn't sent any child support at all yet.

C: What are your children's ages?

SP: Matthew is five, and Sarah is two.

C: I see. And you want to go to college?

SP: Yes. I'd like to start at the community college as soon as possible. I've already contacted them, and have a pretty good idea of what I can do. I have thought about just getting a job, but I don't think I could make more than minimum wage, and that certainly isn't enough to raise my family on. College seems to be the answer.

C: Okay. It sounds like you have investigated your options a little already. If you'd like to get help from social services, though, you'll need to come in to the office and talk with either myself or another case manager.

SP: I thought maybe someone could help me over the phone. I don't have a car, and it's hard for me to get around with the kids on the bus.

C: I understand, but I can only give you general information over the phone. You'll need to see a caseworker in person to discuss your goals and develop an employability plan.

SP: What exactly is an employability plan?

C: It's part of the new JOBS program which has been developed to assist people who are otherwise dependent on social services to become self-supporting. Education and training are two major components of this program. One of our caseworkers will help you develop the best plan for you and your family.

SP: Can I go to college?

C: If we decide together that it would be the best way for you to become self-sufficient, yes. Our office can offer assistance through two years of college.

SP: What if I need to go to college for four years to get a bachelor degree? What can I do then?

C: We can assist you in finding enough support to help you through a longer program, if that's necessary. We can discuss all your options when you come in.

SP: Please tell me about the kind of assistance I can get for at least two years while I go to college.

C: I can only tell you what you would be eligible for after you fill out your application, talk with a caseworker, and agree on a plan.

SP: May I make an appointment to talk with someone in person?

C: Certainly. It might save you time to do that instead of just dropping in. After we finish our conversation, I'll transfer you to the front office again, and the secretary will schedule you.

SP: I appreciate your help. As I mentioned, it will be hard for me to come in with the kids on the bus. Do you have a suggestion?

C: We may be able to reimburse you for the cost of child care while you talk with us. We can provide you with a list of licensed child care providers in your area. If you're really broke, we can provide enough bus tokens to get you here and back home.

SP: That would be great! I am really broke right now. Oh, how long will the interview and form-filling-out probably take? And is there anything I can do before my appointment to help save time?

C: It will take probably an hour or so. To save time, I can mail some application forms to you now, so you can get a head start on completing them before your appointment.

SP: Is there anything else I should bring with me to the office?

C: Yes. I'll enclose a list of items you should bring with you when I send you the application forms.

SP: You've been real helpful. Your name is Mary? Can you give me your last name and your title, please?

C: I'm Mary Simons, the self-sufficiency coordinator for Team 15.

SP: Well, thanks again. I think I'm ready to make an appointment.

C: Goodbye, and we'll look forward to assisting you.

This example may not reflect exactly what *your* social services office will tell you; it's only included to give you an idea of how your attitude and what you say will affect the caseworker's ability and motivation to give you information. Think about those two conversations for a minute. Where did Cynthia go wrong in the first example? What did she do better in the second example?

Most people in social services offices and financial aid offices will be very professional, considerate, and caring—if you provide them with good information about you, ask questions, and act as your own advocate by bringing as much knowledge as you can to your interactions with them. When you are assisted by particularly helpful, cheerful, sensitive, and insightful people, be sure to express thanks and appreciation to them. Some people will do a good, and sometimes great, job of helping you find out what you need to know and will steer you in the right direction. A quick note to the person or his or her supervisor does wonders—for them, and for the next confused, information-needy person who asks for help. If you deal with that person again, he or she will remember you favorably, and will be even more eager to help you next time. So saying a heartfelt "Thank You Very Much" isn't just good manners, it is good policy.

> *Make long-term goals. Know what you're working toward—have a reason for working so hard. Take some child development training so you can deal appropriately with your children when under stress. Know your resources before and during school—know who and what will get what you want. Have people to rely on (for social interaction, to watch your kids when you need it). Know it's going to be hard. Talk to others about what it is like and what they do to cope.*

Plan A, B, C, D, E . . .

You can start planning the "ideal" journey through college for you and your children. Then set your sights for that ideal. Remember, though, to always have one or more backup plans ready in case your first ideal choice doesn't work out. For example, you should probably apply for admission to more than one college, and choose two or three higher-paying careers that would be acceptable to you. You should check out several child-care centers, and be willing to put your child(ren)'s name(s) on several waiting lists.

It will help you a great deal during college if you *always* have a "plan B" waiting to be implemented if *any* "plan A" doesn't work out for some reason. If you always have a second or third choice ready, you won't be tempted to simply give up!

Specific Questions to Ask

On the following pages are some specific questions you'll need to ask on the phone or in a letter when trying to get information from people about going to school. Some of the answers to these questions can be found in the college's yearly publications or social services literature which they can send you in the mail. Check publications first; if you can't find enough answers, then ask.

Admissions Office

1. What do I need to do to get admitted to your school?
2. Do I need to take any tests? Do you need my high school or former college transcripts?
3. Can I enroll as a nontraditional student because I have been out of school for _____ years?
4. What are the deadlines for admission?
5. Where is your office located on campus? Hours open?
6. Can you mail me the materials I need to fill out?
7. My family has a very low income. Can your office waive any application fees?
8. Where can I get a course catalog that lists all the offerings throughout the year? How much does it cost?

9. Should I attend a new-student orientation meeting? When are they held throughout the year?

Financial Aid and Awards Office

1. What kinds of financial aid are available to people in my situation? Can you mail me all the information you have?
2. Can you mail me the forms I will need to complete?
3. What are the deadlines for completing these forms, and when can I expect that my financial aid package will be ready?
4. Do you know of other sources of aid that I might be eligible for? Are there any scholarships especially for single parents?
5. Where is your office located on campus? Hours open?
6. What kinds of proof will I need to give you about my financial status? What receipts or statements will I need to have for your review?
7. May I come in to talk with a financial aid advisor about my particular situation? May I make an appointment, or do you take walk-ins?
8. What are some alternatives that your school offers instead of taking out a large number of loans?

College Nontraditional Student Center or Women's Center

1. Are there any special programs, groups, or services for single parent students on your campus?
2. How do I get involved in a support group?
3. How can I find other single parents to talk to and make friends with?
4. Where are the bulletin boards on campus on which I may put up a flyer?
5. Do you know any persons in offices on campus who are aware of the special needs of single parent students? Is there an ombudsman on campus?
6. Is there a family housing complex on campus? Is there an on-campus child care center? How do I apply?

College Academic Advising Center

1. Do I need to make an appointment with someone in your office if I ever need help, or can I just drop in?
2. What are this school's policies regarding academic probation?
3. What kind of grade point average do I need to hold to stay in good standing?
4. Can I get some help in planning my course of study?
5. I'm undecided about a major—how can I get more information to make an informed decision?
6. Does your office offer career planning, or is there another center on campus which offers career counseling services? Can I get some help before I'm formally admitted?

College Registrar's Office

1. When do I need to pay tuition?
2. If I pay my tuition late, is there a late fee?

3. What hours is your office open? Can I pay tuition and fees by mail?
4. How do I register for classes?
5. How do I add or drop classes before and after the quarter or semester starts?
6. What is this school's policy on withdrawls or incompletes taken in courses?
7. How many credit hours is a full load? A half load?
8. Can I pre-register by mail or phone?

Campus Bookstore

1. What days and hours is the bookstore open?
2. When can I buy my books for the upcoming quarter/semester?
3. If you don't have a book that I need, can I special-order it?
4. What are your buy-back policies?
5. Do you have used books that are less expensive for required classes?

Social Services Office

1. How will we develop a plan for my education, training, and employment?
2. Will going to college affect any aid I receive from social services?
3. How will various kinds of financial aid affect what I receive from social services now? Are there other kinds of help I may be eligible for when I enter school? Please tell me what kinds of aid will affect other kinds.
4. Can you give me a list of community resources that will help me and my family as I attend college?
5. How can I apply to receive day-care subsidy money? Is there a waiting list for this aid for people who wish to enter long-term training programs (college)?
6. Will I be required to register for work under the JOBS program?
7. What forms will I need to fill out for your office in order to get or continue to get aid?
8. Can you mail me a list of licensed day-care providers in my area or close to the college? Do you have any information about after-school programs for my older children?
9. Will I be required to enroll in a particular course of study, or will I be required to declare a major immediately upon entering?
10. May I make an appointment to come in and talk with a caseworker about possible roadblocks to my education?

Those are just the most basic questions for which you'll need the answers at the beginning, and you'll find that you'll need to ask more along the way that pertain to your particular set of circumstances. You'll run into snags and stressful situations sometimes when you're trying to get information; when you do, use those situations as opportunities to use your brains and diplomacy to gather the facts you need. Fine tune your skills; they will serve you well.

> *Is this a time of major upheaval in your life? Did you just become a single parent, just break up, or are you currently having severe financial problems? My advice is to wait and let the dust settle, improve your parenting skills, and ease into school. School can be stressful even if your life is totally together. But if your life is unstable, you decrease your chances for a successful adventure in school.*

A Trial Run of What College Will Be Like

At this point, if you're not already in college, you may want to try an experiment. To get an idea of what you will be required to do in school and how it will feel, do all of the following during one month:

Check out three large books from your public library on subjects you want to learn something about (no fiction allowed). Then, for the next two weeks, require yourself to study ten pages per day out of each of the three books. That's thirty pages a day in all, adding up to an average light two week's worth of work in college. Delegate your time, and be flexible. Think of creative ways to get all the reading done. Try to remember what you read. Rehearse it in your mind when doing routine household tasks.

During the third week, write a five-page theme paper or essay on one of the subjects you read about. If you don't know how to write such a paper, check out a book on how to do it from your local public library. Type your paper, revise it, then type it again. Then, choose another subject you read about, put that book away, and write down all the major points you remember from your reading. Do the above in one week.

At the end of the three-week period, in week four, evaluate how well you think you did, not only in getting the reading and writing done, but in other areas of your life like parenting and household chores. How did it feel? Could you cope pretty well? How did your children react? Did you lose much sleep? Were you motivated to continue and complete all the assignments? Did you think the experiment was stupid or not worth your time? How much of the total assignment did you complete to your satisfaction?

"But! But! But!"—you say you must work during the day or that you're busy with other things? Well, if that is so, it will even better reflect how busy you will be in college—with classes, perhaps a part-time job, and library work. If you don't work right now, and have some "free time" during the day to study, you'll have an easier time doing this experiment.

Now, you probably won't be expert at any of your tasks, and you certainly shouldn't judge how well you might do academically in college life just from those four weeks. After all, it's just an experiment, and the month you choose to do the experiment in might be full of outside problems that interfere with your ability to do it. If that happens, you might want to try doing it again. The experiment will, however, give you a taste for what you will be required to do in school. It will also give you an idea of how you will need to streamline your life in other areas in order to get the school-work done.

Part of the beauty of an experiment like this is that it does test your capacity for self-control and self-monitoring, especially if you have other major demands on your time. No one but you and your kids knows that you have your four-week assignments, and no one but you cares if you do them or not. Well, that's the way it will be in college. You must be self-motivated and self-controlled in order to make it through school, because it is for your benefit, and no one else's, that you are there. Yes, it will benefit your children, and you can do it for them, sometimes—but you must want it for yourself in order to keep up your morale, persistence, and motivation to successfully travel through school.

My advice would be the same as to a person who was not a parent. School is hard and sometimes frantic, but it's not impossible, terrible, or an insurmountable hurdle. A single parent, I would say, has to understand that she/he isn't going to get preferential treatment and really shouldn't want it. I've found it's important to think of myself as a person, as a student, and not just as a mother. Going to school, like going to work, as a single parent poses its own problems, but you have to learn to adjust, to be flexible, and to be strong. Above all you have to love school and truly believe in the benefits of an education. You have to go, not to impress people, or to benefit your child(ren), but for purely selfish reasons—because you want to. Then nothing is too hard.

SPOTLIGHT ON COLLEGE PROGRAMS
Trinity College of Vermont

Trinity College of Vermont has established an innovative educational program. With the help of private contributions and the Fund for Improvement of Postsecondary Education (FIPSE), a federally administered program which granted $60,000 in organizational monies, the college has created the Trinity College Community Service Scholar Program.

The program offers an unusual blend of educational opportunity with work-study experience in community service. It enables single parents who meet academic standards and have demonstrated financial need to receive a college education. Reach-Up, a state-operated program, provides funds for child care, transportation, clothing, and educational expenses such as books. Each student is placed in a service organization closely linked to their academic field of study.

Trinity President Janice Ryan emphasizes the community service aspect of this new program. "This is an extraordinary opportunity for the students and for the community," she says. "It's a once-in-a-lifetime chance for the Trinity Community Scholars to develop career objectives, leadership experience, greater self-esteem, and participation in public affairs."

The program enrolled twelve students in the first year, and seventeen students in the second year. The college has provided over $80,000 in direct aid to students and program support in the first two years. According to Bruce Spector, director of Trinity's Community Service Learning Program, the college works closely with the Vermont State Department of Social Welfare and local nonprofit agencies to match students with community service agencies and provide support throughout the program.

More information from an abstract on the Single Parent Community Service Project:

"In Chittenden County, Vermont, as in the country, there is a growing 'feminization of poverty.' Female-headed households constitute a staggering 85 percent of welfare recipients in Burlington, the largest city in Vermont. Recent welfare reform legislation points to two key elements in helping women break this cycle of poverty: education and community work experience. Increasingly, higher education is seen as a way out of poverty for these single parents. Further, studies have shown that meaningful, productive involvement in community life can lead to enhanced self-esteem and more full participation in civic and social life.

"Benefits of the program will accrue directly to the students involved and to the community. For students, intended outcomes include the development of career and job skills necessary for professional success, development of a positive attitude toward civic and social responsibility, and a continued commitment to community service beyond completion of the program. The community will benefit from a skilled, mature pool of volunteers, an opportunity to train tomorrow's employees, and an opportunity to assist in developing models for peer advocacy and self-help. Beyond these direct outcomes, benefits can be counted in the effect this program can have on the children of those parents involved, on other single parents trapped in poverty, and on the higher education community. The success of this program can help pave the way for similar programs linking service to financial and educational assistance for other low income single parents and their families across the country."

For more information, contact:

Bruce Spector, Director of Community Service
Director, Consortium for Single Parent Scholarship
Mercy Hall / 208 Colchester Avenue / Trinity College
Burlington, Vermont 05401
(802) 658-0337, ext. 331

3

HOW TO FINANCE YOUR TRIP

You're probably wondering how in the world you could afford to go to college, since lack of money is such a major problem for most single parents. You might be divorced and receive child support payments only sporadically, if at all. You might work, but at a low-paying job with no health insurance or other benefits. You might rely on the social/human services (welfare) system to help with cash and food and medical bills, but that is definitely not high living—in fact, it's barely surviving.

When you're in those situations, there is usually nothing left over for a thousand and one everyday things that most families take very much for granted. How on earth, then, could you ever afford to go to college? But an even better question might be, "Do you want to go on living this way?" Because you're reading this book, your answer is probably a resounding "*no!*"

School Financial Aid

First, get $3.50 together, and write to Project on the Status and Education of Women (PSEW) for an excellent, very readable publication called *Financial Aid: A Partial List of Resources for Women* (this publication is useful to men, too). In addition to good information about financial aid, it also gives general information on what to look for in a school, different ways to attend school, and getting college credit for what you already know. Their address:

Project on the Status and Education of Women (PSEW)
Association of American Colleges
1818 R Street, NW
Washington, D.C. 20009

(Note: Many of the books the PSEW lists as resources in that publication can be found in your public or college library.) Another publication you'll find useful is free from the federal government, *Federal Student Aid Fact Sheet*, which is updated yearly. Call toll-free for this booklet or for any questions about federal financial aid: 1-800-333-4636, between 9:00 A.M. and 5:30 P.M., Monday through Friday. This booklet covers information about federal aid only; your college financial aid office has information about state and local aid.

Next, contact the financial aid and awards office today at the college or university you hope to attend. Ask for any and all information about the four major kinds of financial aid available to you: scholarships, grants, work-study, and fairly low-interest, repayable loans. Explain your specific situation, briefly, and ask for information on all different types of aid. They can mail most of this information to you, or you may be able to go in person to see a financial aid counselor. Again, you must apply for most types of aid three to nine months or more before you actually begin attending school. If you're already in school, explore alternative ways to get more financial aid.

Information You'll Need to Gather Up

Before you actually apply for financial aid by filling out the forms and going for an interview (maybe not necessary, but desirable), collect a year's worth of your rent receipts, utility bill receipts, tax forms for last year, medical bill receipts, divorce papers, child support decrees, moving expense receipts—anything and everything that pertains to your current financial situation. (You'll need all this and more to apply for social services help, too.) Figure out how much money and other resources you had to live on last year and how much you expect to have this year. Include any wages earned and any support you received or will receive from someone else, such as child support, financial help from parents, any social services aid you already get, and so on for both years, separately.

Now you can complete the financial aid application forms; your school's financial aid office will provide you with all the forms you'll need to fill out. The forms will have spaces for "independent" students—that's you. Don't fill out any information about your parents if you are independent (you don't live with them, and they don't list you as a dependent on their tax forms). Before you start filling out financial aid application forms, though, ask the financial aid office if there is a workshop at your school on how to fill out the forms correctly the first time, and try very hard to attend it. You don't have to be already admitted to the college to attend these workshops. It will cost you irretrievable time if any parts are incorrectly filled out or you've missed something. It's your responsibility, not the school's or the government's, to fill out the forms correctly and completely, then turn them in on time, to maximize your chances for getting as much financial aid as possible.

[Our local] student assistance program's (Canada) mentality is geared towards an eighteen-year-old student, both parents living, attending school away from home and living in-residence. On their [loan] forms they keep asking about parents' bank accounts, place of residence, and so forth. If you leave them blank they return the form. I long to be really facetious and put down my cat as next-of-kin—Mr. Silvester Katz looks kind of good, doesn't it!

Deadlines, Deadlines

Find out early on when the deadlines are for your particular school for completion of all the forms, and draw a big red circle on your calendar to remind you. Try to get the forms sent in well in advance of the due date. Most financial aid is "first come, first served," and available funds do run out, particularly grants and work-study funds—nonrepayable money that everybody wants. Remember, you will need to fill out the same financial aid application forms each year you are in school, and get them in on time. Aid is allotted yearly.

Changes in the Way Need Is Calculated

In the late 1980s, one major federal change was made in the way financial need and benefits are calculated. No longer can financial aid offices consider your children's day-to-day living expenses as part of your expenses or needs while you attend college. The only expense related to children which can be counted is the cost of child care you must pay while you are in college. This was noted as a "devastating" change for independent single parent students by one college financial aid director in Montana.

Nevertheless, you can still obtain enough financial aid to cover your tuition, books, supplies, *your* living expenses, and part of your child care costs. Any remaining needs can be met by working part time and/or by using social services help. You'll need to discuss your family's financial needs with both your financial aid office or counselor at your college, and your local social services caseworker, if you think you'll need social services assistance. You may need to go back and forth between those offices a few times in order to apply for and receive as much assistance as possible.

Getting Individual Help from the Financial Aid Office

Each financial aid office has some "professional leeway" in the way they can calculate your complete financial aid package. (Federal policies and rules are universal and do not vary from state to state or school to school.) There is no leeway, for example, in the distribution of federal Pell grants, but there is some leeway in the distribution of Perkins loans, work-study funds, and supplemental grants. Go in person to see a financial aid officer at your school, explain your special circumstances, and ask for his or her expertise in helping you design the best package of aid possible.

Also, persistence here is again very necessary on your part. You may be quoted rules and regulations (especially federal rules). Ask for alternatives. Be willing to compromise. Be willing to work for what you get. Be ready to explain the situation, in detail, to more than one person. Ask politely but firmly to speak to people higher up if you are not satisfied with the help or answers you get, no matter what situation you are in. Stay with it until you have explored every avenue open to you. The earlier you do all these things, the better, because financial aid offices at schools do run out of money to disperse, and no matter how worthy or deserving or poor you are, they may not be able to help you unless you apply for aid well in advance of all deadlines.

Again, be aware that some schools (due to increasingly tight budgets) have very few financial aid workers and counselors, and even less time to help individual students. This is immensely frustrating to someone like you who really needs all the information and advice you can get. Don't let this circumstance stop you from applying for aid. Find out when the financial aid counselors *are* available, and go talk to one of them, if it is at all possible. Do not go during the two to three weeks before each semester or quarter starts; that is when the office is busiest. Pick a less busy time, say around the middle of a quarter or semester. A particularly busy time is the month or so before the new school year starts in the fall. You'll get much better service and many more answers and possible alternatives to finance your education if you go talk to them when things are less hectic.

Work-Study Money

Aside from grants and loans, one type of self-help aid in which you might be particularly interested is called "work-study." Work-study means you can get a job on-campus (usually) where your employer pays a small fraction (one-fifth) of your salary and the government pays the rest as part of your financial aid package. (Off campus non-profit employers now must pay one-half of your salary, while the government pays the other half.) A work-study job will give you more money to live on. As of this book's printing, work-study money will not be counted against an AFDC grant, but may be counted against food stamps. Still, you'll end up with more total resources.

Twenty hours work a week is all you are allowed to labor on a work-study program during the school sessions. You may work full time during the summer, though, if you don't take classes then. In addition, most work-study employers are very flexible and willing to work around your class schedule. One of the best things about a work-study job is that you can often find one in your field of interest. The job will help you to learn more about your chosen field. It will give you first-hand experience of what it may be like to be a professional in that area. It also helps you to be able to say later to a potential employer that you did work while you were in school, and kept your skills up and learned new ones while gaining invaluable on-the-job experience. You'll have something besides courses taken to put on your résumé.

One of the biggest drawbacks, though, of having a job (work-study or not) is that working will cut into library and study time that you otherwise might have during the day. It is a trade-off of time and money. Which do you need more? When you fill out your financial aid application forms, mark "yes" to the question that asks you if you want work-study assistance, even if you're not sure right now. You can always change your mind later, and the work-study money that was tagged for you will just go to someone else who needs it.

Other Sources of Financial Information and Help

It is useful in your quest for money to call or write to organizations in your area to see if any offer scholarships or grants to people in your situation. Libraries also have books that list national organizations that give financial aid. Your local chapter of the American Businesswomen's Association (ABWA), Society for Women Engineers, Lions's Club, and so on, are all possibilities for some kinds of help. Any professional organization or service society in the Yellow Pages of your phone book may have a college fund. In addition, go to your public library and ask the librarian to help you find a publication that lists local foundations. Some of these may offer financial aid to folks like you. Ask if your financial aid office at the college publishes a list of private or public organizations that offer money for college. If it doesn't, call your state government's higher education office (your college would have their number) and ask if someone there is aware of possible helping organizations in your area. See also the reference list at the end of this chapter.

You may also be eligible for some special types of state or federal aid if you are handicapped (emotionally or physically), a member of a racial or ethnic minority, a veteran of the armed forces, have been laid off a job recently and need retraining, and so on. Be sure to give your financial aid office counselor as much specific information about yourself as you can, and include the information in a letter attached to your financial aid application. Make sure that the people who calculate and distribute financial aid know as much about you and your financial situation as possible.

Borrowing Money, or the "L" Word (for Lousy, Lethal Loans)

You probably won't be able to get through school without borrowing some money. My strong advice to you is to borrow as little as humanly possible—go without rather than go into debt. Each year you will be given a financial aid "package" from your school's financial aid office after the staff processes all the information about your case. These days, up to half or more of your total financial aid may consist of loans—the dreaded "L" word! Beware, beware! Did you know that college students in the United States borrowed a collective total of $1.5 billion in the academic year of 1970-71, but borrowed over $10 billion in the school year of 1985-86? Increasing cutbacks in Federal nonrepayable student aid (grants, work-study) student aid is partially responsible for this rise in student debt.

Do not meekly accept the offered package without exploring with your financial aid counselor some alternatives to borrowing, especially if you discover that a large part of your aid comes in the form of loans. It may be much better for you to work part time, take fewer classes, take longer to get through school, and borrow less money. Can you qualify for a work-study job? Could you borrow some money from relatives interest-free? (Be aware that this may carry its own set of problems.) Can you get your employer to pay for part of your college costs? The only way you can lower your debt load through school is to contact as many people as you can find to get options for financial aid.

For example, the *College Cost Book*, from the College Scholarship Service (probably available in your local public library or the college library) lists eighty-seven colleges (as of 1986) that offer tuition or fee waivers for adult students, and ninety that waive tuition for the unemployed or children of unemployed workers. It lists ninety-one colleges that waive tuition for minority students.

> *Money is very high on my list of problems and relates to other problems such as stress and anxiety as well as leading to depression. I have learned to live on a very minimal income. Unfortunately, due to the lack of income such things as clothes, school supplies, and dentist bills, etc., for my daughter were purchased through credit cards. Bad mistake! My credit card bills are quite high and are leading me further and further into debt. I have, however, cut up all my cards to stop future debt. On top of that is the fact that through student loans I will owe the government $35,000 by the time I graduate. This is adding a lot of pressure to finding work that will pay enough to allow me to pay back my loans.*

Several schools have tackled the problem of their students borrowing too much money for school by offering programs that help students obtain extra grant aid or jobs, including: Cornell University, Swarthmore, Guilford (North Carolina) Technical Community College, Berea College, University of Minnesota, State University of New York at Brockport, University of Vermont, University of Pennsylvania, and many more.

When One Kind of Aid Affects Another Kind

Be aware that getting some kinds of financial aid through your college or private organizations can affect the kind and amount of aid you get from your local social services department, and vice versa. For example, receiving federal financial aid (Pell grants, work-study) can reduce or eliminate any food stamps you might otherwise get, but it won't affect the amount of your AFDC or ADC grant. If you receive a state subsidy for child care while you're in school, your college financial aid office probably won't offer you any money from their end to help pay for child care. The idea is to not overlap aid already provided.

Your goal, though, is to maximize the amount of aid you can receive from all sources to help you through school. You will automatically be given just a minimum necessary amount of aid, because there are so many people who need it and budgets are tight. So, you must be willing to expend a great deal of time and effort at this, long before you even begin college, or before every new school year. No one automatically offers you information about how to maximize the amount of help you can get. You must be a little smarter and more persistent than the next person to learn about everything you can get, how you can get it, and how you can keep it.

> *The red tape between the college financial aid and county social services offices takes forever to go through just to get an answer to a simple question.*

Still More Sources of Help

You should also contact the women's center, mature students' center, or nontraditional students' center at your school for information they may have on little-known kinds of aid, scholarships, and grants. They might know something a financial aid office counselor doesn't, or they may even offer small grants or scholarships out of their own offices. You can also contact your local office of the Displaced Homemakers Network. They are very helpful when you're beginning to sort through information about going to college. Contact the national headquarters to get the address and telephone number of the office closest to you:

Displaced Homemakers Network
1411 K Street, N.W.
Suite 930
Washington, D.C. 20005
(202) 628-6767

For more help on finding enough school financial aid, consult the following books as well as the references at the end of this chapter:

Working Your Way Through College: A New Look at an Old Idea
Pamela Christoffel
Washington, D.C.: The College Board, 1985

Financial Aids for Higher Education
Oreon Kessler, Editor
Dubuque, Iowa: William C. Brown Company
Updated biennially

Mortgaged Futures: How to Graduate from School Without Going Broke
Marguerite J. Dennis
Washington, D.C.: Hope Press, 1986

The College Cost Book
The College Scholarship Service
New York: The College Board, 1991

Social Services Aid

First, let me tell you a little bit about contemporary social services and single parent college students. This might best be done by providing you with some excerpts from the the Family Support Act of 1988 and the Federal Register (federal rules regarding the new JOBS program now in place in each state are explained in more detail further on) having to do with higher education for "welfare" recipients.

In 1988, the Family Support Act (Public Law 100-485) was passed, and planning and implementation of the Act's federal JOBS program was begun. This JOBS program replaced the old "WIN" (work incentive) program on October 1, 1990, and all states began to implement their JOBS programs as of that date.

Under the JOBS program, individual states are required by the federal government to provide certain basic educational/training services and job-obtaining support to able-bodied people on welfare with children above a certain age, usually three years (this age varies from state to state, and may be as low as one year). Under this program, states are allowed to decide whether some college or university schooling will be allowed for those receiving social services aid.

Specifically, the Family Support Act says, in part:"An Act to revise the AFDC program to emphasize work, child support, and family benefits, to amend Title IV of the Social Security Act to encourage and assist needy children and parents under the new program to obtain the education, training, and employment needed to avoid long-term welfare dependence, and to make other necessary improvements to assure that the new program will be more effective in achieving its objectives." The act also states: ". . . if the parent or other caretaker relative or any dependent child in the family is attending (in good standing) an institution of higher education (as defined in section 481 (a) of the Higher Education Act of 1965), or a school or course of vocational or technical training (not less than half time) consistent with the individual's employment goals, and is making satisfactory progress in such institution, school, or course, at the time he or she would otherwise commence participation in the program under this section, such attendance may constitute satisfactory participation in the program (by that caretaker or child) so long as it continues and is consistent with such goals." That last paragraph means that if you are already in college when you apply for social services aid or become a mandatory JOBS participant, you may already be fulfilling the requirements of your local JOBS Program, and can get some aid, particulary child care funding and help with the cost of transportation to and from school—probably. You'll have to ask about funding availability for "self-initiated" students, students who enter(ed) college without the suggestion coming from social services. This is very important.

The additional information below is quoted directly from the final rules of Title II of the 1988 Family Support Act in the Federal Register, Volume 54, Number 197, Friday, October 13, 1989:

> We interpret the language of section 482(d)(1)(B)(i) of the [Family Support] Act to mean that the offering of postsecondary education is an entirely optional matter for the State IV-A agency to address in its JOBS plan, except that we have limited such education to that which is directly related to the attainment of an individual's employment goal, i.e., to obtain useful employment in a recognized occupation. Within this occupational limitation, the State IV-A agency must set forth in its State JOBS plan the bases upon which it will determine whether postsecondary education is appropriate.
>
> We believe that the restriction of postsecondary education to education related to the goal of obtaining useful employment in a recognized occupation is consistent with the intent of the JOBS program. The program's aim to reduce long-term welfare dependence would not be served by permitting a JOBS participant to embrace the broader, more general educational goals that also fall within postsecondary education but that have a less well-defined occupational connection.
>
> While we do not prohibit the use of JOBS funds for this activity, we are concerned about the potential cost. Thus, we encourage States to use resources that are otherwise available to fund postsecondary education for JOBS participants. A State should consider the wide range of other, in some cases less well-funded, components which must be included in its JOBS program when determining whether to fund postsecondary education as well as the fact that most welfare recipients are considerably more educationally needy and less able to support their families than those who are ready to enter postsecondary education. We will monitor State expenditures in this area for the purpose of determin-

ing the extent to which investment in postsecondary education for JOBS participants produces more beneficial returns, such as longer-term self-sufficiency, than are produced by other levels of education or training.

We are maintaining our original position that the relationship of postsecondary education to the participant's employment goal is consistent with the intent of JOBS. While we concur that broader, less job related education can provide skills related to employability, we believe that a specific occupational linkage more readily assures that the postsecondary education will lead to the employment goal that the Act requires to be part of each participant's employability plan.

That means that if your state has decided to allow people receiving social services assistance (mostly AFDC) to go to college, clients must be in a program of study that will prepare them quite directly for a job. Therefore, you probably won't be able to major in philosophy, English literature, dance, physical education (unless you want to teach those subjects and jobs are available) and other areas that are difficult to directly connect with an available occupation when you graduate.

Becoming Your Own Advocate

Here is some more information that you might find useful to bring up in conversations with caseworkers when you act as your own advocate in trying to attend college *and* receive some social services aid.

For example, the Labor Department has made the projection that between now and the year 2000, "For the first time, half of the new jobs will require a post secondary education" and that jobs will require "higher levels of analytical, problem-solving, and communications skills." In addition, in 1986, the typical single parent female under thirty years old with a high school degree but no post secondary education earned just $3,200. In contrast, single mothers who were graduates of four-year college programs had median earnings of $16,000 in 1986, five times more than the high school graduates.

In "Widening Horizons by Degrees," an article by Douglas North, president of Prescott College in Arizona, that appeared in the Fall 1989 issue of *Public Welfare*, we read, "Single parents in short-term job placement programs often fail to achieve self-sufficiency; those who lack education and employment skills quickly return to the AFDC rolls. Oregon recently found that half of the 15,000 AFDC recipients it places in minimum-wage jobs each year return to AFDC within one year, and nearly 75 percent reappear on the welfare rolls within two years."

If you want to attend a college or university, to gain the kind of education that will truly enable you to become self sufficient, you will have to be your own advocate within the social services system; that is, you will have to stick up for yourself. I strongly advise you to not set your sights too low about the kind of career you want. Even though you might not be able to get the education or training for the ideal kind of career you want right now, you will be able to choose something that will pay you a good wage when you've completed some post-secondary education. You'll need to prepare for a career that will pay you between $10 and $15 an hour, with health insurance, for you to be able to support your family and remain completely independent of social services. Remember that when you plan your career and the education you'll need to get it. (Keep in mind that most states' so-called welfare-to-work programs that previously helped people get off welfare only managed to help single parents get jobs that paid an average of $5.50 an hour—peanuts!)

Before You Talk with a Social Services Caseworker

There are several things you should do *before* you talk with a social services caseworker about help for college. First, you need to find out all you can about financial aid that is available through your college, and be willing to apply for all the types of financial aid that is available to you. Don't expect your social services office to pay your tuition and other such expenses directly related to college attendance; most states need to use their federally-matched JOBS money to help other low-income people simply learn how to read and write, or to learn English if they're immigrants. You can expect, however, that social services may provide help with your child care and transportation costs.

Tell your caseworker that you know that current student financial aid programs can help low-income people like you with tuition, fees, books, supplies, and other costs of college attendance, at no additional cost to the state. In addition, many college and university services, such as career and academic counseling, job placement services, internships, and many other kinds of support services, are also available to assist you. This decreases your dependence on the same kinds of services that your local social services office would have to provide if you weren't in college. Remind your caseworker that state funds pay for only one fourth of your total costs of child care and transportation, with federal matching funds under the JOBS program covering the rest.

Second, you'll need to sit down and figure out how much money (or resources) you and your children will need to live on during your time in school. Be conservative. Figure in the cost of school, rent, food, medical care, transportation, child care, and so on. You might want to ask the college's finanical aid office for their estimate of yearly expenses for a family the size of yours when the parent is in college. They will have good estimates of the expenses you can expect, but might not count in your children's day-to-day living expenses, unless you ask them. Make sure *all* expenses are included.

Third, you will need to investigate and then decide on the kind of job you want to get after your college education, preferably before you ever talk to your caseworker about college. If you read the rules of the Family Support Act carefully in the paragraphs above, you will have discovered that post-secondary education is okay as long as it leads to "useful employment in a recognized occupation." If you have a pretty good idea about what you want to be when you grow up, you're ahead of the game. If you don't, contact your local college's career advising or career placement office, or at least go to the library and get specific information on each kind of job you are interested in. An excellent source of information on different jobs and careers and what they typically pay is the three-volume set of *The Encyclopedia of Careers and Vocational Guidance*, edited by William E. Hopke. More books on careers are listed in this guidebook's bibliography. Take specific information you find from those books with you when you talk with your caseworker. Write down information such as what the job pays, the hours it requires, skills that are necessary, and so on. Before you ever go in to talk with a social services caseworker, it's best to have a clear idea about just what job you want, what it will pay, and what kind of education it will take to get it. Remember, earning $10 to $15 an hour, with health insurance, is your goal.

A job that pays $10 an hour will earn you about $19,200 (before taxes) in a year. Some examples of careers that will pay starting salaries of about that much, on average, are: advertising copy writer, agricultural scientist, bank officer trainee, biological scientist, business administrator, medical records administrator, medical technologist, occupational therapist, police officer, postal clerk, radiation therapist, public accountant, accountant, chemist, computer programmer, economist, FBI agent, hospital dietician, college instructor, librarian, physician assistant, psychologist, or speech pathologist.

Think about the future! According to a major banking/lending institution in the western United States, the income a family needs to have in order to qualify for an average $80,000 home is about $32,000 a year, *minimum*. In any case, the most your house payment could be according to banking regulations is 29 percent of your gross (before taxes) monthly income. Furthermore, when buying a home, you must be spending only 41 percent of your total income for all debts, including a house payment, student loans, credit cards, car payments, and so on. That leaves 59 percent for food, clothing, medical, transportation, recreation, and other expenses.

So, although a $20,000 per year job will allow you to support a small family, you'll need to move up in your profession and earn in the low to mid thirties in order to afford to buy your own home someday (that figure will, of course, go up as years pass). So, be sure to become educated for the kind of career that will provide you with upward mobility, salary increases, and a good opportunity for advancement. Once again, don't set your sights too low.

Assert Yourself

If for some reason you find that you just can't do the three things that were suggested in the preceding paragraphs (find out about financial aid, determine the resources your family needs, and have a good idea of the kind of career you want and need) be willing to discuss those issues with your caseworker the very first time you go in. Bring up those subjects; let your caseworker know that you know what is expected of you, and talk intelligently with him or her about possibilities. Be assertive about your desires, but be willing to compromise, at least a little bit. At the very least be flexible.

If, however, a caseworker tells you that you already are skilled enough to become employed (for example, you could be a clerk, secretary, waitress, ditch digger, etc.) you must be willing to fight like the dickens to be able to go to college and get social services aid. You can't raise your family on minimum wage, or even a wage that is much below $10 an hour. Stick up for yourself and your children. If you have extreme difficulty convincing your caseworker that college is necessary, and the doors just seem to be slamming in your face, you have several options. Call your local ACLU office, legal aid society, college administrators, or any other person or organization that may support your efforts. Ask for a "fair hearing" at your social services office, and gather up as much information as you can that will back up the necessity of a college education for your family's self-sufficiency and eventual complete independence from social services aid.

> *Money has been a problem (lack of it). But I found I was eligible for ADC, so that has made all the difference, believe me. I had been living with my sister and her family, and it became impossible to stay—so I knew I had to move, but didn't know how I'd ever pay for my own place. ADC was the answer. I'll be using it for a total of 5 ½ months.*

Almost any profession, from school teacher to social worker to engineer, computer programmer to biologist, takes at least a four-year college education. Almost all decent-paying jobs that also offer health insurance require a college education, and not just a two-year associate degree. Unfortunately, federal regulations are set up so as to discourage the state social services offices from providing you with complete JOBS assistance (for books, fees, supplies, materials, child care, transportation, and other expenses) through a full four-year program of study that will get you a bachelor degree, and no states offer help for graduate study for single parents at this time. With our increasingly technological society, it has been said that a two-year (associate degree or certificate) college education is now worth about what a high school diploma used to be worth. There you have it.

In short, you should certainly apply for the type and amount of social services aid you are eligible for while in college, but you must plan very carefully and discuss options with your caseworker if you need to go to college for four years to become educated for the kind of job you need. About half of the states will offer assistance for four years, and about half will offer assistance for only two years.

Types of Social Services Aid

So, if you have a low income (and few single parents don't fit in this category) you can probably apply for and get various forms of social services aid for at least part of the time you are in school. The major type of aid from social services for single parents is ADC (Aid to Dependent Children) or AFDC (Aid to Families With Dependent Children). There is a flat base rate of payment for a family of a given number of people, and the amount varies from state to state depending on each state's resources and budgets. To apply for this, you'll need to go in person to your local social services office and fill out numerous forms. You'll need to prove your income level (through receipts, divorce papers, child support decrees, check stubs, and so forth). You'll probably need to provide social security numbers for each of your children. You'll need to see a social services caseworker and explain your circumstances. All this will take time. If you're not currently in college and don't get any social services aid, you should do those things well before you start school if you think you'll need to use social services aid while in college.

You will be advised of your eligibility or ineligibility for help within a period of a few days to a few weeks after you apply. Usually, if you're poor enough, you can get ADC or AFDC (the social services office will then keep any child support payments you would otherwise get, unless they are larger than your AFDC grant). You might get food stamps, medical assistance (Medicaid), energy assistance, a day-care subsidy, and help with transportation. (See Appendix A for social services administrators' answers to my questionnaire for an idea of what exactly is available in your area for single parent college students, how states can differ from one another, and a general idea of the way single parents and single parent students are viewed by such agencies.)

Possible Problems with Social Services

If you go to your local social services office and you are told that you can't go to college and receive social services aid because it is against federal regulations (by a new or uninformed caseworker), you can refer him or her to this statement in the Family Support Act:

> The State may also offer to participants under the program (i) post secondary education in appropriate cases, and (ii) such other education, training, and employment activities as may be determined by the State and allowed by regulations of the Secretary.

So, if your state social services office doesn't offer much help to single parent college students, it's because the state decided they couldn't afford it or it wasn't a desirable activity—*not* because the federal government said they couldn't under the new JOBS program. All states, however, allow some post-secondary education under their JOBS programs, and most allow at least two years' worth. You must be your own advocate, though, when dealing with social services, and have as much information as possible (like the information from the Family Support Act) before you go in for a discussion.

In addition, if at any time you don't understand something a caseworker tells you, you are well within your rights to ask for additional information, written rules and regulations, and a full explanation of your rights and responsibilities as far as their office is concerned. Stand up for yourself.

> *Many social service people are openly contemptuous of those of us on AFDC who are going to school, especially because I am going to a private college. They think I'm getting a "free ride"—but I'm graduating with $8000 in loans to repay. I've been lucky to have an understanding financial worker who doesn't hassle me. I wish they'd go after my ex-husband for more support. He works part-time and pays $50 a month—why doesn't someone push him to do a better job of supporting his children?*

"They" Want You Off Welfare Soon

Remember that obtaining AFDC *before or after you start school* puts you on a list of people to "help" through the state-administered federal JOBS program. This means your name will go into the computer and you will be targeted to become "self-sufficient." In other words, you may be required or encouraged by your local social services office to obtain employment or short-term job training in order to get an entry-level job and get off assistance, quickly.

Talk with your social services caseworker about your plans for college. Ask if it is possible to go through your desired program of study at a college or university for the amount of time it will take to earn your degree, and still get enough aid from social services to help you through. Again, you may need to ask for a "fair hearing" at your local social services office, and provide written documentation and witnesses who will support your goals for long-term education and success. Or, there may be *another* way around the rules and regulations.

You might be able to apply for social services aid *just for your children* (taking yourself off an AFDC grant, for example), taking less social services aid. This would enable you to make your own choices about school and your career future. Ask your caseworker if this is a possibility—you probably will not be informed about it unless you ask. Explore your options! Like my favorite Star Trek character, the one with the pointy ears, says, "There is always an alternative!"

Energy Assistance Aid—"HEAT"

Another type of aid you may qualify for (even if you don't use social services aid now) is government energy assistance money (HEAT) to help you pay fuel bills (gas, electric, wood, or coal heating) during the winter. You don't have to be on public assistance to get this, but your income must be low enough. Receiving AFDC, though, automatically qualifies you. You must apply for the energy assistance at your local social services office; even though you receive AFDC or other kinds of help, you won't get the HEAT help unless you specifically ask for it.

Payments are usually made in one lump sum, and will help you heat your home in the winter. The payment will help, but it won't cover the total cost. Apply during the first week the application process is opened, probably in late fall or early winter. The money does run out. This is one of those programs that no one may tell you about. It is in effect during the winter months—no money is offered to air condition your home during the summer!

Rent Subsidies

There is another aid program that can subsidize your rent if your income is very low. Call your local Housing Authority office (look it up under your city or county government pages in the phone book, or ask the social services office for the number). Be aware that there is probably a waiting list for this kind of help, but it's worth it to get on the list as quickly as you can. There are a couple of programs that you may qualify for. One subsidizes the amount of money you pay for rent at a place you choose to live; another offers you the chance to live in a subsidized housing complex for reduced rent. These housing complexes may or may not be close to your school. Ask about both programs.

More Social Services Aid and Other Kinds of Help

There will be several federal, state, local, or private programs in your area for which you may qualify while you are in school. Call your local Information and Referral agency and/or your local social services office for specific information on the ones in your locality. Some of them I've mentioned already, some you'll find mentioned later in this book:

AFDC—Aid to Families with Dependent Children
Food stamps
Medicaid

Utilities and fuel help—"HEAT"
Weatherization Program
Housing Outreach Program
Housing and Financial Counseling

WIC—Women's, Infants, and
  Children's food program
School Lunches and Breakfast
  (children)
Summer Food (children)
Emergency Food (families)
Medical Assistance Only (MAO)

(HUD)
Child Care Subsidy
Legal Services
Legal Aid Society
Government School Financial Aid
County Mental Health Centers

Cheap Booklets to Help You Save Money and More

Another good thing to know is where to send for free or inexpensive booklets (usually between $1 and $5) from the government about all sorts of things, such as "Tomorrow's Jobs," "Handbook on Child Support Enforcement," "Help Your Child Do Better In School," "Higher Education Opportunities for Minorities and Women," "Student Guide—Five Federal Financial Aid Programs," "Dietary Guidelines and Your Diet," "Making Food Dollars Count," "Your Money's Worth in Foods," "Walking for Exercise and Pleasure," "Plain Talk About Stress," "How To Protect Yourself Against Sexual Assault," and many, many more. Write for a free booklet catalog to:

Consumer Information Catalog
Pueblo, Colorado 81009

Challenge and Beat, Don't Cheat, the Social Services System

If you now rely, or are going to rely, on the social services system for help while you're in school, be prepared for some rough roads. As mentioned before, some states only offer assistance (AFDC, child care subsidies, etc.) to single parent college students for two years or less, with no exceptions. This means you will have to either go through a two-year technical or business school, or community college, to gain employable skills, or you will have to depend on other resources during two or three years of a traditional, four-year college or university. (It actually often takes most nontraditional students more than four years to get a bachelor's degree, since most work while they go to school.)

Some states (see Appendix A) with enough resources and enlightened, forward-looking administrators will give social services aid to students like you throughout a traditional four-year degree program. Hurrah for them! I was lucky to live in one of those states.

You'll have to plan very carefully in any case. If you believe that an education program of two years or less will get you what you want in the way of a good job, go for it—then maybe go on to a college or a university later, when your children are older and you don't need help with child care, or when your children are old enough to work and contribute to the family's income. If you truly believe that only a four-year or more program of study to prepare you for a profession now, rather than just a job, is what you want and need and are capable of, regardless of your financial status at the moment, you'll need to talk this over very carefully with your social services caseworker. Certain rules will always apply, and you may or may not be able to circumvent them. Other rules are more flexible, and they may be able to help you get what you want. You must sometimes learn how to beat the system. Start talking with a social services caseworker now about options and alternatives for support for you and your children through school. If you are told that you must "sign up" for your state's JOBS program, do it—and go to college for the maximum allowable amount of time. (A hot tip: social services thinks highly of those who volunteer to participate in the JOBS program, and sometimes funds are made available first to volunteers.)

> *My biggest problem was with social services. When I was separated, I had no job and my ex-husband agreed to pay $400 per month child support. I had moved into a one-bedroom apartment (with two kids) and was paying $185 for rent. I went to social services to apply for help. Because I was just separated and had no legal papers to prove we were officially separated, they treated me like I was there to apply for help while I still had a husband to provide for me. They wouldn't do anything for me until I got a lawyer and had a court order stating what I would get in child support and alimony. Plus, they didn't support any training that requires more than two years of schooling and they also thought that I had enough job training and experience that I could get a "good" enough job to support me and the kids ($5/hour). I was very upset. The day care services were much better. They enrolled me for day care, but they told me that they'd only allow me to be on the program two years—because they also don't accept schooling that requires more than two years.*

Is getting social services aid for a couple of years or more while you get through school worth all the hassle and stress involved? Only you can answer that question. If you learn how to "beat" the system, it will be bearable.

Temptations to Cheat

Now, some people would say that beating the system is the same as cheating the system. I disagree. Beating the system means learning the rules and regulations of any institution, using your powers of investigation and diplomacy, and acting in legitimate and honest ways to get as much benefit as you can possibly get, without stooping to fraud, dishonesty, or cheating. You'll constantly be dealing with honesty, morality, and basic issues of integrity (yours) if you become involved with social services. You'll be coping with power (theirs) and lack of power (yours). If you have had any contact with the welfare system at all, you know that the rules are set up in such a way that they can actually encourage cheating, lying, and the giving of mis-information by clients. I'm sure this wasn't the intent of those who started these major social benefits programs, but it is a negative byproduct of the unwieldy institutions. The system is also set up to punish those who do cheat, but it is often not clear as to how much cheating is really cheating, and when or how you might get caught if you do try to cheat.

If you were raised in a family where integrity, honesty, and rule-follow-ing were major values, you'll probably report everything to everyone you need to report it to, and fill out forms completely and honestly. Doing so, however, will sometimes cause you emotional pain, loss of funds and other resources, and anger at what is all too often an insensitive and truly unjust system. One such example: During her third year in school a single parent student (on AFDC, working part time, and carrying a full load of courses) received a scholarship from a private, outside-of-the-university organization in the amount of $200 per quarter for one school year (a total of $600). This scholarship was based both on need and on achievement. Being the honest, risk-averse soul that student was, she reported receiving this amount of money to both the financial aid office at school and her local so-cial services office. Both offices now counted this money as "income," and she had benefits reduced from both sources. In effect, it was as if she had never received the scholarship at all, because what one organization gave, the other organizations took away by reducing their aid packages! Yes, that student was me, and was I mad! It was very demoralizing.

I share this disturbing story because it illustrates the nature of the sys-tem. I could have really used an extra $200 per quarter (less than $100 a month) for children's school clothing and winter coats, a pair of good walk-ing shoes, car repairs, groceries, extra and sick child care, household items, and countless other things that were really needed and most unfrivolous. The money could have been spent on whatever I or my children needed, as long as it helped me get through school, since the scholarship-giving orga-nization made no stipulations about the particular ways I could spend it. I let this scholarship organization's president know about the situation and my predicament. She was saddened and angry, but was also helpless to change anything. I asked myself back then what might have happened if I had kept the fact of receiving the scholarship money to myself. This is how the system encourages cheating—but you probably already know that.

Even though you may have several similar experiences during your years in school, I still advise honesty in dealing with and reporting to agencies and organizations that you receive financial and other help from. Why? Be-cause morality and integrity notwithstanding, the consequences and costs of cheating outweigh the possible benefits of cheating. You can be cut off from receiving any aid from social services for a certain length of time. You can lose school financial aid. You may become marked as a cheater—even if the system is truly unfair to you, and even if people working in that system recognize that fact. They must work within the rules, too. You could go to jail. Since most if not all of the agencies and organizations you will deal with are now tied together by computers, and your social security number as well as your name is used for identification purposes, the probability of "cheaters" being caught has risen dramatically from what it was even a few years ago.

> *Social services cuts food stamps because of school loans and grants. That means I have to come up with money for food, money I don't have or foresee having. Usually bills are only paid one-half so we have enough for food.*

Getting Your Facts Straight

You will, undoubtedly, face difficult and frustrating financial situations during your time in college. What you must do, then, is find out as much as you possibly can about how the regulations do work. Find out how you may work within the system to maximize the amount of aid you can get from all sources. Get the information in writing. A sad but true fact is that few people volunteer all the information you'll need, as I indicated before. You must persistently inquire about everything. You must be willing to spend enough time on the telephone and in person with workers from all helping agencies you interact with in order to get reliable, concrete, useful information. Write it all down and date it!

Be advised, also, that any information or rules may also change from year to year as federal and state regulations and budgets change. You must ask for current information at least yearly, and it's even better if you give people a call every quarter or semester. You are also perfectly within your rights to ask at any time if the worker thinks anything might change, and when.

You must find out from your local social services office and your school's financial aid office how resources from both places interact, and how they affect each other. Ask what kinds of resources do not affect resources from other places. Ask about hypothetical situations. If you work while you go to college, what will happen? Will work-study money still not be counted against an AFDC grant? Will you lose some daycare assistance if you work? Will you lose food stamps? How much money can you earn and keep it? If you share a house with someone, but don't share income, will you suffer decreases in aid? Regulations may differ from state to state (on nonfederal issues), and you'll need to get all the information about your situation in writing, so that you may refer to it as you need to.

Another example of financial difficulties: A specific problem can arise if you work during the summer and receive AFDC benefits. (Yes, this also happened to me.) You might work full time during all the summers—part of the time at "real," non-work-study jobs. The non-work-study money you earn may then count against the social services aid you receive in the fall (especially AFDC) when classes start, since there is often a two-month lag in the way the social services office calculates benefits.

For example, if you earn money in July and money in August, the income you earn in July would decrease the amount of your AFDC grant you get in September, and the income you earned in August would decrease the amount of your AFDC grant you get in October. The amount of the AFDC money would be substantially reduced during those two fall months, even though you then go back to working only part time when classes start, and actually have a much lower income when starting back in school! In effect, you receive much less money working part time, and much less money from AFDC, for two whole months when classes start again in the fall. In this situation you would not receive a full AFDC grant again until November.

You must plan for circumstances like these and try to save just a little for times when rules and regulations will decrease your income for what seem to be nonsensical and unfair reasons. Fall quarters will probably be the most financially poor ones for you and your family, just because of the way income is calculated by aid offices. This time is especially hard because children need school clothes then, and most of the major holidays with gift giving occur between September and January.

I don't feel that social services (or the public) supports a college education for single parents. They want to get you trained in some skill so you can get off welfare—but they don't want to support you while you get a degree. They feel that a college education is a luxury, something that poor and/or single parents are not entitled to. And how do you change public opinion?

Organizing for Positive Change

Challenge the system by organizing single parent students on your campus. Find others in your situation by advertising with flyers or in the school newspaper. Get sympathetic people in power in the university or college or other locally respected organizations behind you. Or, encourage your college's women's center or nontraditional student center to bring people like you together to start effective changes. Call your local legal aid society to find out if you can challenge the system through litigation. Get the word out, and you'll find support, sometimes in unexpected places.

You and some other single parent students at your college or university might effectively organize together for a few years and educate both social service personnel and financial aid personnel about your circumstances. Your organization may manage to get a better dialogue going between those two organizations (essential if the states' JOBS programs are to work) and better coordination may result. If you continue to challenge the system in your area, it is very possible that more equitable allowances for you and other single parent student families will be possible, and that people like you might actually be able to get a scholarship or two and keep it without penalty!

> *Social services should take us seriously and treat studying for a better future as a truly viable pastime. Be there with help when needed. Crises tend to happen between Friday night and Monday morning.*

You can also challenge the system in individual, subtle ways. If you are having a discussion with any caseworker, and the answers you are getting are not acceptable to you, you may ask to speak with that person's supervisor or another worker. You may find someone who is a little more aware of possibilities or who is more willing to stretch the rules to their very limit in order to get you as much aid as possible. My rule is: "Never take '*no*' as an answer the first time (or even the second time) you talk with anybody!"

Challenge your caseworkers to come up with alternative solutions! Challenge the rules by submitting written complaints to heads of offices and organizations, spelling out in as much detail as possible your circumstances, the rules, and possible alternatives. Ask to see written rules and regulations; you never have to take anybody's word for *anything!* Come up with some creative solutions of your own, and suggest them to people in power. Impress them with your ability to be professional, diplomatic, calm, persistent, and resolute.

Mistakes You Can Make Under Stress

What shouldn't you do in your attempts to challenge and beat the system? The following things don't work, and most of them actually make things worse: crying, screaming, angrily arguing, ranting and raving, giving up, bad-mouthing, cussing, storming into someone's office without an appointment, storming in with an appointment, demonstrating, jumping up and down, blaming, and so on. You get the idea.

The only way to get people in charge of anything to listen to you and become supportive is to be diplomatic, calm, professional, and persistent. Bother them, but bother them politely! (You probably think I'm harping on how you should behave with other people. I probably am, but just because your behavior is so critical when you're not the one with the power.)

The Other Side of the Desk

Always remember that the people on the other side of the desk are just that, people, doing a job. Most aren't out to get you, most aren't out to be unfair. They work within large systems that are slow to change and which usually are not very outwardly responsive to rapidly changing social circumstances. There is an extremely high rate of job turnover in the human service professions, and I believe that many people who leave are just as frustrated as you are because they can't change things fast enough from their side of it, either. They went into their profession because they do care about people!

One of the troublesome side effects of this high turnover rate is that caseworkers and "front-line staff" will change regularly. New people who don't know all the rules and regulations may be trying to help you; therefore, much confusion and many mistakes can result. If you find yourself talking with a seemingly incompetent or uninformed person, ask to speak to an old-timer, someone who's been around for at least a few years and who knows what to do. But realize that sometimes even old-timers can have trouble, since federal and state rules and regulations change often. It can be hard for anyone to keep up with it all and maintain ever-increasing caseloads. Have you ever peeked at a social services book of rules, regulations, policies and procedures? It would be a full-time job to just read it and keep up with all the amendments and changes.

Social services and financial aid workers must work within a system that was set up years ago, long before most single parents even thought about attending universities and colleges. "Welfare" used to be mostly for widows with young children to support, so they could stay home and be mothers without having to be breadwinners, too. Now "welfare" is mostly for young single parents, most of whom are divorced or widowed, but many of whom were never married at all. Social services must try to distribute assistance to more and more people all the time, usually with less and less money allotted to their organization by increasingly conservative political bodies and reluctant taxpayers. If a single parent student hollers at a social services caseworker or financial aid officer, all he or she ends up doing is make it more stressful for the worker and less possible for the person to really help.

Am I defending the system? No, but I am speaking from some small experience from both sides of the desk, now. I know what it is like to need aid, I know what it is like to have to give out aid from a limited amount of resources. In our frustration with "the system" we want to find scapegoats, we want answers faster, we want life to be fairer instantly. It doesn't work that way. It works much more slowly, much more erratically. If you learn anything as a single parent in college, you will learn patience. You will also learn that the world is even less fair than you thought it was! But, you will learn ways of dealing with the world that can maximize the benefits to you and your family as you struggle through college and through the years after you graduate. You will leave school with a fair amount of cynicism, but with enough knowledge and skills to enable you to survive on this imperfect planet.

What Money Goes Where?

Next are some hints to help you more wisely spend the money you have obtained using the suggestions above, and some more forms of help you might not know about. You may also be able to find a course (either at your college or through community education in your area) on money management. If you can take one, it will help you learn how to budget and stay within your very restricted income. If you can't take a course, the following suggestions may help.

First, take care of necessities: groceries, rent, clothing, transportation, medical bills, tuition, and books. You probably won't be able to save any money while you're in school, but you'll usually have enough to get by. Sometimes bills might have to wait a couple of weeks to be paid, but between working, school financial aid, and some help from social services you will be able to afford the necessities of life.

> *I do pay all bills on time, and then I go crazy with any extra money. Usually I feel okay with what I have bought, and yet I know that my spending is a way to give myself temporary pleasure. What works with this is making a list of needs and one of wants, and getting one thing off each list a month.*

Buy your clothes at local thrift shops. Set up (or encourage others to set up) a children's clothes swap at the child care center you will use. Many times children will grow out of clothes that are still good and have a lot of wear left, especially such items as coats, boots, sweaters, shirts, and pajamas.

Don't buy junk food at the grocery store or at school. This includes soda pop, candy, ready-to-eat stuff, and highly processed foods. If you stick to whole grains, lean meats and fish, fresh or frozen vegetables, fruits, and low- or no-fat dairy products, you and your children will enjoy an excellent diet at a lesser cost than if you buy junk food (and you'll all feel better and stay healthier, too!). Try to find a store that has bulk food for sale, and when you have an extra dollar or two stock up on things you always use, such as rice, pasta, and beans. Also, find a refrigerator on campus that you can use—maybe one in your major department's office, a student lounge, or wherever. Then you can pack a good lunch and snacks from home, keep them fresh, and save money.

I recommend that you don't buy anything that is disposable, except of course facial tissues and toilet tissue. Don't buy paper towels, paper napkins, disposable razors, disposable diapers, paper plates and plastic cutlery, etc. Use the rule, "wash, don't toss." This will save you money.

Consider having your milk delivered to your door. I mention this elsewhere, and it may seem like an extravagance, but it really will save you money and time because you won't always be running to the store for milk. (Most dairies that deliver will also bring eggs and other perishables.) When you go to the store "just" for milk, you might end up buying more than that (especially if you're feeling hungry at the moment) and you'll spend more than you should—not to mention bus fare, time to walk, or gas for and wear and tear on your car. It will cost a few extra cents a gallon for this delivery service, but believe me, it's worth it. It's worth your time alone, will spare you endless hassle, and will cut down on "impulse buying."

Find out if there is a food co-op in your area. Religious organizations (for example, Catholic Charities) or women's groups would know about one, as might the student center on campus. You can usually buy wholesome food at lower cost because you supply some labor or other support to the enterprise. You may not, however, have enough time to devote to such an organization while you're taking courses, but you might be able to help out during school breaks or during the summer.

Call your community's local food bank (social services or an information and referral center would have the number) and see if you can get some food from this source if things are really tight or on an emergency basis.

Also, use the age-old barter system. Swap your skills or possessions for those of others. Do you have a sewing machine, and can you fix tears and patch clothes? Do your neighbors lack a sewing machine but know how to change the oil in cars or fix leaky faucets? You could fix their clothes, they could help you maintain your car. When you don't have a lot of money, bartering works great. Exchanging child care is also something to consider, or you may use something else in exchange. Is there a retired person close by who would watch your children for a few hours a week while you study, in return for you cleaning his or her house or doing light repair work? Just because you can't always pay for a sitter doesn't mean you always have to go without. Be creative! Can you put up flyers on campus or at your day-care center or your children's school to find another single parent to swap child care and other activities with? Perhaps someone close by could take care of your children while you go out Friday night, then you could watch his or her kids so he or she can have a break on Saturday night. (You'll need to find someone with about the same number of children and the same number of hours needed so neither of you will feel put-upon or unfairly treated.) If you can find someone with children the same ages as yours, it might even help to have extra kids around to keep yours busy and interested while you catch up with housework or paperwork.

> *What would be really nice is to get together with other single parents with kids the same age as mine, to trade babysitting, allowing the parents to study or have leisure time without expense.*

You can usually sell back most textbooks to the campus bookstore after a course is over for a variable percentage of what you paid for them (usually 50 to 75 percent). This helps you save a little money. However, I do recommend that you keep basic and important texts, especially ones in your major field of study, because you'll need to refer to them later, especially if you are going to be taking a graduate record examination (GRE) for application to a graduate school, if you choose and are able to go on. (Be advised that most social services help is not currently available to graduate students—probably only food stamps are available to this group.)

What are some other things you can do to help make money stretch while you're in school? One of the best things to do is to not isolate yourself. This may seem like it doesn't have a lot to do with saving money, but the more you talk to other people (especially other struggling single parent students) the more information you will gain from them. Maybe they know of a great little discount store somewhere close by, or a new social services program that could help. Maybe they're members of a church that offers some assistance to folks like you. Maybe they know of a car repair shop that does great work for a lot less money, or a discount clothing store you haven't heard of. Talk to people!

It will seem that you never have enough money while you're in school—but you probably don't have enough now, and you wouldn't have enough even if you were working full time at a job because it probably wouldn't pay much. All the financial planning and money management in the world won't change these facts. You and your kids can, however, survive on what you will have for a few years while you're in school, knowing that you won't be this poverty-stricken forever. (You just have to remember this when times get really tough.) I know it seems like forever! I thought my five years in college would never end. But, you know, being in the "poor house" isn't nearly so bad when you know you are smart, motivated, and getting yourself prepared for a career that will boost you out of it.

Selected Resources

American College Testing Program. *Applying for Financial Aid.* Free from:
American College Testing Program
P.O. Box 168
Iowa City, IA 52243

Brunner, S. (undated) *California Student Financial Aid Workbook.* California: California
Student Aid Commission.
Information on applying for aid and evaluating aid from different colleges and universities.

College Board Publications. (1985) *The College Board Guide to Going to College While
Working.*

College Entrance Examination Board. (1983) *Paying for Your Education: Guide for
Adult Learners.* New York. $7.95.
Comprehensive information on how to obtain financial aid, opportunities for part-time study, and comparative shopping for financial aid. Order from:
College Board Publication Orders
P. O. Box 886
New York, NY 10101-0886

Consolloy, P. (Editor) (1981) *After Scholarships, What? Creative Ways to Lower Your
College Costs—and the Colleges that Offer Them.* New Jersey: Peterson's Guides.

Hawes, G.R. (1984) *The College Money Book: How to Get a High-Quality Education at
the Lowest Possible Cost.* Indiana: Bobbs-Merrill.

Higher Education Opportunities for Minorities and Women: Annotated Selections.
(1989). Superintendent of Documents, U.S. Government Printing Office, Washington, D.C., 20402. $4.25, includes postage and handling.

Jawin, A.J. (1979) *A Woman's Guide to Career Preparation: Scholarships, Grants and
Loans.* New York: Anchor Press.
Detailed information on traditional and nontraditional financial aid sources and making career choices.

Leider, A. and R. Leider. (1990-91) *Don't Miss Out: The Ambitious Student's Guide to
Financial Aid.* Alexandria, Virginia: Octameron Associates.

National Science Foundation. *A Selected List of Major Fellowship Opportunities and Aids
to Advanced Education for United States Citizens.* Washington, D.C.: National Science Foundation.
Sources of aid for undergraduate, graduate, and postdoctoral study and a publications list.

Peterson's College Money Handbook. (1991). Gives costs and financial aid information
about the country's 1700+ four-year colleges.

Project on the Status and Education of Women. (1990) *Financial Aid: A List of Resources for Women,* obtainable from the Association of American Colleges, Project on
the Status and Education of Women, 1818 R Street, N.W., Washington, D.C.,
20009. Cost: $3.50 per copy. Checks payable to AAC/PSEW.

Schlachter, G. (Ed.) (1989–90) *Directory of Financial Aids for Women.* Los Angeles:
Reference Service Press.
Scholarships, fellowships, and loans intended primarily or exclusively for women;
women's credit unions; sources of educational benefits; and reference sources on financial aid.

Schlachter, G. (1989-90) *Directory of Financial Aids for Minorities.*
More than two thousand financial programs designed for minorities are listed.
Women's Educational Equity Communications Network.

Educational Finance Aid for Women: An Information Packet. San Francisco: Far West Laboratory for Educational Research and Development.
Ways to finance education.
Mudrick, N.R. (1980) *The Interaction of Public Assistance and Student Financial Aid.* Washington Office of the College Board, Washington, D.C.
Available from: The College Board Publication Orders, Box 2815, Princeton, New Jersey, 08541 ($3.00 Prepaid)
Neglected Women: The Educational Needs of Displaced Homemakers, Single Mothers and Older Women. (1977) National Advisory Council on Women's Educational Programs.

SPOTLIGHT ON COLLEGE PROGRAMS
Ohio State University, Columbus, Ohio

The goals and objectives of the ACCESS Program at Ohio State University are:

1) To provide resources and environmental supports that will enable Black and other underrepresented minority single parents to achieve the undergraduate degree and to find employment suitable to their academic preparation;

2) To increase enrollment and graduation rates of minority students at Ohio State University by examining barriers that prevent full participation in the university for these students;

3) To coordinate a package of university and community support services to meet their needs as students and as heads of households;

4) To help make student and family arrangements that will best support their academic program;

5) To provide a peer-support network to help each other solve their problems and reach their goals;

6) To serve as an advocate, resource, and information source for all single parents who are trying to complete an undergraduate degree at The Ohio State University campus. (Author's note: nonminority single parents are referred to the Women's Program in the Student Life Department for assistance with their problems and needs.)

ACCESS personnel realize that when single parents try to negotiate the university bureaucracy without assistance it can be an overwhelming experience. Therefore, ACCESS personnel maintain frequent contact with the admissions office, financial aid office, child care center, and residence and dining hall offices to ensure that ACCESS participants "receive efficient and the most expeditious care in resolving admission, financial aid, housing, and child care needs."

More information about the ACCESS Program at Ohio State University is taken directly from their pamphlet about the program, September 1989:

The Challenge. America must have a well-educated work force in the twenty-first century if it is to remain competitive in the global marketplace. A critical role of a college education is to help students learn to be adaptable and self-sufficient and to prepare them to meet the challenges of a service-oriented, technology-based society.

For many people, however, a college education is a difficult, if not impossible, goal to obtain. Among them is a growing number of households headed by single parents, especially minorities, who live near or below the poverty line. These single parents often find themselves trapped in entry-level positions and unable to obtain the education and training necessary to advance their employment prospects. They and their children face a constant struggle to build their lives with minimal resources.

Ohio State's Response. The ACCESS Program at The Ohio State University seeks to help minority single parents develop their potential by offering the opportunity to pursue a college education at Ohio State. The purpose of ACCESS is to increase enrollment and graduation rates of minority students at The Ohio State University by examining the barriers that prevent full participation in the University for these students. The program's primary goal is to help students to obtain a coordinated package of University and community support services to meet their needs as students and as heads of households. The program also assists minority single parents in identifying career opportunities compatible with their undergraduate program of study.

How the ACCESS Program Works. The ACCESS Program is open to all minority single parents, both male and female, who have custodial responsibility of their children and have not yet completed an undergraduate degree. Criteria for acceptance into ACCESS include a commitment toward receiving a degree, academic promise, and potential for future success as shown in prior experiences, including leadership, scholarship, or community service. Each participant's family situation is evaluated to determine his or her need for financial aid, child care, family housing, and support systems. Participants also are assisted in making the kinds of student and family arrangements that will best support their academic program. Program participants have access to parent education, child development programs, academic and career development counseling, family life education, and other University support services and resources they need. ACCESS participants also form a peer-support network to help each other solve their problems and reach their goals.

Program Benefits. The obvious beneficiary of this program is the single parent who obtains a college degree and enters a promising career. The parent's children also benefit through the availability of quality child care and family development programs. And having seen their parent succeed in a college environment, they will also be more likely to aspire to college themselves and obtain a degree.

By extension, society as a whole reaps considerable rewards from the ACCESS Program. Because it is designed to increase the proportion of single parents who are college educated, the program will strengthen the labor market and add to the professional, managerial, and technical expertise necessary to support a growing economy. The university will benefit from the diversity that ACCESS participants bring to campus and from their strong motivation to succeed.

Find Out More. You can find out more about the ACCESS Program at Ohio State University by writing or calling:

Dr. Jacqueline Wade, Director ACCESS Program
Office of Minority Affairs
The Ohio State University
115-A Independence Hall
1923 Neil Avenue
Columbus, Ohio 43210
(614) 292-1035

4

RULES AND REGULATIONS

"Tuition must be paid by the end of the second week of the quarter, or a late fee will be added." "Classes can only be added or dropped during the first two weeks of the semester." "You must officially drop any courses you do not wish to take by the second Friday of the quarter or you will be required to pay tuition for them as well as applicable late fees." "If you do not register by telephone, you may register during Late Registration. You must pay a $20 Late Registration service charge." "Students who miss the deadline but who are admitted prior to the end of Telephone Registration should call or visit the Registration Service windows to obtain an assigned registration time."

Long, Long Ago in a University Far, Far Away

Keep in mind that many of the original Musts, Shoulds, and Oughts in college regulations were written an awfully long time ago for 18- to 22-year-old students, mostly well-to-do white males. These students had no one else besides themselves to worry about. Unfortunately, the descendants of many of those original rules seem still to be written with that kind of student in mind. (Grandchild-of-Rule-Number-Nine-Hundred-and-Thirty-Two written in the 1800s may still be unfair to you in the 1990s!)

> *This institution [a state university] fails to recognize anyone who is older than eighteen or nineteen as a freshman undergraduate.*

The administrators of more enlightened institutions are aware that their population of students is and has been changing; the average student now is older (over 25), has at least a part-time job, and maybe even has a family to support like you do.

But, and this is a big BUT, even though administrators of colleges and universities are aware of their changing populations of students, and know that things must change, some rules and regulations will change very, very slowly in a positive direction.

Long tuition and class registration lines still exist during normal office hours, hours when you are supposed to be in class or working. Penalties and fines are still given for tuition paid late, no matter what the reason—even though you may have a very good reason why you couldn't pay it by the deadline (such as your child support check was late and you had to use the funds on hand to pay for rent and groceries). Most required classes and seminars are taught during the day (when you might have to work) and some are taught either very early (7:00 A.M.) or late (5:00 P.M. or later), before and after your child care center is open. There might not even *be* a child care center on your campus or very close to it. The campus counseling center might likewise be unavailable for weekend problems or after-hours emergencies, and the academic advising center also probably operates only during normal office hours, 9 to 5.

Your college or university isn't set up to be unfair to you, and one shouldn't place blame; however, it was probably set up for a different kind of student.

Preventing Administrative Problems

All those constraints and more make it harder for you to get through even the mundane, routine technicalities of going to school. Large educational institutions appear to sometimes assume that all their students have all the time in the world to stand in line and very few other responsibilities other than going to school. Part of the problem these days is that most colleges and universities are on ever-tightening budgets. One of the first things to go is "excess staff." Now you don't think they're excess when you're standing in line for two hours to get to a financial aid window, but the college does. They have to cut somewhere. Unfortunately this leaves fewer and fewer people to help more and more students, just like there are fewer social service caseworkers to help more and more clients. What can you do?

Administrative problems are difficult, but not insurmountable. One of the best ways to minimize problems, at least with tuition and registration lines and deadlines, is to try at all times to get administrative things done as soon as you perceive that they will need to be done by a certain time. Obtain and fill out financial aid forms early, early, early. The day you get your class pre-registration materials in the mail (if your school does it that way) sit down with your course offerings book and fill out the forms. If your school only has in-person registration, try as hard as you can to go the first day and get it done. Realize that this registration process will need to be completed every quarter or semester, and arrange your time accordingly. Let your employer know when you'll need to go stand in line, and make arrangements beforehand to get the morning or afternoon off. Supervisors are usually very helpful if you give them enough lead time.

> *My college could be more understanding about the extra burden and real problems of the single parent student and take this into account when grading. We really don't compete fairly with the younger, single student. Perhaps the type of assignment could be varied more to fit the student. [They shouldn't] preach about priorities. Single parent students know very well what these are.*

More rules and regulations that pertain to the "traditional" student at your school won't fit your nontraditional circumstances very well. You'll just have to learn to live with these constraints (until they are changed and made more realistic) and work within the system to your advantage. This means you'll need to do things early, keep on top of your paperwork and form filling-out, let people in charge know as soon as possible if you have a problem, and ask for help at all times even when you have what you may consider to be small, inconsequential problems. Take care of small problems before they become big ones. Use the system—there are some people left in it who are just there to help you, the nontraditional student.

Social Services Regulations

The social services office's rules and regulations can be even more inane and bothersome than the school's. These offices require proof of everything; your progress in school, receipts for expenditures, proof of employment, proof that your children really do live with you, proof you even have children, and so on. The best way to deal with these folks also is to do things early—don't wait until something becomes a real problem or crisis.

For instance, you might get a letter in the mail saying that if you don't turn in Form XYZ by tomorrow, your aid will be cut off entirely. Well, you probably received Form XYZ in the mail a couple of weeks ago, and thought you had plenty of time to fill it out and return it, then you got busy and forgot, or put the paper in a pile with all your other papers, and it got buried. (Out of sight, out of mind!)

My advice (and this I really learned the hard way) is to fill everything out *the day you receive it*, even if this means getting a half-hour's less sleep, or missing out on some study time. The most important things are those you'll need to do to ensure that you receive enough financial and other aid to survive, and this takes precedence over almost everything. You'll kick yourself if you don't get a check because you forgot to fill out and return a stupid form! Get a shoebox, a large envelope, or some other container and put it in a conspicuous place in your house, a place that you can't possibly miss. Then put important and urgent paperwork in it, and go through it every day or at least every other day, clearing it out and doing whatever you need to do to get the paperwork out of the box and into the mail or into the hands of clerks and secretaries. Don't put paperwork in a stack on the cupboard or a shelf, and then think you'll go through it when you have time. You'll never have time! So, go ahead and do it now. Do it before it becomes a problem.

> *Social services will only pay child care for the hours I'm in class, not for research, library, or study time. Between housework, child care, chauffering the kids, and classes, study time is hard to sandwich in—usually late nights and weekends.*

Changing Some Rules

If you ever run into a rule or regulation that just isn't at all fair to someone in your circumstances, by any stretch of the imagination, you can try to get it changed. This may mean finding other people with the same problem and getting together to approach a dean, an administrator, or someone else in authority. You may, of course, approach people by yourself, but I've found that if you can prove that an unfair rule affects many people adversely it's more likely to be changed, or at least amended. Use the advice given in the section on "Challenge and Beat, Don't Cheat, The System" in Chapter Three, and you'll be able to make some important changes.

> *Many times when I had an hour between classes I yearned to be able to lie down and sleep. I could have got through the days a lot better if there was somewhere I could just collapse in private and relax completely for a while. Classes began at 8:30 or 9:30, five days a week, in my community college, and sometimes the last class didn't end until 5:30 at night. The campus was severely overcrowded; sometimes at lunch it was difficult to find somewhere even to sit! So what I would wish for was some sort of little dark cubicles with cots where one could just sleep for a bit. I used to get so exhausted.*

In summary, if you go to school, you've got to follow some rules. If you can get some changed to be more fair to you, by all means do so. If you can't, make sure you follow them so you don't get in trouble — even if you think they're unfair or unreasonable. If you don't follow them, out of a feeling of righteous indignation or stubbornness, you'll just hurt yourself (and your children). Your college or social services office is probably much too big to take much notice of your solitary indignation and couldn't care less if you drop off the face of the earth—but, if you get together with other folks in the same boat, people will sit up and take notice. (If you're interested in an excellent history, read *In The Company of Educated Women, A History of Women and Higher Education in America*, by Barbara Miller Solomon, Yale University Press. Get it from your library.)

SPOTLIGHT ON COLLEGE PROGRAMS
The University of Tennessee at Martin

Project Success is a program enabling single parent welfare recipients to earn a baccalaureate degree at the University of Tennessee at Martin. The program is a model of cooperation between state and federal agencies and a public institution of higher education to provide complementary means of financial and social support for selected families. In the pilot effort for academic year 1989–1990, nine participants were selected from six counties in west Tennessee. By the second year, 1990-91, eighteen participants from seven counties were enrolled.

In August 1988, representatives of key agencies formed a Task Force and planned the program. Task Force members represented the University of Tennessee at Martin; the Tennessee Department of Human Services (AFDC and food stamps); the Tennessee Department of Labor (Job Training Partnership Act); and Tennessee Housing Authority (HUD, Section 8 Rental Assistance). The clients selected had to meet admission standards to the University of Tennessee at Martin, and had to be first-time students at the institution. The clients were enrolled in the Department of Home Economics for at least the first year.

Essential to this model program, and critical to the successful transition in lifestyles for families, are the ready resources available on the campus at the University of Tennessee at Martin:

1. Counseling for financial, social, psychological, and health needs
2. Housing for independent family living
3. Child care services for preschoolers
4. Proximity to commercial services such as grocery stores, laundromats, pharmacies
5. Academic advising and career orientation

Given that the participants of Project Success are technically "wards of the state," the University's present role is clear and evident in enabling their shifts to becoming economic contributors, supportive parents, and well-adjusted individuals. Home economics has a direct role to play in facilitating our society's welfare reform. Having in place the means to meet fundamental needs with an array of essential services and compatible personnel are keys to success in the model for assisting welfare-dependent families. Providing a well-rounded education, career preparation, and career follow-through with today's single parents are unique and timely opportunities for higher education in general, and for home economics in particular.

A newspaper article by Mary S. Reed, published in *The Jackson Sun*, December 13, 1989, further illustrates the program:

Moms Schooled Off Welfare
Project Success offers education, job challenges

A year ago, Irene felt she was at life's bottom: three kids, divorced from their father, on welfare, no way to better herself. Today, the 29-year-old woman is a freshman at the University of Tennessee studying to be a registered nurse. She's part of Project Success, a test program at the university to help single parents on welfare get a college education.

"The whole region is looking at us," said Dr. Anne L. Cook, UTM chairwoman of the department of home economics, which oversees Project Success.

More colleges and agencies are considering similar programs, she said. They can offset declining college enrollments. They also help meet the challenges of a new welfare reform act that calls for training moms so they can get jobs and get off welfare.

Project Success, started this fall, is a joint effort by several agencies:

- The university, which provides counseling and support.
- The Job Training Partnership Act, which pays for the women's books, tuition, child care costs, and a monthly stipend to help them meet expenses.
- The U.S. Department of Housing and Urban Development, which made some of UTM's student housing eligible under Section 8 so part of the mom's rent is subsidized.
- The state human services department, which continues to give the women Aid to Families with Dependent Children and Medicaid coverage.

For Cook and JTPA operations supervisor Lafayette McKinnie, Project Success is a logical step for the state to help its welfare mothers become self-sufficient. "Better-paying jobs—attainable with a college degree—will lessen their chances of falling onto the welfare rolls again," McKinnie said.

"Once you add up what the welfare mother gets in AFDC, food stamps, and especially medical help through Medicaid, minimum-wage jobs just don't represent a lot of incentive to get out of the system," said McKinnie.

"The project's most measurable effect will come in four to five years when these women become wage earners and start paying taxes," Cook said. For Irene, Project Success is her ticket to a better life.

"I do not wish to stay on welfare," said Irene, married at 19 and a mother at 20. "Once I accomplish my goal (of a nursing education), this money I'm taking can go to someone else."

Before the program, Irene sometimes felt like giving up. "But I looked at my kids and I started picking myself up."

Paula, 19, another mother in the program, agrees: "The most important person in my life is my son. This program is benefiting him."

She always had plans to go to college. But when Justin was born after high school, she said, "I thought I would be in a minimum-wage job the rest of my life."

"Mothers in the program know the benefits of education—and their children are growing up in that environment," said Cook. "Ten years from now, these children are more likely to be successful, too," she said.

At Cook's suggestion, UTM Chancellor Dr. Margaret Perry called a meeting of several agencies in August 1988 to see whether the program was feasible on Martin's campus.

"UTM turned out to be a natural place for the program because it already had day care on campus and its student housing permitted the women to live independently rather than in a group dorm setting," said Cook. "Another plus was the university's home economics department, which philosophically feels it should help single parents who are on welfare," she said.

For more information, contact:

Anne Cook, Ph.D., R.D., C.H.E., Coordinator, Project Success
Chair and Professor
Department of Home Economics
340 Gooch Hall
University of Tennessee at Martin
Martin, Tennessee 38238-5045
(901) 587-7101
        or
Stephanie Mueller, M.S.
Campus Director, Project Success
Office of Student Affairs
University of Tennessee at Martin
Martin, Tennessee 38238-5045
(901) 587-7702

5

WHAT ABOUT YOUR
TRAVELING COMPANIONS?

One thing is certain—you're not going to be traveling through college alone. You have at least one child who is going to be your companion on the journey, step-by-step right along with you. How can you make the trip as interesting, pleasant, secure, and comfortable for your child(ren) as you can?

Child Care

A recent, super good book on choosing child care is: *The Complete Guide to Choosing Child Care*, by Judith Berezin, published by Random House. Consult this truly excellent guide for specifics on choosing and using all sorts of child care. Call your local library to see if they carry the book; if they don't, ask that they get it, pronto. Read on for some general advice about child care.

To find a good child care setting, start as early as you do to find financial aid. It is important for you to know that your children are well cared for while you are in school or working. At the end of this section you'll find a listing of national organizations related to child care; a listing of child care resource and referral (R&R) agencies and organizations in each state is found in Appendix B. (The book recommended above also lists child care R&Rs.)

As of 1991, about 38 percent of all colleges and universities in the United States had on-campus child care centers providing some form of child care. Call the college you plan to attend and ask if it has an on-campus center that takes children of your children's ages. Sometimes on-campus centers are the best because there is a real mixture of children of different nationalities, ethnic and racial backgrounds, and religions. In addition, the people staffing these on-campus centers know about your concerns and pressures as a student parent. Many of these centers also give first priority for space to children of single parent students, especially students who live on campus in family housing or apartments.

Most often these on-campus child care centers are your best bet, too, for convenience, reliability, and security for your child. Your kids will be able to play with the same children they live by, if you're in on-campus housing. This helps them adjust to the child care center, among other things. You will also probably be close enough to drop in on occasion, and it won't take a lot of extra time to take your children there and pick them up. If there is a waiting list to get your children in and you like the center, get on the list fast!

If your college doesn't have an on-campus child care center, another good place to start is to call your local social services office, family services or child care division, and ask them to send you a list of licensed day-care providers located close to your home or to your college. Ask each child care center or home-based care center about staff qualifications, number of children per caretaker, hours they are open, ages of children they take, fees, special activities, space, playground facilities, and if there is a waiting list to get in. Think of more things to ask them that are important to you.

Take the time to drop in on one or more centers. Don't call ahead! You want to find out what the situations are like when they aren't expecting company. A good time to drop in is mid-morning or mid-afternoon. What are the children doing? Do they seem relatively happy and busy? Are there enough adults to go around to take care of their needs? What is being prepared for lunch or snacks? How is the noise level? Are the children busy or do they all stare at you as you enter? Is anyone crying, and why? Another good time for a drop-in is in the late afternoon. Everybody is more than a little tired and bedraggled by then, and you'll want to know how the fatigued adults handle cranky kids, naptimes, and afternoon activities.

> *My daughter's day care is good, the best of eight I looked at, but it is overcrowded. There is very little good day care in my city, and the campus day care hasn't been able to get funding to expand from the university.*

Child Care Subsidies

Also ask your local social services office, division of family services or child care division, about whether help with child care costs is available to people in your situation. You may have a child care place in mind that you would like to use, and you might know how much it costs. If child care subsidy money is available at this time in your area, find out in person how you might qualify for such aid, if no one tells you. You must provide documentation of your financial situation to receive child care subsidies, like you do for other kinds of social services help. Almost all the documentation you used in applying for school financial aid can be used in your quest for child care assistance. The caseworker will tell you (if you ask!) what you need to bring with you to the office if you are unfamiliar with the social services system.

When Your Children Start Going to a Child Care Center

When you start to use a child care center, and your children aren't used to going to one, try the following things. Take your child there for just a half-day, if you can, the first couple of times. Ignore crying, screaming, and flailing arms and legs when you leave your child, if he or she acts this way. Those are just signs of separation anxiety and will go away quickly if the center is a good one and can distract the child away from you. Don't let the staff, though, trick your child into becoming interested in something else when you're going to leave, and then let the child discover that you are gone a few minutes later. That just breeds mistrust and anxiety in your child. Hug your child, smile, and let him or her watch you walk out·the door.

Sometimes, though, it seems like it's more painful for us parents than it is for our children when we leave them at a new place with new people! Kids will pick up on your anxiety, so it's best to give your child a quick hug and kiss with a smile, let him or her know exactly when you'll be coming back, then scram. If your child isn't old enough to tell time, you might want to say something like, "I'll pick you up right after afternoon naptime," or "I'll come back just a little while after you have your afternoon snack."

> *I've had to change child care arrangements about four or five times in the last year and a half—it's been a problem to find new places to take her that I felt were good for her to be. One place I had to take her out of because I felt she wasn't physically safe.*

It will take a couple of weeks or so for your young child to get used to a new place and new people and stop crying when you leave. The time it takes for this to happen depends a lot on your particular child's temperament. If crying continues beyond a week or two, you should drop in (when you can pick your child up early and go home—you don't want to leave him or her crying twice in one day!) and check out how your child is doing at that moment.

Is he or she involved in an interesting activity? Are the adult caretakers paying attention to the children? Or is everything just chaotic and noisy, with the children wandering around aimlessly or picking at each other? Check these things out, and you might decide to change centers if it looks like the first one won't do. You'll run into waiting lists again, probably, so it's really best to check out a center as thoroughly as possible before you leave your child there in the first place.

Positive Effects of Child Care

You might be interested to know that scientific studies of children in good child care situations show that the children do very well. The children don't show any more or worse or different problems than do children who are at home all day with a parent. In fact, it has been shown that going to good child care centers (this includes good home-centered child care) is actually a very positive experience for children.

Your children will learn that you are not the center of the universe. They will make more friends. They will learn how to cooperate with others. They will gain self-esteem and self-reliance. If the center is a particularly good one, as the on-campus center that I used was, and offers preschool education, your child will be that much more prepared when he or she starts school. If your child care center offers transportation to and from school for kindergarteners, and after-school care for older children, that's even better.

If Problems Do Happen

If at any time you have a concern about the center, the staff, or how your child is doing, for heaven's sake talk with your child and the provider about it. Don't ever let your worries interfere with your ability to be an effective student or employee. Most of the time your concerns can be addressed quickly and to your satisfaction if you discuss any concern with your provider as soon as you start to feel uncomfortable about something.

Organizations on Child Care Issues

You might be most interested in an organization specifically involved in on-campus child care, called the National Coalition for Campus Child Care, Inc. (NCCCC). Here is a brief sketch of the organization, quoted from an open letter from the chairperson:

Dear Colleague:

After ten years as an informal network of campus child care providers, teachers, administrators, and other supporters, the National Coalition for Campus Child Care became incorporated as a membership organization in 1982.

National in orientation and representation, it exists to promote and provide support for both the concept and the reality of high quality accessible child care on campuses of higher education institutions throughout the United States.

Membership in the organization is open to campus child care centers, higher education institutions, and any individuals with an interest in campus child care. At last count our diverse membership included faculty, administrators, staff, programs that were half day, full day, flexible scheduled, evening, just starting up, struggling as well as successfully expanding into new buildings.

NCCCC encourages participation on committees and at conferences. Members benefit from professional workshops and extensive peer support.

We hold a conference once a year in different parts of the country and a half day session at NAEYC in order to be accessible to as many persons as possible. [Author's note: 1992 NCCCC conference will be held in Breckenridge, Colorado, from April 8 to 11.]

Members also receive three newsletters, a membership list, an updated bibliography yearly, policy and strategy papers, and reduced rates for conferences and publications.

If you, your center, or your higher education institution is interested in promoting child care or receiving future information on our national conference, please write to us today.

Sincerely,

Jane Ann Thomas
Chairperson

Their address and phone number:

National Coalition for
Campus Child Care
c/o Charles Boulton, Office Manager
Box 258
Cascade, Wisconsin 53011
(414) 528-7080

More organizations:

Child Care Action Campaign
330 7th Avenue, 18th Floor
New York, New York 10001
(212) 239-0138

Child Welfare League of America, Inc.
440 First Street, NW
Suite 310
Washington, D.C. 20001-2085
(202) 638-2952

Children's Defense Fund
122 C Street, NW
4th Floor
Washington, D. C. 20001
(202) 628-8787

The Conference Board (information on Employer-Supported Child Care)
845 Third Avenue
New York, New York 10022
(212) 759-0900

National Association for the Education of Young Children (NAEYC)
1834 Connecticut Avenue, NW
Washington, D.C. 20009
(800) 424-2460
(202) 232-8777 (local)

National Association for Family Day Care
c/o Children's Foundation
725 Fifteenth Street, N.W., Suite 505
Washington, D.C. 20005
(202) 347-3300

National Women's Law Center
(child care and tax issues)
1751 N Street, NW
Washington, D.C. 20036
(202) 872-0670

School Age Child Care Project
Wellesley College Center for
Research on Women
106 Central Street
Cheever House
Wellesley, Massachusetts 02181
(617) 431-1453

The Non-Sexist Child Development Project
Resource Center for Non-Sexist Early
Childhood Education
c/o Jo Sanders, Director
Women's Action Alliance, Inc.
370 Lexington Avenue
New York, New York 10017
(212) 532-8330

Being a Parent

What else can you do for your children, besides finding an excellent child care or after-school care program? You are in school, or thinking about entering school, partly in order to become better able to care for your children and provide them with more opportunities and just a better life. But your schooling and working can interfere with your ability to be an effective parent much of the time, simply because you will be so pushed. And the fact is that while you are in school your children are growing up.

How can you reconcile all the conflicts and be an effective student and parent? How can you keep in touch with your children, and give them what they really need from you, their single parent? How can you keep from losing something precious while you're trying to improve your own and your children's lives? How can you make certain that you are being as good a parent as you can be, when you are so busy and frazzled?

This section will help you learn some positive parenting techniques you can use while you are in school (and always) that will help your family life a great deal. You'll also learn some different ways of being with your children, so that you can get everything done that needs doing and still spend time with them. You will learn how to help them feel good about themselves, such a very important obligation of any parent. You'll learn how to stay in control of your family situation, so the whole world doesn't seem so overwhelming. You'll learn that positive discipline and rewards work so much better than punishments. You'll also be teaching your children good parenting skills that they will use when they become parents.

> *It is an illusion (not to be encouraged) to think that you can have everything. If you go to school full time, there will be sacrifices and there will be losses. A lot of the losses will be for your children—in fact, I think it might be accurate to say that most of the losses will be for your children. I believe that if you choose to give birth to children, you should, with that choice, understand that with it goes a commitment—of time—of large amounts of availability, not just bits here and there. A child deserves the time of a parent. Not necessarily to be doing things with her/him all the time, but to be an example—to be available to listen, or discuss, or help, or guide, whenever the need arises. If you choose to go to school, you understand that a commitment of large blocks of time goes with that choice. The same steadiness of commitment should apply for choosing to have a child.*

The Big Catch-22

First of all, there is one main thing which you will need to be able to acknowledge and accept if you are going to make it through college successfully. (If you're already in school, you've probably come to realize this.) The fact is that you will not always be able to live up to your own standards or abilities in your major roles, including parenting, while you're a student. This fact can be more problematic and painful the more intelligent and capable you really are.

You know, for absolutely certain, that you are capable of being a wonderful parent, a wonderful employee, a wonderful friend or companion, and a wonderful student. But not always all at the same time! And, given the fact that each of these endeavors can be a full-time job, you will be stretched to the very limit while you are in school.

Let's face it: the more children you have, the harder it may be. And most often your young children won't understand; they won't be able to set aside their needs just because you are so pressured as a student parent. Even older ones can feel resentment and irritation. Your children are a big part of the reasons why you are in school; they are the major reason why it is all so hard. Talk about a Catch-22!

Managing the Chunks of Your Life

The best you can do, then, is to carve your life into manageable parts—areas in which you don't expect yourself to be perfect, just pretty good. That is, when you are a student—at school, in class, in the library—just be a student. Don't think about your children. Don't think about your job. The theory also applies if you work at a job. When at work, don't think about your children or school.

If you allow all your responsibilities to weigh on your mind all the time, you will become exhausted just thinking about them! Don't spin your wheels. This will take practice, but learning the skill is worth it. This separating of activities and roles allows you to enjoy each of them without feeling like you should be doing something else whenever you are doing anything. (More information on this is found in Chapter Six.)

> *Having enough time to spend with my son has proven difficult this year since I have been carrying an overload in my courses. I feel guilty about not playing enough with him, but often when I play with him I find my mind is thinking about school. I've tried to ignore other mothers who seem to spend exhorbitant amounts of time with their children, and concentrate instead on what is enough for the two of us. There is so much unneeded advice going around it seems regardless of what you do someone will tell you how to be better. This is a problem that I've created, I think, from my beliefs of what constitutes a "good mother" which I can't live up to and also be in school.*

Back to your children. When you are with them, and they need time, conversation, food, or anything else from you, just be a parent. Forget about school. Forget about work. How can you do this, especially when you have so much to do all the time? You don't have to cater to every whim of your children whenever something strikes them, nor do you need to be a slave at their beck and call. What you do need to do is spend predictable, pleasant time with them—time they can count on and feel good about. More than almost anything else they need this from you, especially when you are pulled in so many different directions, and they know you are and sometimes feel uneasy about it.

Divide and Conquer

For most of us, the time from when we and our children get home in the early evening until dinner can be the most conflict-ridden and awful of the whole day. If this period of time is very unpleasant, it sets the tone for the rest of the evening, and conflict becomes almost routine and habitual. Everyone is tired and hungry, has been around a lot of people, and has been told what to do all day by teachers, day-care workers, employers, office workers, and others. One way to get around this early evening conflict and fighting is to use solitary play agreements (also discussed below under "Keeping the Peace").

A solitary play agreement is used to separate people, to lessen the chances of conflict, and to provide everyone (even you) with some winddown time after coming home. These agreements can also be used for periods of time on weekends. The agreement, whether verbal or written, simply states that each person will do something alone during the same period of time, say a half hour to an hour, while you prepare a meal or rest for a short while. This works with children about three years old and older.

Your children go to different parts of the house or room, and must play by themselves without talking or interacting with anyone else for a certain period of time. It's better if the television is not turned on, and the children are separated as far apart as possible. A good part of the trouble with television, especially when people first get home, is that it bunches everyone together in a small space, and fights about what to watch, who gets to change channels, and who bumped whose leg are likely to result. In addition, during solitary play running around is not allowed, nor are the children allowed to bombard you with any requests or talking. You may require that they write down anything they need to tell you that they might forget, or have an older brother or sister write it down for them, or simply wait until you can really listen effectively.

It is necessary (if solitary play is to work well) to provide yourself and each child with a nutritious snack right when you get home, right before solitary play time. This keeps everybody from becoming irritable from hunger and helps you and your children get through comfortably until meal time. It takes some of the pressure off of you to fix dinner fast. It's almost a truism that the faster the dinner, the less nutritious it is, especially if you find yourself relying on ready-to-eat foods a lot. Before you send each child off to a different part of the house (of their choosing, if possible), give them each a big hug and kiss, and tell them you love them.

You might need to use some kind of timer with a bell for younger children during solitary play since it's hard for them to keep track of time. Older children and teens can read a clock, and can be told when they can expect solitary time to be up. It is also important to let your children choose what they will do during this time, within normal family limits of course. The children should not be allowed to do anything that will interfere with what other family members want to do—for example, one child can listen to the radio, if it is turned down low enough so it doesn't disturb another child reading or doing homework.

What is your children's incentive for cooperating with this plan? Their motivation is that you will then spend pleasant, predictable time with them later on in the evening—time and contact that has not been marred by earlier conflicts before dinner. Of course, tell them that you will be spending special time with each of them later on in the evening, and that the time will be so much nicer if they cooperate with you now. Don't keep it a big secret!

By separating people with solitary play, you have greatly decreased conflicts, and you don't have to play referee or policeperson when you get home—one of the most unpleasant things a parent has to do. You are not immediately put in a difficult position when you are tired and stressed from your day. Research also has shown that when children are taught to use solitary play they are then much more able later on in the day or evening to interact with other people and family members in positive ways! It really does help.

So what do you do if your children don't cooperate with your grand plan for solitary play? You can use time-out for young children, and a work penalty for older children and teens. (See "Keeping the Peace" below for specifics on how to use these techniques.)

It is most important, however, that even if there does happen to be some conflict during solitary play time, that you *do not* take away your children's special time with you later on in the evening. It will probably take a while, a week or two, for your new system to work, because children react against new rules and test you. This special time can be spent all together as a family, or it can be spent with you and each child alone for a while. Pleasant time during dinner is a nice whole-family activity, and clean-up and other household chores can be an after-dinner group thing, too. Throw in a little conversation. I found that this time was plenty for my family's togetherness, and that spending a little time alone with each child (fifteen minutes to a half hour or so each) worked well (I have three kids—they were five years, three years, and eighteen months old when I began college).

Your children, especially your older ones, will have their own activities in the evening, too, and you can schedule around these in order to spend some time with each of them alone. While one does homework, you can talk with another one about his or her day or take a look at schoolwork brought home. While one child runs off to a friend's house, you can play catch with or read a story to your little one. While your oldest takes a bath, you can help another with a school project.

You can use your and your children's imaginations to come up with things to do. Remember that you don't have to do anything that costs money or that takes you away from home in order for your children to feel loved and important. All you have to do is be there with them, not just around them. Again, it is very important to force yourself to forget about all the homework or household chores you have to do for a while—just be a parent.

> *People are shocked I have a child—it makes me feel separated from my friends sometimes because I have a child.*

While you are reading this you are probably asking yourself, but what about *me*? What about my need to study? What about my social life? Look in other chapters (such as Chapters Six and Seven) for answers to your questions; you'll find that they won't contradict what is said here. Also, my examples above presume that you work and attend school during the day; if you have a different schedule, simply use solitary play and together play at times that are compatible with your particular needs.

The Benefits of Predictable Time with Your Children

The benefits of spending predictable, pleasant time with your children are profound. Each of your children will come to feel unique and loved, and will believe that you really care for them even though most of the time you are crazily, frenetically busy. If you practice your own brand of personal thought-control, if you can keep school and work and money problems out of your head while you're spending time with your children, your kids will become convinced that you are indeed their parent and that you are invested in them emotionally, spiritually, and otherwise. Your children will become less likely to fight with each other, they will become more cooperative with you, and your whole family life will be much more enjoyable for everyone. You will see a gradual change over a period of a few weeks to a couple of months using this system—nothing happens overnight.

Parents sometimes wonder why their children don't seem to feel loved, when the parents do in fact love them very much. Maybe it's because parents think they are spending time with their children when they're really not, and their children feel it. Just being around doesn't quite do it; you must be truly available to your children.

> *Be careful to give children your time—plan family fun and be available to your kids, even if you have to cut back on school hours a bit. Do as much schoolwork away from home as you can. Kids have to see where you go to school and where you spend your time. Enlist their help and support.*

Keep Discipline Separate from Special Time

If you must discipline a child for something, don't make it part of your interaction during your special time with them. Always keep discipline separate. Don't use the opportunity of your alone time with your child to scold, counsel, reprimand, punish, expound, or lecture on any wrongdoing of your child that happened earlier in the day or week. If you need to discipline during the special time, because your child has disobeyed you or broken a rule right then, do so as quickly after the offense as possible making the discipline brief, fair, and fitting the offense (time out or a work penalty works well) and then forget it. Try as hard as you can to use your alone time with each child only to interact in a positive, pleasant way with him or her. If your children just aren't behaving very well during dinner or early evening, use a quick, effective discipline, and then go ahead and spend time with them later on, forgetting earlier conflict.

If you don't do it that way, and if you take away positive time with you as a punishment, your children will start to feel helpless and hopeless, something you certainly don't want to happen! And you may simply start looking at your children as liabilities, not as people to love.

Actually, each child is quite unlikely to misbehave during your alone time together, simply because your attention is focused on him or her and there is no need to misbehave. If misbehavior should happen, however, do some quick discipline explained under "Keeping the Peace," and try again with the child later on.

If other children interfere with your alone time with their brother or sister, again use some discipline with the interfering child, and go on. But don't take away the interferer's time with you later. Use a disconnected discipline procedure (time out or work penalty) and don't allow yourself to be baited or get angry. Keep your temper, and stay in control. Don't yell, don't spank, don't threaten.

You may be surprised to find that when you are focused on your children and are doing something with them that they value too, their behavior improves a lot—it improves not only while you are spending time with them, but it improves at other times as well. Since you have explained to your children that they each will get their turn to spend time with you in the evening, there will be less motivation for them to fight or compete for your attention. This, however, may not be the case the first few times you use the new strategy, since any major changes in routine bring about uncertainty and testing. Your children will learn, however, and peace will gradually replace most conflict. Sometimes children fight, I believe, just to engage their parent in interaction with them. Like the old saying goes, even negative attention is better than no attention at all. When you start providing predictable, positive attention to your children that isn't based on their behavior but that just happens because they are your children and you want to be with them, their behavior will dramatically improve.

> *When I took my daughter to class, she contributed to a psychology discussion on childhood. She was generally received well by instructors and students. My daughter has gained self-confidence and a greater understanding of the world.*

Of course you would never force a child (especially a teenager) to spend time with you if he or she would rather not, but you can always hold out the opportunity for your child to be with you. In addition, do not allow the telephone or other interruptions to interfere with your time with your children. You can always tell callers that you are busy (you are!) and that you will get back to them. Maybe you can even unplug your phone for a while, and put a "Please do not disturb" sign on your door.

Points to Remember

Some of the most important points to remember are:

1. Divide your life activities—practice thinking about only what you are doing at any given time. When you are with your children to spend time with them, be a parent and friend only, and allow yourself to enjoy it!

2. Use solitary play agreements to divide and conquer and keep the peace, even at times on weekends.

3. Each child needs predictable alone-time with you in order to feel loved and cherished.

4. Do not use this special time to reinforce discipline by counseling, scolding, and such.

5. Do not allow anything (short of fire, flood, or tornado) to interfere with your special time with your children.

If you use these skills and suggestions, you will be much less susceptible to guilt about not being a very wonderful parent, and you will worry much less about how your children are affected by your being in school. These techniques will not solve all of your family problems, but they will lessen conflict, improve each child's self-esteem, and allow you to be as much as possible the kind of parent that you would like to be. You may become an even better parent *because* you are in school, because you'll try different and more workable ways of being with your children.

Keeping the Peace with Positive Discipline

First, children need a good deal of routine and predictability in their lives. This means eating meals at the same time and place every day, going to bed with the same routine at the same time every night, knowing where you are and when you'll be home, having chores to do on a daily or weekly basis, and so on. With your incredibly busy schedule you'll need to try to keep as many things routine and predictable for yourself and your children as possible. I haven't ever seen happy, calm, well-adjusted children in chaotic families with haphazard ways of doing everyday things, have you? So don't be afraid to set limits, schedules, rules, and family routines—and then stick to them. Your children will be more secure, happier, and better behaved because of them.

Next, each of your children needs to feel like he or she is a special, loved person in your life. They not only need to feel loved as a group or bunch, they need to feel individually special and cared for. It is only possible for them to feel this way if you spend regular, predictable time with each of them on a daily or weekly basis. You may need to set up appointments or "dates" to do this when you're in school, but set them up. When you make a date with your child, don't break it.

> *I don't spend as much time with my children. I used to think and do more for them than I did for myself. Now I allow them more freedom and I make good use of the time we have together. We live around other student families so they don't have friends who receive a lot of toys and such. Otherwise they might compare our lifestyle with other kids' lifestyles. They can see how important school is to me, so they also think school and learning is important.*

A Few Words about Babies

Love them, hold them, attend to them, nurture them, feed them, and don't worry that something you do will spoil them. You won't. During the first year or so of their lives, babies learn how to trust and how to communicate. The way they learn to trust is by your quick and loving attention to their needs. You'll learn to communicate with each other.

Think about something silly for a moment. What if the only way you could communicate your needs to other people was by crying, whimpering, fussing, or, at last resort, screaming? This is what young babies must do, because they can't talk. You *will not* spoil your baby by tending to his or her needs as quickly as they arise. Hold your baby a lot, stroke your baby, lightly massage your baby all over when nothing else seems to help, sing to your baby, rock your baby while you study.

You will learn that different cries and different types of fussing mean different things. Give yourself time to learn; give your baby time to learn to communicate what he or she needs from you.

One thing your young baby does *not* need from you is discipline, simply because babies don't know any rules, they just have needs. A baby doesn't do anything "wrong." Now, this doesn't mean that your baby will never annoy you! Sometimes you'll be terribly angry, or frustrated, or exhausted, and your baby's cries will become extremely irritating. At these times you *must* set aside your negative feelings, and simply tend to your baby's needs in the kindest, calmest, most loving way you can.

If you are a new parent, I strongly encourage and urge you to take parenting classes from your local community education center, hospital, university, community college, high school, or other place. If you can't find a class right away, call your pediatrician's office, a local hospital, or college and ask about one. These classes will be invaluable to you, especially if you are alone with no friends or family to help you with parenting problems. You'll be able to find a free class, or one you can afford. Some of them even provide child care right there, while you are in the class.

House Rules

It's perfectly reasonable to post rules where children old enough to read can see them. It's also a good idea to have your children help make up the rules; let them be a part of the rule-making process. Of course, your house isn't entirely a democracy—you must always have final say about what goes or doesn't go. When rules are broken, use one of these techniques:

Time-Out

This is very effective with younger children (preschoolers about two years old through school-age kids up to age ten or eleven); with older kids it just doesn't work and they think it's silly and rebel against it. Time-out is simply that—time out from interaction with other people and enjoyable activities. To use time-out in the best way, you'll need to do the following things:

1. Use it as fast as you can after your child breaks a rule or does something inappropriate and unacceptable to you.

2. Say to your child, briefly (don't yell) that a rule was broken and you are sending him or her into time-out for a few minutes.

3. Send your child into a *safe, boring* place in your home for two to five minutes, using your watch or a kitchen timer to time it. A chair in the cor-

ner of a quiet room, the bathroom, or another suitable place will do. Don't send the child into his or her own bedroom—too many fun things in there.

4. Leave your child alone, and when the time is up let your child out of the time-out place.

5. Do not mention the broken rule again, but do require your child to make restitution or apologize to someone else for the behavior if necessary (for instance, if your child hit a younger brother, your child must apologize to his or her sibling). If your child made an awful mess with something, he or she must now clean it up. Then drop the subject, and don't mention it again.

There are a few things you must *not* do when using time-out. Do not raise your voice, do not touch your child. You may gently guide a young child into the time out place. Do not send a child into time-out for more than five minutes at a time, but do add one minute (tell them you will do this) for each time your child fusses or complains or resists the discipline. *Do not* put your child somewhere which will be frightening to him or her; a closet, a dark, dank room, somewhere that there are scary things like spiders. *Do* use a room such as the bathroom (with hazardous things placed well out of reach or locked up), a corner of the living room, or somewhere else which is safe and boring, boring because there are no toys there, no television, no radio, and so on. Your child doesn't necessarily have to be put in a place where you can be seen, but you should be within hearing distance. Don't leave the house.

Do not use physical restraints of any kind. Have your child just sit down on the toilet (lid down) if you use the bathroom, on a special "time-out" chair, or on the floor. Again, after the discipline is over, don't harp on the misbehavior or talk about it again. The time for rule instruction and teaching right from wrong is some time not connected with discipline. Most parents harp on rules and regulations right after a child has done something wrong, but this is a time when their child is actually least likely to really be listening. He or she is too busy feeling bad or guilty or fearful to really take anything in or remember it. Teach your children what you expect from them at times when nobody is in trouble. Also pick a time when the children are rested, fed, and reasonably calm. Then do it.

If Your Child Doesn't Obey Time-Out

What do you do if your child, especially a little bit older child, refuses to go into time-out? Then you move one step up, and restrict a privilege, activity, or valued object. You may give your child one or two minutes within which to comply with time-out. Set a timer with a bell. You may indicate to your child what he or she will lose if time-out is refused. You may restrict television, the use of a toy or bike, or anything else that is prized by your child that will happen that day. Don't threaten to take away something that he or she is looking forward to in a few days or next week—your children know you might change your mind, and your promise to restrict something later will be meaningless to them. Use something that will have immediate impact or at least impact that same day. Then follow through with your promise (not threat) if your child doesn't comply. For example, if your eight-year-old doesn't go into time out after one or two minutes, you may take away television watching that evening, or playing with a friend, or something the child was planning to do. (If you were planning alone-time with your child that evening, don't take that away.)

You may certainly use time-out with more than one child at once, just send each child to opposite points of the house or room. You can also certainly use time out when you're away from home—the same rules apply. Find the most safe, boring place you can and have your child sit there, alone, for a few minutes. You can use time-out in the grocery store, in a park, in a restaurant, at school, in the library, at the movies, or almost anywhere. Whenever you're tempted to yell at or spank your child in a public place (or at home!), remember time-out and use that instead. Don't worry about what other people around you will think; they'll appreciate your quiet handling of the problem, and your nonviolent discipline. Aren't you disturbed when you hear a parent yelling at or spanking a child in a store or somewhere? It always makes me cringe.

Never, Never, Never Play Referee

Time-out as a discipline strategy is especially effective if all your children are fighting with each other and you cannot know who "started" it. Actually, parents should never play referee—if your children fight, *all* of them immediately get disciplined with time-out or a work penalty. This will save you endless time that you probably spend now trying to play policeperson, judge, and jury in trying to figure out just who should be disciplined, who is being the "bad guy." Pretty soon all your children will figure out that it doesn't pay at all to fight.

Use time-out as often as you have to. Don't be afraid to use it over and over. Kids don't like to feel bored and isolated from people and activities, as they are in time-out. Use time-out consistently and as quickly after a rule violation as you possibly can. This takes what a psychologist once called "off the butt discipline"; get up off your butt, and don't touch your children's! Get up and deal with the problem. Then go back to what you were doing. Remember, use other calmer times and places to go over rules, regulations, and expectations you have for your children's behavior.

Be Quick About It

Above all, *do not* get sucked into long, drawn out, whining, yelling interactions when you use time-out (or any other discipline procedure, for that matter). You should interact and talk to your child during a discipline procedure for no more than thirty seconds to a minute at the very, very most. Tell your child, calmly, exactly what it is that you are unhappy or angry about, tell your child what discipline you are using and what he or she will have to do, then carry out the discipline and be quiet. Did you know that attention and conversation with you at a discipline time can actually reinforce bad behavior?! Your children might learn that to get your undivided attention they need to act badly. So, be brief, be to the point, then *ignore* your children while they're in time-out. Then let them out and pay some positive attention to them later, when they're behaving well.

Work Penalties

A discipline technique quite different from time-out which works well with older children is a work penalty, mentioned above. Older children means about age ten or eleven and above. You can judge how mature your children are, and if they are ready to switch from time-out to work penalties.

A work penalty is a job that can be done around or near the house, an icky job that doesn't usually get done, a job that is unappealing and which will really be useful to you to have it done. (Don't use regular chores for work penalties.)

Some examples of good work penalties are: stacking and bundling newspapers for recycling, washing windows, cleaning the inside and outside of a car, scrubbing a floor, getting rid of cobwebs and dust in out-of-the-way places (if your child is afraid of spiders and bugs, certainly *don't* give him or her this job), cleaning the inside of the refrigerator, sweeping sidewalks or a garage, and so on. You can think of other things that need to be done around your home that would qualify as "icky" jobs.

Next, the work penalty should not last more than one hour; two hours is the very maximum and should only be used with older teens for more serious offenses (minor stealing, lying, destructive behavior). There are also four important rules for your child that go along with a work penalty: there will be (1) No Food, (2) No Fun, (3) No Phone, and (4) No Friends for your child until the work is completed, and completed to your satisfaction.

While your child is doing the work, do not stand over him or her or comment on how well he or she is doing. Also, don't let your other children or neighbor children hang around, pester, or tease the worker. Leave your child alone, and only inspect the job when the time is up. If you find that the job was done very sloppily (even for a child), carelessly, or that an even bigger mess was made than was supposed to be cleaned up, the same job can be expected to be done right the next day, right after you get home or, if it's a weekend, before your child gets to do anything fun. Your child still does not get to see friends, use the phone, or have any fun until the job is done right. Of course, you cannot and must not take away regular food for that period of time until the next day! (You can and should take away any goodies, pop, sweets, or dessert.) Feed your child regular meals, but do not allow any fun, phone calls, or friends.

Your children, though, will probably do their icky jobs pretty well the first time (but don't ever expect perfection, or that the job will be done exactly as you would do it), because they will want those valued privileges back. They won't want to spend all their free time doing unpleasant work. Of course you will have told your child that if the job is not done right the first time that it will be done again the next day, and no privileges will be restored until then.

The final step in this work penalty process is forgetting the rule violation (that led to the penalty) after the work is done satisfactorily according to your child's abilities. Don't talk about your child's bad behavior that caused you to impose the work penalty—not today, not tomorrow, not even in the far future. Wipe the slate clean, and do not harp at all on the subject. Remember to use another time to reinforce household rules or remind children of them. Allow your child the dignity of having worked off the penalty and let him or her go on from there.

Grandma's Law

Another child discipline procedure is called, simply, "grandma's law." You know this one—your child can do something that he or she wants to do *after* doing something that needs to be done that isn't particularly fun. You know, a child can watch television after homework is done. Or, a child can have dessert after dinner is eaten, or can play with friends after chores are done. You can apply this technique to all sorts of things, and you can model it to your children yourself.

When you need to read a chapter in a textbook (and you might do so when your children are busy with their own homework) talk out loud, saying something like, "After I get this chapter read, I'm going to take a nice walk around the block—would anybody like to come with me?" Now, walking around the block isn't usually that exciting to kids, but they'll get the message that you can also do routine or necessary things before you do more enjoyable activities. Your children will be more likely to follow "grandma's law" for their own behavior if they see you applying it to your own life. You'll need to bring it out in the open, though, by talking out loud. Most of the time children just don't notice a lot of what we do, nor do we pay attention to what they are doing, until a problem comes up.

Solitary Play

The next discipline procedure is solitary play, discussed briefly earlier. This is a good thing to use especially when you first get home from school and work, and everybody is milling around, hungry, and annoying and picking at each other. You may set up a household rule that for the first half hour to hour after everybody gets home in the evening (or whenever you all get home) every person must go to a separate place in the house and do something of their choice, quietly. Remember to give them each a big hug and a good snack first! This allows you time to fix a meal, read your mail, put your feet up for a little while, or go through the newspaper. It also allows all the family members to "come down" after a hard and hectic day at school, work, or daycare. Sometimes we don't realize how jazzed up our children can get and that they need some quiet time alone to unwind after their hard days, just like we grownups do.

This technique works well for children who are older than toddlers, starting about three or four years old. If you have a baby or younger child, you certainly won't be able to expect that young of a child to play quietly by himself or herself, especially when your toddler hasn't seen you all day. If you have a very young one and older ones, though, you can keep the baby or toddler with you and send the others off to different points in the house to unwind.

What if your children don't cooperate with this solitary play plan? Then use time-out (for young kids) or work penalties (for the older ones). Your children will soon discover that it's much more pleasant and fun to be able to do something alone of their choice for a half hour or hour than it is to be sent into time-out or do an icky job.

After this half hour to hour of solitary play, after everybody has had a little time to relax, then talk with your children, ask them about their day, have them help with dinner, or whatever. If they happen to be particularly cooperative, cheerful, and quiet during the wind-down solitary play time, praise their behavior or give them a bonus of a special treat or activity later on that evening. Rewards always work so much better than punishments.

Solitary Play on Weekends and Holidays

You can also use this technique of solitary play at various times on the weekends or days off from school. Just announce, when things get out of hand, that there will now be solitary play for an hour. You might even want to get an old cow bell, whistle, or another not-too-aversive-sounding but loud item to get their attention on your announcement of solitary play time. Save your vocal cords—don't scream at them. Then enforce solitary play with the above discipline strategies. You don't need to yell, or spank, or cry. Just divide and conquer!

Please Be Quiet, Please Be Quiet, Please Be Quiet

Finally, I recommend that you do not, with your school-age children, ever repeat yourself. (It is very *normal* for parents to have to repeat things to preschoolers or learning-disabled children—go ahead and do it). How many times a day do you ask or tell your normal, school-age child to do something, over and over and over? The same request!! Well, that wastes an awful lot of your time, you end up getting really angry and frustrated, and your children learn to tune you out. Use *consequences* instead of repeating yourself.

To do this correctly, you need to make absolutely sure your child hears you ask or tell him or her to do something the first time you say it. Get your child in front of you, watching your face. Say it once, slowly, quietly. Then say that if the activity or whatever you've requested is not minded or completed by a certain time, something else then will or will not happen.

For example, you might want your child to clean up his or her bedroom before dinner, but your child is watching television. Wait for an advertisement, then turn the sound off on the set and get your face in front of your child's face. You do the moving. Tell your child that you expect the bedroom to be clean (your version of clean, not your child's) before dinner is served. Tell your child that if she or he does not accomplish this task by the specified time, that there will be no dessert that evening, nor any more television after dinner, nor any fun at all that evening. The child will spend the rest of the time after dinner, alone, in the messy bedroom. (If other children share the bedroom, the same can hold for everyone who needs to help clean it up.)

Don't watch the clock or nag your child to hurry up and get the work done. If you're sure your child understood the request, don't say it again. Check the child's bedroom once, quietly, right before dinner. Don't say anything to your child. Then feed your family, and don't say anything about the bedroom yet if it wasn't cleaned up. Have a normal dinner with normal conversation. Then, after dinner, if you noticed that the bedroom hadn't been cleaned like it was supposed to be, simply state that fact, in a matter-of-fact tone of voice, and then enforce the consequence. Don't yell at your child. Don't get upset. Simply state that the unappealing consequence will now occur, and accept no excuses for poor behavior. Do this *every* time you ask your child to do something. If your child says, "But I forgot!" you may simply say that you are very sorry he or she forgot, but that the consequence still applies. You can express your belief that the child will remember what you say next time. Then drop the subject.

If your child did lean the bedroom as you requested, reward your child with a big hug, kiss, and maybe a special treat or privilege.

Another example: you're trying to study, and your kids are supposed to be doing their own homework. Instead, they're talking, fussing with each other, or just playing around. Tell them once to sit down and do their homework quietly (it helps if each child has a separate place to do this). Give them as many minutes as you choose to comply with your request. If they don't do what you ask within that period of time, use time-out or a work penalty for them all. If, as a result, they don't have time to complete

their homework before bed, tell them they will get up early the next morning to finish it. Wake them up! They won't like that, and next time will
probably do their homework quietly when you ask.

> *My children seem to be proud of me for my endeavors, but sometimes they
> can't help but be a little jealous of the time I spend away from them. The
> divorce has been more of a source of adjustment for them than my school
> has been. But all in all, they are adjusting very well to both.*

Remember, Don't Nag!

Some of us have gotten into the awful parenting habit of nagging, nagging, nagging our children about ⹂verything, and we end up being an un-
paid, unappreciated policeperson all the time! How unpleasant a task that
is for parents, and especially for single parents. Start now—instead of nagging, yelling, cajoling, begging, or whatever, tell your child once what is expected, make sure he or she understands exactly what that is (perhaps you
can ask your child to repeat the instruction back to you), explain the consequences for appropriate and inappropriate behavior, then leave your child
alone and later simply enforce the appropriate consequence. (Rewards are
fine when your child actually does what you ask and does it when you want
it done, in the best way that your child can). Be absolutely sure that you enforce any consequences; if you back down, forget, or "go soft," your children won't learn anything.

Staying in Control of Your Family

Single parents can often end up feeling out of control when it comes to
child behavior and discipline. Since we're the only ones who do the day-to-
day parenting, sometimes we find ourselves trying to be good guys and being as easy on our kids as possible, for a while. Then, when we reach the
end of our ropes and patience, we come down too hard on them. Then we
feel guilty, and try to be easier on them again, and the cycle just goes
around and around. However, if you use the techniques described above,
they will help you get back in control, smooth out your family life a great
deal, and help you be a better parent. This, in turn, will help you be a much
better student and employee.

Be aware, though, that with any change in household routine or discipline strategies or in how you treat your children there may be some back-
lash. That is, your children might react to the changes by acting worse than
before, *for a little while.* This isn't because these strategies discussed above
don't work, it's just that it's human nature for children to test any new system to see if you really mean business and to see how long the new rules

are going to be enforced. So don't give up! After a couple of weeks to a month or two your children will fall into line with these new techniques (if you use them consistently—that is, all the time and every time you need to) and your family atmosphere will improve greatly. Your children will become more cooperative, get along with each other better, and will be generally nicer to be around (so will you!).

It's so very important for you as a single parent to feel like you have control over your family life in general, but it's especially critical to be in control of yourself and your children while you're in school. When you feel like you're back in control, you'll yell and threaten less, and your children will feel like they are loved and cared for when they see you relax and enjoy them—instead of frantically trying to maintain control and discipline all the time with truly negative and ineffective strategies like yelling, nagging, threatening, spanking, over-reacting to everything, and so on. You'll be able to better concentrate on studying, too, when you're away from your children and being a student. You will also be able to relax more and actually spend much less of your precious energy at home on child discipline. You'll become a calmer, more effective parent, and your children will respect you more.

Professional Help for Your Child and You

If your children, after a couple of months of your consistent and proper use of these simple discipline techniques, don't start to behave better and you find yourself just hating being a parent most of the time, certainly get some professional help, for you and them. You may want to send your problem child(ren) to a social worker, psychologist, or other professional to be "fixed." Well, it doesn't work that way! Families are dynamic, and you must be involved in the process.

A friend, your child care center's staff, a school psychologist or social worker, or a social services caseworker will probably be able to refer you to someone helpful. A good rule is to never let things deteriorate to the point of a crisis before you get some help. For more advice and information on consulting a professional, see Chapter Ten: Just Stress, I Guess.

SPOTLIGHT ON COLLEGE PROGRAMS
College of Saint Catherine

Saint Mary's Campus of the College of Saint Catherine of Minneapolis is planning a Single Parents Program to open in the winter of 1992 with housing near campus for ten single parent families. The purpose of the program is to provide housing and other services in an environment of mutual support to encourage single parent students on welfare to start and complete their educational programs. Single parents often start, drop out, and never return to their academic programs due to problems with child care, transportation, or lack of supportive friends and family. In addition to housing, students will qualify for child care subsidies and receive assistance in child care placement. Support networks will be provided and the Single Parents Program coordinator will serve as a liaison to appropriate community programs.

Saint Catherine's has traditionally educated women in an atmosphere sensitive to women's needs and concerns. Saint Mary's is a small urban campus designed to help students with special needs succeed; special admissions programs, financial aid, individual counseling, and learning assistance programs are made available. Two-year associate degrees in health care and human services are offered. The need for professionals in these fields throughout Minnesota will aid recruitment of students from around the state. Ninety percent of Saint Mary's students secure positions within six months of graduation, at an average salary rate of $11.00 per hour.

For more information, contact:

Kathy Heinzen, Director of Student Services
St. Mary's Campus
2500 South Sixth Street
Minneapolis, Minnesota 55454
(612) 332-5521

6

TIME MANAGEMENT ON YOUR JOURNEY

In addition to money, another resource that will always be in short supply for you while you're in school will be time. You won't have less of it than anyone else, since everybody gets twenty-four hours a day, but you will always have too much to do. You will be a parent, student, and maybe even an employee all at the same time. This can be as overwhelming as it sounds, but you'll be able to handle all of these responsibilities if you use good time-management skills.

Keep It Simple and Organized

The first time-management technique is simplification. How can you simplify your daily activities? First look at what you normally do everyday. Second, decide how important all the activities really are. Third, look at how much time each takes. Fourth, decide how much time you must or want to spend on them (most of us do things and don't even think about these considerations).

Cut down on the amount of time you spend doing chores that are just habits, but that don't need to be done as often or as well. Remember "The Odd Couple?" Be a little more like Oscar Madison the slob than Felix Unger the neat freak. You can learn, through practice, to not let a semi-messy house bother you so much.

Not only should you look at what you do, you need to look at your environment to make it more organized. Can you make it more streamlined and efficient? Is there a lot of clutter around your house you could easily do without? Does every person in your family have a little space, a cardboard box or shelf, for their own stuff? Are often-used items placed in areas where someone can always find them, or do you or your children have to hunt around for half an hour for a pair of scissors? Are useful items kept in your house someplace where children can easily reach them (given that they are old enough to use the objects), or do your kids always have to ask you to fetch things for them? Do you always "lose" your tape, glue, safety pins, and so on? Get organized, and it will save you minutes which otherwise would add up very quickly to hours and days of wasted time.

Household Chores

Another time-management issue is household chores. Are your children given age-appropriate tasks to do, so that you don't end up doing everything to keep your household going? Are you teaching them how to do household tasks and clean-up activities so that they really are becoming responsible for their fair share of the work? (I'm a firm believer that boys as well as girls should learn how to do everything it takes to run a home.)

There will be times, of course, when you'll need to do some major chores yourself, just to do them fast and well. On a day-to-day basis, however, your children should certainly do their share. It takes a little time to teach them how to do jobs right and to your minimum satisfaction, but the time spent teaching them will pay dividends in the future. If someone doesn't do the job right the first time, he or she gets to do it over—a natural consequence of sloppiness.

> *As one person, I cannot do everything, and cannot be everything to everyone. So, my children have learned to cook, clean, and put out more effort so that we have more team work. This means accepting the way they do things and not expecting them to be perfect, either.*

After you've taken a good hard look at your life and daily activities and surroundings, be ruthless in your streamlining and simplifying. Give away old clothes that don't fit you or your children. Give away "junk" sitting around the house. Call a local thrift shop to pick up big items. Sell whatever is semi-valuable that you don't need or want anymore. Have a rummage sale before you start school or during a break in your courses. Besides bringing you a little extra cash, this can be a fun family activity and will help you cut your household down to size.

Place the furniture and household items that you decide to keep in spots that are easiest to clean and manage. If you haven't already, start making lists of household chores that you expect your children to do. Get a system of household management going.

Plan simple menus so that you must shop for groceries only once a week or, better yet, only twice a month. Consider getting milk delivered to your door. This costs a few extra cents a gallon, but will save you time and money in the long run. Slow cooker, stir-fry, and one-dish casserole dinners are great time savers; your kids will like them if you keep the number of ingredients down and only add ingredients they like.

Do laundry only once a week. Encourage your children to wear outer clothing that isn't too dirty twice. Try using a clothes brush (an old clean floor scrub brush can work) to get rid of surface dirt and dust. Even if you have a washer and dryer, it may be more time-effective to take all your laundry to a laundromat and do it all at once. You might even volunteer to take a friend's laundry and do it too, if your friend will care for your children for a couple of hours while you do it. Take a textbook to study and go at an off-hour when the place is not busy.

Personal Care

Get a haircut that is flattering and easy to take care of (go to your local beautician school for a cheap but good one). Same for your kids.

Make a schedule for bathroom use, if it is a problem at your house. Stagger getting-ready-for-bed activities, so that one child is in the bathroom, one is getting into pajamas, another is finishing homework.

Any time your kids come home grumpy or really tired, encourage them to take a nice, long bubble bath if they're old enough to be in the tub without your supervision. Right after school is fine. That gets one person alone and quiet for a while, so you can do other things. Pull the shower curtain closed around the tub to afford some privacy if others need to get in the bathroom at the same time. I recommend that you don't put more than one kid in the tub at a time, unless you are certain you can spend time supervising and staying in control of the situation. Never put your kids together doing anything if one or more of them are grouchy or aggressive at the time.

Encourage your children to be assertive about their feelings, and be assertive about your own. That is, if they feel like being alone, or going for a walk, or laying on their bed in a shared bedroom to read for a while, encourage others in the family to respect their wishes. Personal care begins with an awareness of the changing needs of one's self and others. This respect builds a large part of the foundation that enables everyone to manage their own time effectively. When people in your family begin to respect each other's time and space, it will help you stay in control of your own.

The "While" Strategy

After you have streamlined and simplified your daily activities and surroundings, one time-management strategy that works wonders is this: While you are doing a task, or waiting for something, do another thing at the same time. For example, while you wait for the water for spaghetti to boil, wipe down the cupboards and kitchen table. While you talk on the phone, do whatever needs doing that is in reach of the phone cord—dusting or straightening up, for example. While you walk from room to room in your home, always pick up and take things back to their proper places. Seldom walk anywhere in your home without taking something that doesn't belong in the room you're coming from, and transporting it to the place it does belong in the room you're going to. Make sense? While you do dishes or laundry or scrub the bathroom, turn on your tape recorder and listen to the class lectures you taped during the week again (see Chapter Seven: Studying in No Time at All). If you've just used a cloth to wipe up a spill of water, use the same already damp cloth to wipe something else close by. While you're waiting in the grocery store line, get your note pad out and write down anything you need to remember. While you're watching TV with your kids, rub each other's shoulders. And on, and on, and on.

There is one major exception to this strategy. That is, when you are paying attention to your children, either listening to them talk, looking at something they've made, helping them with a problem, *don't* do anything else at the same time. Look them in the eye; really listen to what they're saying. This will go a long way in building your children's self-esteem.

As you practice the "while" strategy, it will soon become a habit and you'll be surprised just how many extra things you can get done without them taking up a lot of extra time.

Just Say NO

Another area ripe for time management is what you do outside your home. Is your time taken up with activities that you don't enjoy but feel obligated in some way to do? Are you someone who can't say no? Are you always the one who supervises outings, bakes cookies, shepherds children hither and thither, delivers flyers, and on and on? When you become a single parent student you will have to learn to say no to a great many outside activities or your home life and schooling will suffer.

Announce to any persons who demand time and energy from you (that you now are unwilling or unable to give) that you are a college student and must streamline your life in order to make it through. You now have at least two full-time jobs, children and school. You probably work, too, which gives you another half-time to full-time job. Maintain ties with people and organizations that you value only, and don't get caught up in the "yes, of course I will" syndrome; try saying "thank you for the opportunity, but no." You'll have a whole bunch of time after your children are grown up in which to volunteer for things. Keeping that in mind will help you feel less guilty now.

I think one of the hardest things for us to do if we were raised to "do unto others" is to say no, especially if we don't have a whole heck of a lot of self-confidence and self-esteem. It is almost like we have to say "yes" all the time so people will like us and think well of us, when all the time we are seething with resentment inside, and then feel guilty because we feel resentful! I don't think living like that is good for anybody, especially single parent students. It also teaches a lousy lesson to our children because they see the hypocrisy.

Since it's hard for most of us to say "no," you can practice by changing the way you deal with people slowly. It helps to take a deep breath and let yourself think clearly about any outside request for about three to five seconds before you automatically answer "yes" to someone you're speaking to. For example, if your child's teacher asks if you could go on a half-day field trip with the class to help herd the kids around, you might consider doing it if you think you could skip your classes or take a little time off work. (It's very peculiar, but people who know you are a student often don't think you are really busy and think you can be on call all the time.) After all, you probably would like to spend more time with your child, and this is one way to do it. Can you do it, though, without worrying excessively about what you're missing in school or creating problems at work? If you feel you can't, after a few seconds of thought suggest an alternative to the teacher. Are there phone calls and other preparatory work that need to be done before the class can go on the field trip? Is there something else connected with this field trip or another class activity that you could do at a time that is better for you and that won't make you resentful of the time you're spending? You don't have to say "no" and just leave it at that; you can come up with alternatives. Maybe you could do something else for your child and your child's teacher or class during a break in your own school schedule.

Another way to say "no" easier is to say it fast—soon after your three to five seconds of think-time. The longer you delay saying "no" to someone, the harder it will be, and the guiltier you will feel. Take a deep breath, and if you have decided you must say no, do it. Don't say, "I'll get back to you." Say "no," then forget it. Go do something you need to do.

Time Demands From Your Children

It will also help you to streamline your life and your time if you start making appointments to spend time with your children. Does this seem silly? It really isn't; it's a practical way of spending special time with them. They feel like they're more important to you, too, if you make special arrangements to do something with them.

Bargain with your kids. Say, "Let's make a deal. If you play quietly together for an hour now, then at 7:00 before bedtime we'll pop some popcorn and I'll play a game with you." Or say, "On Saturday right after lunch I can take you to the zoo or a movie, if you can play outside during the morning, without coming in and bothering me, so I can study." Let your children choose, as often as possible, what you do together. Then do it. Pretty soon your kids will figure out that you, their incredibly busy parent, can still make time for them. Once a week is probably a minimum goal to reach for in spending special time with them when you start school and you're still trying to work out a schedule you can all live with.

Do you have the problem of being bombarded by children's needs, wants, and requests constantly? Do you find yourself spending much too much of your precious time playing referee and consoler and recreation chairperson? This may be because you are putting your children off, unknowingly and unconsciously, most of the time. We get busy as single parent students and don't even realize that we aren't really listening to what our children are saying. We're always telling them to go do something else, away from us. So they end up coming back again and again, because they feel shortchanged.

Another simple fact is that nobody likes being a parent all of the time, or is even very good at it all of the time. If you never get a break from being a parent, you can end up feeling resentful of the fact that your children even exist, even though you love them dearly and can't imagine what you'd do without them. They'll pick up on your resentment. This may make them act out worse. The cycle of resentment, bad behavior, more resentment, more bad behavior has begun.

If you find that your children are demanding your time and attention in all sorts of ways far too often, try the strategies outlined in the previous chapter in the section on "Keeping the Peace." Start making appointments to spend time with them and use bargaining techniques to elicit their cooperation. And try to trade child care with another single parent student to give yourself a break.

Your children will figure out, like everyone else will around you soon, that you are not someone who is at their beck and call every single moment of every day, but that you will make special time for them. They will come to respect your time—if you also respect their need for interaction with you.

Sometimes you'll get home and all of your school-age children might bombard you with different things: "Mom, I need an old shirt to paint with tomorrow—I need help with my homework—I lost a tooth, do you think the tooth fairy will remember tonight?—Dad, I need a costume for the play next week—You said that I could sleep over Friday night at Sarah's house and play on Saturday and you need to call her mom—Can you wash my football uniform?—I have to take a treat to school on Wednesday for our class party"—and on and on.

You can make a rule that your school-age children must not bombard you with requests and demands right when you get home, but that they must write them down right after you all get home so that you may look at them later when you can. An older child can help younger ones with their comments and requests. Post a blank sheet of paper on the fridge or a bulletin board once a week for these requests. One added benefit of their writing requests down is that you'll actually remember them.

Another idea you might try is to make sure your children let you know about things they need or places they need to go well in advance. The only way to get your kids to do this is for you to refuse to scramble around desperately to do things for them if they ask you at the last minute to do things they knew about earlier. Too often we try to be super parents and move heaven and earth to make life nice for our children. That's not a good idea any time, but especially when you're in school. Require that your children treat your time with respect, and they will learn to do so. If your child pleads and begs, "But I just forgot to tell you!" you can put your arm around his or her shoulders and say you're sorry, but that you fully expect him or her to give you more notice next time. Then stand firm, and don't give in to the unreasonable request.

Your child will be mad at you for a while, but will also have learned a valuable and painful lesson—that you are not a slave, that your time is valuable, and that you are a person to be respected.

> *Finding the time to clean my apartment (and the energy to do it) is difficult. Actually, finding the energy to do anything beyond my schoolwork and caring for my daughter is difficult. I've found you just have to focus on what's important and ignore the rest as much as possible.*

Keeping Track of Everything

Another good idea is to get or make a large calendar on which to write all the important things you must do every day, and then post it in a place that you walk by all the time. Buy the biggest calendar you can find, or you can use a large piece of construction paper or tape blank pieces of paper together to make a large enough one yourself. Get out a ruler or yardstick, make the squares, pencil in the numbers of the days and stick the calendar up.

It helps to put a calendar up that covers the whole school term or semester. You can mark down when tests will be given, when papers are due, special appointments with your kids, when you and your children need to see the doctor or dentist, school holidays, social service paperwork due dates, financial aid paperwork due dates, registration and tuition due dates, and on and on. It's best to write things down somewhere the moment you become aware of them and quickly transfer the information to your calendar, because it's so easy for very busy, stressed-out folks like you to simply forget. Can you expect your children to become organized and remember things when you don't yourself?

Dividing Large Jobs into Smaller Ones

Whenever you have a big job to do (such as spring cleaning, a large assignment, a complicated job at work) learn how to divide the job into manageable parts. This idea was mentioned before in terms of separating your life into the various roles you must play, and paying attention to only one role at a time, such as parent, student, or employee. Now we take this idea one step further.

If you don't practice thinking about big jobs in terms of their smaller parts, you'll find yourself overwhelmed most of the time. For example, it's spring break, your house is a catastrophe, and you have a week to catch up on it before the next term starts. If you let yourself think about the whole job, you might very well feel overwhelmed and rebel against this feeling by actually not doing anything useful at all! So, pick a room a day to clean. Or, if that chunk is still too big, half a room. Then let yourself only think about that little chunk on the day you're supposed to do it. Then get up off the couch and do the first part.

You can even break up your first job into smaller tasks. For example, the bathroom can be broken up into sink, toilet, tub, floor, shelves, walls. Begin with the smallest task that you least like doing (cleaning the toilet?). It will feel so good to get started, and get something done, that the next few jobs will go much better. Use this strategy with any big project you have, and you'll feel much less overwhelmed and will be able to get everything done.

You can use the same divide-and-conquer technique with almost any big job, including long research papers for a college course. It works especially well when you have to write something. For example, get five references a day from the library, or write one page a day, or read one chapter a day, or sit down and force yourself to write a rough outline when you have a good idea of your main point. It helps when starting to write any paper to think in terms of paragraphs. When you sit down with the blank paper or blank computer screen staring at you, don't think about the whole dog-gone paper. Think about the first paragraph, or a middle paragraph, or an end paragraph. Then write it in the approximate place it should go. Don't expect it to be wonderful (you are going to go back to revise it later.) Then work on another paragraph, and so on. Pretty soon you'll have one page, then two, then the whole thing will be done! You can teach your children this strategy, too. It will help them get homework done, finish projects, and keep all their own activities under control so they don't always come running to you for help when they're running out of time. Teach them how.

Keeping Up Instead of Catching Up

The best time management technique anyone could offer you is quite simple in theory but very hard in practice: keep up—don't play catch up or let things pile up all the time. This is usually possible, if you use self-control and develop some good organizational skills, though it won't always be. Keeping up takes an incredible amount of self-discipline while you're in school. It is something that no one can teach you but you, and you must practice it on your own with your own will power.

If you find yourself putting off homework again and again, ask yourself what the problem is. Is the assignment boring? Are you feeling too tired? Are your children demanding your time? Are you distracted by a messy house? Does the assignment seem too hard? Are you afraid you won't do a good enough job in the time you have? Sometimes when we put things off a lot, we need to take a good hard look at *why*. Sometimes the underlying reason for our procrastination needs to be taken care of before we can jump in and get something done.

If the assignment seems boring, so what? Some of your assignments in school will seem as silly and irrelevant to you as some of mine did to me. Try to find a way to liven them up a bit. For example, don't write a normal, dull essay or paper. Be a little creative or off-the-wall. Look at the assignment from a different angle. If you're afraid you don't have enough time to do a great job, you're going to hurt yourself even more if you put off starting. If you need to sleep before you can tackle something, go to bed when your kids do and set the alarm for very early in the morning. Then do the assignment. If your kids are out of control and you find yourself constantly after them, reread the chapter before this one. If the assignment seems to big to handle, break it down into little chunks. Last but not least, while you're in school you'll have to satisfy yourself with doing the best job you can, given the limited time and energy you have. You'll probably rarely feel like you have enough time or energy to do the kind of work you'd like to do. That's just the way it is. The time will come in your life when you can focus your energies on what you want to do. Don't fight uncontrollable circumstances now and use up your emotional energy feeling bad about them.

If I follow the schedule I plan out for the day, things get done. I even schedule "nothing" time. Every so often I don't plan my day on purpose as a sort of treat. Usually every day there are things which give me a structure for my day—school, appointments, etc.—then the remaining time I divide up into study, housework, "nothing" time, and play time. There are many things to do in any given day. What hasn't worked is to have no plan.

It's particularly hard (if not impossible) to keep up when you or your children get sick and you simply must take some time off from everything to recuperate or take care of them. But, at all other times under the usual stresses, keep up spending special time with your children, keep up with your text-reading, keep up with paperwork, keep up with bills (as much as your budget will allow), keep up with your must-do housework, and keep up with doing preventative maintenance activities to save yourself from crises later.

If you practice the "keep up, don't catch up" strategy regularly, and learn self-control, then when something does go wrong you won't be overwhelmed by everything else, too. Being a single parent in college can be overwhelming enough—don't let things fall apart around you, and you'll stay in better control of your entire world.

SPOTLIGHT ON COLLEGE PROGRAMS
University of Utah, Salt Lake City

The Women's Resource Center (WRC) provides programs and services to women and men from the university and community. Needs of nontraditional students, single parents, limited income women, and students over fifty years of age receive special emphasis.

The Women's Center offers several services:

1. Referral and resources: information on university and community services, a library on women's issues, a book of current job listings, and a new bulletin board.

2. Two noon event series, "Sack Lunch Seminar" and "Lunch With A Lawyer," are open to women and men, faculty, staff, and students, and members of the community. Participants bring a sack lunch and enjoy the speakers while learning something new or discussing current issues.

3. Nontraditional student orientation: for students thinking about coming back to school, this workshop is offered on the second Tuesday of every month.

4. Conferences and workshops.

5. Individual short-term counseling and ongoing support groups.

6. The Project on Single Parent Students investigates university and governmental policies affecting single parents, reaches out to single parents in the community, and provides services, including:

- "How to be a Successful Single Parent Student at the U," an 80-page booklet free to single parents who pick it up
- Telephone and in-person consultations with a Single Parent Student Advisor
- Workshops on topics of interest to single parents
- Recreational activities for single parent families

For more information:

Women's Resource Center
293 Olpin Union Building
University of Utah
Salt Lake City, Utah 84112
(801) 581-8030

7

STUDYING IN NO TIME AT ALL

This guidebook certainly doesn't pretend to be a "How to Get A's" book. There are many excellent books on study skills available in your local public library and your college library, and college courses designed to help you learn more and obtain better grades. Look in the bibliography for some good books. The following hints are some techniques and creative ideas that will help you get through school much more easily as a single parent student.

Tips for While You're at School

• What the heck is a syllabus? I remember going to my very first class of college and hearing the professor say that she would pass out the syllabus at the end of class. I was mortified! Was it a test? Was it a big assignment? Just what was it? It turned out to be just the schedule of the things that were to be covered in the course and dates of tests and such. I was too embarrassed to ask anyone sitting by me if they knew what a syllabus was, and sat through most of the class too worried to pay attention! This is included here to prod you into asking someone about anything you don't understand to save yourself a lot of anxiety and wasted time. It's always best, I think, to ask the professor about an assignment or test if you don't completely understand what's going on. (The person sitting next to you might not understand, either.) You can ask a fellow student, though, about syllabi and other such things. (Why don't they just say course outline?!)

• If you know what classes you will be taking in the next quarter or semester and who will be teaching them, you can always contact those professors after finals and ask them if you could get the course outlines and schedules (syllabi) in advance (sometimes they have them ready before class starts). Or, you could ask them what chapters you should look at in the textbooks for the first couple of weeks of the course. Anything you can do to give yourself a head start before each period of courses will help.

• Beg, borrow, or buy a small, portable tape recorder and tape class lectures rather than take volumes of written notes. Write down only major points, and listen. Think about what you are hearing. You will learn a great deal by relaxing and really listening and letting your recorder do the rest.

• Always exchange phone numbers early with another person in each of your classes, each and every semester. That way if you miss a lecture or two you'll have someone to call to get an assignment, to find out about an upcoming test, or to ask if you can borrow their class notes. Chances are that your phone friend didn't miss the same class you did.

• Take only a minimum full load of classes, if you must take a full load to qualify for financial aid. If you are going half-time, take a minimum half-time load. Don't try to take all hard science courses at once. Use your head and schedule yourself a mixed roster of courses every semester that consists of, for example, one hard class, one really easy class, and one or two medium-hard classes. Just remember the "Three Bears" story—you know, one bed was hard, one was soft, and one was just right for Goldilocks! Use this strategy whenever your course sequence and major's requirements make it possible and you'll do much better. If you have to take two difficult courses at once, make sure your third is a real slider. It also helps to take different types of courses at once—one English course, one math course, and one self-improvement course, for example. That way the topics you study won't interfere with each other in your brain.

• If you find yourself absolutely swamped during a semester and you just can't finish one of your courses, it may be possible for you to be given an "incomplete" or "work in progress" grade for that course. You'll then be given some time (maybe up to one year) to finish the course requirements. It's always best to try to complete them during the next break between semesters, though; that way your incompletes won't pile up and seem impossible to finish.

> *Being a single parent is a problem because I find myself trying to spend so much time with my kids that I let my school work slide sometimes. This procrastination causes me a great deal of stress when I wait until the last minute to complete assignments which I should have had plenty of time to complete.*

When You're at Home, in the Library, or Elsewhere

• Since you've used a tape recorder to tape class lectures, you can now study while you wash dishes, do laundry, exercise, cook, bathe, or do just about anything else you can think of. Just turn on the tape machine and listen again and again. You'll be amazed at how well this will work for you. Instead of having to sit down somewhere to read and review your notes, you can go about your household chores, get them done, and study at the same time.

Of course, this takes a little cooperation from the kids to be reasonably quiet so you can hear the machine, but if you get a cheap set of headphones you can do pretty well even with the kids in the same room. Just be sure to not make them feel like you are shutting them out. Arrange to spend a little one-on-one time with each of them later when you are done "studying," or spend some time with them before you get started.

• I recommend studying most of the time only when your children are outside playing, when they're asleep, when they are engaged in solitary play, or other times when they are unlikely to interfere with your quiet and concentration. It's much better to not always be hollering at them to be quiet so you can study. You'll end up feeling frustrated, angry, and resentful of the fact that they exist if you always try to study while they're up and about.

Try studying very early in the morning, before they get up. Go to bed when your children do so that you'll get enough sleep. Then study from 3:00 or 4:00 in the morning until it's time to get everybody ready to go somewhere. You can also use solitary play agreements with your children at night and on weekends to give you a little more study time.

• Study at odd moments, even if they don't last very long. Memorize just one important point. Always take a textbook or notebook with you wherever you go. You can read a page here and there and pretty soon you'll be through a whole chapter if you just do this all through the day. Read while you wait for a lecture to begin, read while you're standing in line for something, read on the bus, read at any odd moment. Practice reading a little faster each day.

• Learn how to skim texts. This will take you a while to get the hang of it, but if you practice you'll save yourself lots of time. I don't recommend underlining or highlighting passages out of books either—it takes too much time and you don't know if what you're marking is important. Just read, and review major points or concepts. Always spend time with conclusions of chapters; introductions are less important. I recommend a quick run-through of each chapter, then a thorough study of its major points. You might just quickly make check marks with a red pencil in the margins of the book next to important-seeming paragraphs when you run through a chapter the first time. Then, when you go back to really study, you'll have marked what you need to go over extra carefully.

• Try to read the first parts of textbooks before a course even starts. There is always some "break" time in between quarters or semesters. I recommend that you buy your textbooks, whenever possible, right after you take your final tests for one semester, then start reading them during the break before the next bunch of classes begins. Then you'll be ahead of the game. Even if you don't know which chapters will be required first, you'll get a feel for how the book is written and how hard you'll have to work at understanding the prose; some books are just easier to read than others.

> *Be realistic in your course load and study requirements. Hours out of class spent studying should be at least double the time spent in class.*

• Cramming is okay if you do most of the reading and studying for the course at other times. Cramming should consist of just review, not trying to learn a quarter's or semester's amount of material in a night or two. Cramming has the unfortunate attribute that you'll only remember what you cram (if it's only the first or second time you've seen the material) for a very short period of time, maybe just for the test, if you remember it at all! To retain material longer and be able to integrate it with other things you've learned, you'll need to study it over a period of several weeks and review it regularly. Cramming is especially ineffective in courses where you'll have a comprehensive final test—that means that everything in the course will be fair game on the final exam. If all you've done is cram during the course, you won't remember much for that final big exam.

Writing Papers

• When you are assigned to write a term paper or research paper, get started doing the library research for it right away. Many times the books and journals you'll need will be checked out or otherwise missing, and this will give you time to request that they be recalled or found. If you start out in college not knowing much about how to use a large library, take advantage of any guided tours given by library staff, or attend such seminars as "How to Use the Reference Section" as soon as you can in your college career.

• Pick a narrow topic for any research paper. For example, if you're taking a social psychology course and you are to write a paper about some aspect of social psychology, don't try to discuss more than one theory on the subject (unless you've been told to do an overview of the field). For example, pick one famous or not-so-famous social psychologist and discuss two or three major experiments done by that person. Or pick a social phenomenon, such as mob behavior, and put it in a context (perhaps the 60s race riots, or the uprisings in China and Eastern European countries in the late 80s). Talk about one particular riot, and how a social psychological theory might explain the participants' behavior. If you think you have a narrow enough topic, write it down and reduce it further. Do you know how to reduce mathematical expressions? Use the same concept to reduce research topics. Make the topic small, then write a concise, informative paper on it.

• Write papers with a personal slant, or try to write to educate or inform—don't just write in generalities. Your professors and others who will be reading your paper don't want to read something they already know—dig up particulars, write about something novel or unique, look at the problem from a different angle. This will get your paper noticed, and if it's well thought out and well-written, will get you a better grade. Be a little adventurous in your writing and most readers will respond positively.

• Go over what you have written to find spelling errors, grammatical errors, and lack of continuity and flow. Then rewrite the paper at least once. Rewriting doesn't mean changing everything, just work on those sentences or passages that are confusing, misleading, or unclear. Never, never expect to be able to write an "A" paper at one sitting—believe that you'll always need to rewrite at least a portion of it.

• Leave your paper alone for a day or two; let it "sit," then go over it again. You'll notice dumb mistakes and sentences that don't sound like you want them to. You'll take out entire passages that are irrelevant or unnecessary. You might add something you forgot. It's important to give yourself some time in between readings of your paper. If you're too close to it (maybe you just wrote the last five pages) you won't be able to see what needs to be changed. This is another reason why it's important to get started early.

Keeping Up

• Keep up, don't try to catch up. As I mention elsewhere, this is very critical, yet so hard to do. Study a little each day, even if you don't do a lot. Then have some days where you concentrate your efforts and get through several chapters of a text, or do lots of problems for a science class. You will have an incredible amount of reading to do, guaranteed. Then pick one day a week when you won't study at all, and give yourself a break. If you save all your studying for the weekend before a big test, you can be sure that most of the time something will happen to prevent you from studying very much that weekend!

> *When trying to find enough study time, I sometimes become overwhelmed with everything around me. So, to get the quiet time I need, I go to bed when my children do, early, and then set the alarm for 12:00 or 12:30. I get up then and study for two to three hours and then go back to bed. It's a good thing that I only need 4-6 hours sleep a night most of the time.*

College Courses to Help You Study and Learn More Effectively

If your reading, writing, math, or study skills are rusty, don't hesitate to take college refresher or remedial courses that are offered. Even if you've been in school for a while, if you find that you consistently get poor grades on papers, it would serve you well to take a course in manuscript writing or editing, or basic composition. Of course, it's best to take these kinds of classes when you start off in college; they take time at first, but will save you lots of time, effort, and aggravation later.

Those courses and others on test taking, test anxiety, or schedule/time planning which may be offered by your school may seem to pertain mostly to folks who have much more time than you do to study. So, take the parts of what the courses offer that you can use in your situation, and disregard the rest. Try not to be offended if the instructor tells the class members to not party too much, or to set up a time and place to study that is the same each day (since when were any of your days the same!), and so on. If you're lucky, you'll be able to find classes such as those listed above which are targeted specifically for nontraditional, older, hard-working students with families to take care of. These are the best, but if you can't get them, take second best.

> *The older my son gets the later he goes to bed—particularly in the summer—I find that I used to get a lot of work done in the evenings, but now I must stay up later to accomplish the same.*

Help from the Library

As mentioned earlier, most colleges and universities have a section in the library with books on building study skills, reading skills, math skills, writing skills, test-taking skills, and so on. Even before you start college, visit the campus library and read some of these books. (You may not be able to check books out of the college library unless you have a student card, or buy a special nonstudent card.) Once you're a student you can check them out and study them in more depth. Your local public library will have some of these guidebooks.

SPOTLIGHT ON COLLEGE PROGRAMS
Community Colleges of Spokane

The Community Colleges of Spokane, including the Institute for Extended Learning, offer several services that benefit single parent students.

The first is a "Help Line." Single parents (and other low-income or disadvantaged people, or displaced homemakers) can call this number for assistance with all sorts of concerns, and for referral to appropriate college and community services. This is also a walk-in service; call the help line number for the address: 459-3755.

The second is a resource guide called "The Single Parent Outreach Connection Resource Directory," available at no charge. This little goldmine of a guide offers information about child care, food banks, low-cost health services, low-income housing, and a myriad of other topics that are extremely useful to single parents and others. This resource guide lists services and organizations throughout Spokane County.

A third program is called "Project Self-Sufficiency" which is particularly for young single parents on AFDC. Call the number below for more information.

The Institute for Extended Learning is a "college without walls" bringing educational opportunities to people who live outside the Spokane city limits. "Change Point" is a program especially for displaced homemakers. For more information about any of these programs available in the Spokane and surrounding areas, contact:

Brenda VonBrock, Director Life Skills
Community Colleges of Spokane
Institute for Extended Learning
West 3305 Fort Wright Drive
Mail Stop 3090
Spokane, Washington 99204-5228
(509) 459-3218
Help Line Number: 459-3755

8

THE PERFECTIONIST TRAP

Don't try to be a perfect anything—especially while you're in school. Be very aware, at the outset, that you will most often have to accept much less than perfection from yourself in all areas in order for you to be reasonably good in any of them. Was one of your parents a superperson who tried to do everything perfectly and who expected the same from you? Then you'll have a tough belief system to conquer, and you'll need to tie your self-esteem up with something else (perhaps persistence, courage, flexibility, tolerance, creativity, reasonableness, or fairness).

What Have You Got to Prove?

Are you trying to battle feelings of having to prove to the world that you can do anything, no matter what? Sometimes those kinds of feelings can spur us on to do wonderful things; however, sometimes those same feelings can be carried too far and cause some problems. Do you remember Indiana Jones running from the eight-hundred-pound boulder in the opening scenes of "Raiders of the Lost Ark?" You'll feel just like he did then if you try to do everything perfectly; everything will soon become like that massive boulder, and you'll have to run faster and faster to keep from getting squashed by it all!

> *My problems are generic: time, energy, money. If an adult student returns to school, she/he has to balance the adult responsibilities of supporting a home and/or dependents. There is simply not enough time, energy, and money to have a standard of living or standard of intimacy that would be desirable to the average person.*

Re-examine Your Expectations

It's extremely difficult for some of us to have a less than spotlessly clean and neat home, get less than all "A" grades, raise less than wonderfully well-behaved and brilliant children, enjoy less than a full and exciting social life, have less than . . . you name it. But accepting less than what we want, and especially less than we know we are capable of, is something that single parent students have to do all the time. When we refuse to let our expectations for most areas of our lives come down a couple of notches while we're in school, we end up feeling frustrated and angry at ourselves, our children, and the whole world a good deal of the time.

Okay, I'll admit that I tried to be supermom, superstudent, and supereverything for the first few quarters I was in school. I ended up feeling exhausted and getting sick all the time, and my expectations were brought down with a thud to an even lower level than they had to be by my own overwork. I could have managed to get A and B grades, keep a reasonably neat house, raise reasonably okay children, perform reasonably well on the job, if only I had been reasonable!!

> *When I first started school, grades were very important. I had my eye on a 4.0 (A) constantly. It didn't take long, however, to see this as unrealistic. When taking into consideration all of the responsibilities that I have, and the course of study I am pursuing (science), I came to realize that I have taken on a monumental task, and that completing this task is what is important to me—whether it be with a 4.0 GPA or a 3.0 GPA. I had to drop a lot of "perfectionistic tendencies" in order to cope with everything from housekeeping to homework.*

When you try to be superanything, what usually happens is that you wear out yourself and people around you. It always turns out that something suffers from your overzealousness. Usually it's your good humor, but sometimes it's your children, studies, work, or friends. It is simply the case that you are now or will be in a situation where it is absolutely impossible, without doing undue damage, to be a perfect anything. You must settle for less, maybe not a great deal less, but less. You must also learn to do this fairly early on in your college career in order to save yourself and your children much trauma.

This doesn't mean that you *always* have to settle for second best. Sometimes you can be very, very good at certain things, at other times you'll switch and be very, very good at others. Just don't expect yourself to be able to do everything awfully well at the same time. For instance, during the beginning of the quarter or semester, you can keep your home neater, pay more attention to your children, and keep up with homework. Then, as midterm tests and papers come up, you'll spend more time on them (doing pretty well) and less time on your housework and children's wants (not needs). As the quarter or semester draws to a close, you'll be spending even more time catching up with homework, and your house may be a real mess. (Hopefully you haven't totally ignored your children at this time—but you've put off some of their wants for your break time.) Then the break between courses finally arrives, and you take your children to a movie like you promised them when you were busy, and you spend a little extra time with them. You can work on getting your home back in order.

Give it a try, but be realistic with your expectations of yourself. I have had to come to terms with the fact that if I am to be what I consider to be a "good" parent (i.e. involved in my son's life) then I cannot expect to also make "A" grades all the time.

Allow yourself to put some of your children's wants (but not needs) off at times when you are extremely pressured by schoolwork. Also allow yourself to occasionally put schoolwork off to be able to enjoy your children, friends, and the world away from school and work.

If you let yourself believe that you must be completely competent and wonderful in every facet of your life at every moment, you'll become a pretty unhappy person. If you realize that things ebb and flow and change almost minute by minute, you'll get through easier and with much less guilt and bad feelings.

SPOTLIGHT ON SUCCESS

Ms. Joan Otting
Traer, Iowa

My advice to any OTAs (Older Than Average) single parents contemplating going to college? Do it! Of course, my initial thoughts on pursuing a college degree were not this definite. In fact, I dithered, one day thinking I'd go, and then changing my mind overnight.

I was married at age eighteen right after high school graduation, and for the next twenty-seven years I had a great time, raising eight children with a great husband in a great big house, and doing a lot of volunteer work for great organizations. One winter evening in that great life, my forty-eight-year-old husband dropped dead in the kitchen from a heart attack. Life was not so great then. I was a panic-stricken woman with six children still at home to support, in a thirteen-room Victorian house in constant need of repair.

I had no marketable skills, I thought, and there were few jobs available in the small town where we lived. Job Service told me they could place me as a hotel maid when I went there two weeks after the funeral. I attended a Displaced Homemaker class at the YWCA in a large town twenty-five miles away which was very helpful. Against the leader's advice, I decided to take a three-month secretarial course. She told me I should go to college, but I was too afraid and too insecure to try such a big step at that time.

The course turned out to be very easy for me and very boring, but I did find out I could do something beside cook and change diapers. So, I decided to do something I had dreamed of doing, go to college and become a social worker. I was then forty-six years old.

During my secretarial course I had to be home by the time school was out, as the children at home were more dependent on me than they had been previously. By some odd coincidence, considering how many activities they were in, all were home the evening my husband died and were now aware of how quickly they could lose a parent. They were reluctant to have me out of their sight too long.

We didn't exactly have a family "conference." It was more of a pep rally with all eight children urging me to go to college. I wanted to go, but was still very hesitant and afraid, but did know from the secretarial course that I could study. Traer, Iowa, where I live, is a small town (1700 people), twenty-five miles from the University of Northern Iowa in Cedar Falls.

I had commuted daily for the secretarial course, so that obstacle had already been overcome. I'd already talked to myself about that (I found myself giving "Me" frequent pep talks over the next three and a half years). It went like this: "What if you have car trouble, at night, alone on the highway?" "Me" answered, "You used to go shopping at night to Cedar Falls, alone, while Link (husband) was alive and didn't worry about this; why worry now?" I also prayed, a lot!

During the family discussion my oldest son pointed out that using some of the insurance money to get a college degree was a wise investment, as I would be doing something I wanted and would, hopefully, have a job to show for it. In August 1980, I enrolled as a freshman, shepherded from department to department by my two oldest daughters who were then both seniors at UNI. They both lived in Cedar Falls and showed me the campus, where each of my classes were, and then told me, "You're on your own now, Mom!" The phrase "ungrateful brats" did come to mind for a few seconds, but as one of the things I'd been trying to teach them for twenty and twenty-six years, respectively, was individual independence, I decided to keep quiet and go to class.

During my first day of classes, in the huge Student Union, an older student (my age exactly, God is good!) approached me and we struck up a conversation. We spotted another OTA student who had also been in one of my social work classes, and we all got acquainted. She was ten years younger. They were both just divorced, and while my first new friend had had a year of college twenty-five years earlier, two of us were freshman. But, best of all, we were all social work majors and single parents.

These two persons became, and still are, two of my closest friends. And you do need some kind of a support system! We were very supportive of each other and could freely talk, laugh, or cry with each other and did all three often. In my last year and a half, a student group of OTAs met weekly at lunch time in the Union. Shared worries are easier to work with, and many times another older student would have had a similar experience and would have some valuable insights to share. If you have the opportunity to attend a group like this, I would urge you to try it.

Driving fifty miles daily, juggling my schedules, my children's schedules, my normal responsibilities (grocery shopping, cooking, cleaning, washing, etc.) with my new responsibilities of class assignments, term papers, and research was, at times, overwhelming. I couldn't "gripe" to my children *all* the time; they were having enough of a change in a mother who was now not there for them every day. We were also sharing reduced financial circumstances. I found the housework was the first thing that didn't get done "like it used to." We had previously attended each child's school events, band, vocal concerts, plays, and games. When we had two at different schools, I would go to one, and my husband would go to the other. I attended most of them the first year and a half, and then had to schedule night classes my last two years. Again, a discussion; my children were all very supportive. At times an older brother or sister could attend in my place. That didn't help the guilt that seems to be built into this kind of situation. When I talked with single parent fathers, I found they, too, experienced these feelings of guilt. Talking with each other helps, as all student single parents were in the same position.

One of my problems, that not every older student experiences, was my weight. I still haven't overcome it. I am fat. College campuses are not designed for fat people whose ankles swell up when they have to hurry between classes and have many blocks to cover! Nor are most classroom chairs designed for fat people! But I figured, "I got here, I'm too pooped to leave, I'll wedge myself in and worry about the permanent crease across my rib cage some other time." Later, I learned to schedule classes with enough time between, and was much happier knowing I wouldn't miss the first ten minutes of the lecture because I was trying to catch my breath and start breathing again!

On winter mornings when it was –20 degrees and I was walking up from the parking lot in my boots, stockings, long-johns, sweaters, scarves, and mittens, with frost on my eyebrows, I would mutter to myself, "What in heaven's name am I doing here like this when I could be home?" And my answer would always be, "Having the time of my life!" I enjoyed the classes, absolutely loved learning, and to get affirmation of all that I did, in the form of grades, was too wonderful to miss a day!

I did miss some days, though. Kids still get sick when Mom's in college. I would stay home with them, call the professor to explain why I wouldn't be in class (something they were not used to!), and catch up on the notes from someone who had been in the class. If a test was scheduled and it was at all possible, I would have one of the older children stay at home with the sick child until the test was over and then rush home and be "Mom" instead of #185062, my college ID number.

A by-product of my studying every evening was the children doing their studying with me in the family room. A further bonus was that their grades improved. I never did get the hang of studying with the TV and the stereo on like they did, and would usually wind up reading in bed long after they were asleep.

I also cried myself to sleep some nights. College was fun, but it was hard work. Except for parent-teacher conferences, I had not been in a classroom in twenty-eight years. Not all classes were enjoyable (statistics comes to mind), not all professors were helpful, the children were not always angels or accepting of what I was doing. I was often feeling alone, tired, and afraid I was never going to graduate or get a job.

I had grandchildren, and once overheard my oldest son telling his son, "Grandma can't babysit with you this weekend. She has to study for a big test." I would much rather have babysat.

The biggest obstacle was trying to live up to the "Super-Mom" image I thought I had to fill. My freshman year I kept on teaching a catechism class weekly at church, did my normal volunteer work, I had been elected to the School Board two years earlier and continued that (I have since been elected to two more terms and am still on the Board), did two to four loads of washing daily, cooked, kept up on my antiquing hobby-business, and made the Dean's List both semesters. By June I was exhausted! I planned on attending summer school and did all three years, so I stopped the teaching (I still miss it), quit most of the volunteer work, stopped most of the antiquing, assigned the three oldest children at home different nights to cook dinner (and ate it quietly, unlike some of the other family members!), and showed each child how to run the washer and dryer. Later I told them pink-tinged towels and underwear were my favorite kind. (Parents who sort clothes will understand.) Things got much easier.

I found my age a plus in most of my classes. My history professor called me a "valuable resource" in class one day as we discussed "history," the 40s and 50s! I decided it was a compliment. Life experience with many of the subjects was an added advantage. For the past five years I have served as a speaker in a "Family Development" class at UNI when widowhood and single-parenting is discussed.

As I mentioned earlier, I had feelings of inadequacy to cope with. My daughters, who showed me the ropes, also urged me to take some exams to try and test out of some subjects, as I had been an avid reader all my life. I did, and tested out of fifteen hours, a semester of classes. This was a boost to my ego, and is an option every student should explore.

My first year was harder than it needed to be by my trying to maintain all of my former activities *and* take the place of two parents for my children. When I finally realized I was a *single* parent and could never be two parents, I was able to assess what I could reasonably expect of myself and not set myself impossible goals that I could never meet, as I had been doing.

In May, June, and July of 1983, I did my field placement as a Medical Social Worker at a hospital by working forty hours a week for nine weeks. At the end of that time, my supervisor at the hospital asked if I would consider working half time in the fall, starting September 1, while she took a maternity leave. I rearranged my classes, with a great deal of help from my professors, and my last semester I worked twenty hours a week on Monday, Wednesday, and Friday at the hospital and carried fifteen hours of classes nights, Tuesday and Thursday. I graduated with honors in December 1983, almost four years to the day from my husband's death. I had a B.A. in Social Work, and minors in Gerontology and Women's Studies.

One of my professors had recommended me to take his place as a Social Work Consultant at a nursing home eight miles from where I lived. I graduated December 14, still working twenty hours at the hospital. That job ended January 1, 1984. However, I had started work on December 1, working sixteen hours a week as a Social Work Consultant at the nursing home (Christmas was a blur that year!), and in the next month accepted part-time jobs at two other nursing homes as a consultant.

In July 1984, I started to work full time as a medical social worker in the nursing home where I am still employed. It is twenty-one miles from Traer, but I am well used to the driving. I enjoy what I am doing, and in all my job interviews my age was a definite asset. I emphasize that, as one of my fears all through school was that I would have my degree and no one would hire me because I would then be so old! The administrator who hired me for my present job (I was then fifty years old) told me my going to school at my age was what made him decide to hire me. He said, "I figured if you could do that, you could do anything." And you know what, he was right!

9

FINDING THOSE OF YOUR SPECIES AND OTHERS ALONG THE WAY

When you begin college, you might be sure that you're the only single parent on campus. Almost everybody else looks so young and unencumbered, and you'll probably feel out of place for a while. But you'll soon discover one person, then two, then more like you, both men and women. (It's like coming home after being away on a long trip—at first you don't notice the spider webs, but once you see one spider web you're going to see a whole bunch!) There are many, many folks like you struggling through school with similar responsibilities, problems, dreams, desires, and motivation.

How Can You Find Them?

If you don't want to wait to run into people in similar circumstances one at a time, you might want to contact the student services center, the women's center, or nontraditional student center on campus. Attend support groups, and go to seminars geared toward nontraditional students for help with financial aid, study skills, and stress management. These on-campus activities are often advertised in the college newspaper, and on flyers around campus and on bulletin boards in the centers mentioned above. You'll meet people like yourself at those kinds of functions. Even if you're not ready to involve yourself socially, learning that similar souls exist on campus will help you to feel less alone and can help you emotionally. When you attend such activities, you'll probably be surprised to find out how many students like you are on your campus. There are more than you might think.

Advertising Strategies

If you have small children, you can put up a flyer at your daycare center to advertise your desire to exchange babysitting with other single parents for study time or recreation. You can take your child to class or the library with you sometimes; this can make other people in similar circumstances aware that you are a parent as well as a student, and a glance at your bare ring finger will tell them you're probably single.

Talk about your family situation in casual conversations with other people. They, in turn, might tell you about someone they know, or mention you later to a single parent friend they have.

Open your ears and listen. You may overhear someone else talking about their single parent lifestyle; then you may introduce yourself at an opportune moment. Pay special attention to other students in your classes—look for the ones that look the most exhausted at times, the ones with a little gray hair, and the ones that get the best grades and seem the most motivated to be there, in spite of their tiredness. When you identify someone in your classes to approach to be a phone pal (someone you can call for assignments or information if you miss a class or two), you'll probably choose someone who seems similar to yourself. That person might very well be a single parent student, too.

On-Campus Activities

Some campuses have already organized activities for students like you. If they haven't, you might want to approach certain groups (such as the school of social work, the women's center, the nontraditional students' center, or the associated students' organization) to see if they would be willing to sponsor educational seminars or recreational/social activities for single parent students in the near future. In addition, you can approach the campus office pertaining to student organizations and activities; the staff there will have a list of all student organizations. You'll find something you're interested in.

> *I'm involved in on-campus acti..ities such as lobby groups for more day care, better family/student housing, etc. I believe in striving for goals that are attainable.*

Organizing a Single Parent Students' Group

If you're highly motivated, and want to organize people like yourself into an on-campus group for social activities, mutual support, child-care trading, and/or political action, go for it! It helps if you know at least five other people who want to help you start up such an organization, and then delegate tasks to each. One person might be in charge of advertising, another could meet with university officials and professors, another could explore fund-raising possibilities, someone could brainstorm for ideas for activities, and so on. This can take as much of your time as you are willing to give.

You might try to get some advertising funding from any of the student centers mentioned above, or pool your own resources to put an advertisement or two in the student newspaper about your group. You could scrounge scratch paper from the computer or copy center to make flyers to put up around campus, if you can't afford to put an ad in the paper. You could have brown-bag lunches at a certain spot on campus or in the cafeteria, at a set time and day of the week that never changes. Single parent students could then attend when it's possible for them.

But, you say, "I won't have time for any of that!" Okay, you may be able to get through school just fine on your own, with very few contacts with other people in your circumstances. Then again, you may be short-changing yourself. It takes about five minutes to make up a flyer something like this:

ATTENTION SINGLE PARENT STUDENTS
Need a friend? Stressed-out? Looking for other students like you on campus to trade child care with, to talk to, or just socialize with? Leave your name and phone number with someone at the front desk of the _____ center. We are organizing a single parent students' group for mutual support, help, and maybe even political action. Stop by today.

You could make up ten or fifteen of these flyers. Put one in your day-care center, and pin up a couple on bulletin boards around campus. You'll find someone in the nontraditional student center, financial aid office, or other office on campus who would be willing to let you have a little counter or desk space for your sign-up sheet. Although women's centers are great places, you might not want to choose that place at first for your sign-up sheet, because it might scare off single parents who are men! Try first for an office without a gender connection. If the women's center is your only possible choice, just make sure that you encourage men to sign up too, by indicating this on your flyers.

What if you don't get a large response? Well, you could go back and put a big red border around your flyers so they're more noticable, or you could put up more of them, or change their locations. You don't have to make special trips to do this, just put them up while you're on your way to various classes or offices around campus. The more flyers you put up, the more likely it is that they will be noticed by someone like you.

Once you get enough people involved and interested in keeping the organization going, you might want or need to register your group with the associated students' or student services organization's office on your campus. Once you have developed a bona-fide student organization, your group will probably be eligible to apply for funds through your college or university which are available for such student-run groups. Talk to the advisors in these centers for advice and instructions on how to register your organization and apply for aid.

One of the best advantages of getting a single parent group going—or joining an already existing one—(especially if it's advertised that the group is open to single parent students whether they have complete custody of their children or not) is that you'll have regular contact with other people like yourself. You'll be able to socialize with folks who well understand what you're going through and who might become real allies in your life.

It's just easier to start making friends with people in similar circumstances. They're the most empathetic and understanding, and their friendship will help you build up your self-confidence enough that you will be able to expand your circle of acquaintances to include all sorts of people in all sorts of circumstances. I don't recommend, though, that you associate only with other single parents all the time, even at first. This is important because you need to get different views of the world from other people, and because it's too easy to get bogged down in the traumas and problems of single parenting.

Are You Terribly Shy, Distrustful, Hurting?

Maybe you're shy or self-conscious and have an awfully hard time meeting people. Maybe you just don't trust anybody anymore. Maybe you're afraid of getting hurt or disappointed by someone. Okay, well, so what? That sounds pretty harsh. But you know, you can choose to carry around your emotional baggage forever, and stay alone and afraid, or you can choose to try to meet different people now—some of whom may become just the kinds of friends and lovers you want.

> *I don't have any dating relationships for now. There is no time. Something has to give, and it can't be the kids or school, and I have to work. But I would like to date and it's lonely too much of the time.*

Somebody to Hug, or More

Water, water everywhere, and not a drop to drink! It will seem like that sometimes in terms of people to get together with while you're in school. You're surrounded by hundreds, if not thousands, of people at school all the time. You might not have a clue as to how to go about getting to know any of them intimately. A large campus can be a very isolating place even though, or maybe because, there are so many people. Everyone's schedule is different, everyone is terribly busy, and almost everyone is lonely at least part of the time. All students, especially when they begin school, battle loneliness and feeling isolated on college campuses; it certainly isn't just a problem for single parents.

You probably know what it is like to have a life partner, even if the relationship wasn't very wonderful. You probably know what it's like to not have to sleep alone. Now you're going to become (or you already are) a student with little time and energy to meet people and get together once you meet them. You just have to get organized enough and practice good time management skills so you'll have a little time to socialize, while at the same time mustering up enough courage to allow yourself to be just a little bit vulnerable and socialize.

Dating and Intimate Relationships

Most single parent students I've heard from rank "dating and relationships" as being major problems for them while they're in school. The ones who seem to have the most trouble are those recently single, and those just starting school who are still really bogged down with juggling their various responsibilities and maybe lacking in self-confidence. It's the most difficult for those who haven't learned how to manage their time well enough to make time for at least minimal dating and time with friends.

The single parent students I knew personally dealt with this problem in lots of ways, from staying absolutely socially isolated, celibate, and/or lonely, to working hard at maintaining friendships and contact with potential dating partners, sometimes even at the expense of their studies or time with their children.

> *It's good that my daughter's father takes her on the weekends, but it's hard to cope with, too. I feel so alone and isolated when she's gone. No excuse to go out. I'm generally pretty shy, unless I have to be outgoing.*

Now, no one has all the answers to finding and keeping people as friends and lovers, especially all the answers for you. This section will only offer a few suggestions about how you can get started with your social life, if you haven't already, and how you can create time and room in your life for other people while you're in school. Short of advertising in the school newspaper, hanging a sign around your neck, or beating a drum around campus, what can you do?

Getting Started

For starters, you should set aside one morning, afternoon, or evening a week for just you and a friend or dating partner. This time is sacred, and you can allow nothing short of dire emergency to take this time away from you. Then you can't use the excuse of never having any time to see people (that's an easy excuse to use, especially since it seems so true!). Even if you take yourself to a movie, out to dinner, or somewhere else, you are using this set-aside time for you. Trade child care with someone else.

Second, you can ask someone for a date. If you're a woman and haven't ever done this before it will be hard. You'll get a taste of what it has been like traditionally for men. Men lay their hearts and self-esteem on the line, and most of them have to get up a considerable amount of courage before asking anyone out. It's not easy even for the ones who seem slick and smooth and practiced. When you ask someone for their company, you don't have to suggest something exotic. Just meet for sack lunch out on the lawn after classes, walk though the campus museum, or visit a little restaurant just off campus. Make it easy on yourself, make it easy on them.

Sometimes the best way to go about doing this is to suggest an activity in just a casual way to someone you've met in a class, lab, at work, or anywhere. It's easier if you've had a chance to talk with the person a little during the normal course of your days; that way the person doesn't seem like a total stranger, and you both know a little bit about each other's lifestyle. I do suggest that you go "dutch" whenever you go out with another student, and make it as inexpensive a date as possible. Most students, be they single parents or not, are quite poor and will appreciate your thoughtfulness and insight into their financial situations.

> *The worst part about being a student and a single parent is the feeling that you are constantly juggling things—your family, your job, studying. I couldn't even imagine trying to develop a relationship with someone on top of everything else. I simply don't have the energy!*

If you're shy (most people are) and not very adept at starting conversations and are afraid of looking foolish, start small. If the thought of asking someone out gives you a major case of nerves and makes you think about asking your doctor for Valium, read on.

When You're Terribly, Painfully Shy and Quiet

One of the things you can try is to make small talk with people who are standing next to you in bookstore lines, tuition lines, and other places. (I tried this after I was at the university a couple of quarters and was tired of feeling so interminably alone in a sea of people.) You could start out making comments to various other people waiting in a long line like you on the lack of enough personnel to take care of everyone's business when enrolling for classes or buying books. Or, comment on something good that is happening. You'll find that most people will respond quite well—some other people are bored and feeling lonely in line, too. It is a rare person who won't respond with a friendly comment in turn, or who acts totally uninterested in conversation at all.

This strategy will probably help you if you're someone who is too independent, too isolated, or too shy. After you practice talking with complete strangers for a few minutes every day it will become easier to talk to people in general, and to start longer conversations in more conducive circumstances. You will gradually lose your fear that people are looking at you negatively, and you'll just go ahead and talk to people.

If you've been a stay-at-home parent for a good number of years, you could have lost (or may never have learned) the fine art of conversation and interacting with people who are as tall as you are and around your same age. Some people are never taught how to initiate and sustain conversations as children and teens, and trying to do so then becomes even harder as adults. Even if you were married or lived with a partner for some time, you might have spent most of your time in front of the television or doing separate things at different times. After we've parented for a good number of years, we wonder, too, if we can even have a normal conversation with another adult after years of interacting mostly with children, or being stuck in jobs where we are really pretty isolated from people and don't have much chance to be sociable.

> *It's hard work but rewarding. Don't feel sorry for yourself—think of it as a challenge and that you are doing something positive for your children. Ask for help (from counselors and others) when you need it. Realize that you will not have the time to do all the household tasks like you did before. Enjoy the process and not just the end result. Make friends with other single parents, help each other out.*

Many people and magazine articles tell you to just get out there and do things, but many don't tell you *how*. Try these specific things if you're dissatisfied with your social life:

• Look people in the eye from time to time. This sounds kind of silly, but some of us who are shy and really lonely just don't do this, so other people assume that we're just not very interested in them. You don't have to stare; just make eye contact with someone who seems interesting, whether as a friend or lover. If you go around looking unapproachable, always looking everywhere but at people, it's unlikely that people will approach you.

• Assume a relaxed bearing. People tend to avoid other folks who seem real anxious, "uptight" (I really do hate that word), or nervous and worried all the time. Even if you feel those things most of the time, practice looking like you don't. Take a deep breath, relax your forehead, hands, arms, and hunched shoulders, quit moving nervously, and then be a good actor or actress and look relaxed. You may think this is being false or not real, but you will find that doing those things actually helps you to relax on the inside, too.

• Start talking to and with people. A couple of times a day, ask anyone for the time, comment on the weather, moan about an upcoming test, anything to get your mouth open and someone to listen to you for a minute. You don't have to say anything profound, witty, or very intelligent. Just start talking. (Getting started talking is a lot like getting started writing—start small and almost anything will do!)

• Take college classes in assertiveness training, conversation skill building, test anxiety management, time management, or child development. You'll find people in those classes who are like you and with whom to do things (maybe practice the skills you learn in class?).

• Try to attend your major's department seminars, lectures given by guest speakers, political or other kinds of meetings on your campus once in a while. Then use the strategy of talking to someone, briefly, and you'll be able to find comrades with similar interests.

• Sit in public places (if you can stand the commotion) to study and read. Look up from your book or notes now and again and look at people. Make yourself visible—don't go away and hide. Someone might approach *you*.

• Bring your children on campus sometimes for activities or just to a class now and then if they can behave themselves. You'll find that other folks in your classes that you know in passing will come up and say, "I have a daughter about her age, too," or something like that. Bring your lifestyle out into the open—I always loved seeing children on campus. It made me feel like I wasn't the only one with that responsibility. It opens up commonalities with people.

• Use the campus recreation facilities, the gym, and other places where people congregate. Take a P.E. or recreation class, such as tennis or hiking. Try to get involved in an activity where you'll need to communicate with other people to do the activity.

• Get to know your neighbors. The more people you have contact with, the more you will find that they have friends and relatives who are single and who would like to get together with someone like you. You don't have to be "fixed up" or go out on blind dates, you just have to be aware and say "hi" to them when they visit your neighbors. You may be invited to dinners or get-togethers, and find that there is someone there you want to get to know better.

• Do not look for perfection in friends or lovers. It doesn't exist. Don't wait for Prince or Princess Charming to come along and reject all others. You don't have to accept all opportunities for companionship, surely, but don't be too picky, either. Give yourself at least one chance with a person during a lunch or daytime activity (much better than evenings for "first dates") and then see how you get along.

• Don't let your loneliness put you in awkward or dangerous situations. It's better to spend some time during the day with a potential date than it is to go out at night for the first few times. That way you don't have the awkward "should I invite him/her in?" dilemma at the end of an evening, and you're less likely to be pressured into something you don't want. (Of course, typical nighttime romance can be arranged for daylight hours, too, if you desire!) When checking someone out, attend places and do things around a lot of people—meet him or her there and then take yourself home or wherever you go next.

• Let people know, right off the bat when you're engaged in conversation, about your lifestyle and family responsibilities. I always kept everything right up front and most people really appreciated it. You don't have to explain everything at once, but be sure and indicate that you have children and that you are obligated in serious ways. A quick mention will do. That lets people know, in general, how much time and energy you may have to spend with them, and they won't have to guess. They'll probably be relieved that you won't be expecting them to be always at your beck and call!

• Ask someone in one of your classes to have a snack with you in the student union after class, or something equally nonthreatening and easy.

Stretch Marks and Saggy Breasts, Receding Hairlines and Paunches

Oh, to be older, in college, and surrounded by young people! Although there are many mature students on campuses now, there are still a lot of young hard bodies running around there that we unnecessarily compare ourselves with. Some of us end up trying to compete both sexually and aesthetically with these young people who aren't even aware that we are envying their physiques and surface qualities. Are you going to compare yourself to the unencumbered eighteen-year-olds and, worse yet, try to look and act like them? There's nothing wrong with trying to look as well-preserved and attractive as you can, but there is danger to your perhaps already faltering self-esteem in comparing yourself to the hordes of students who have young bodies and young energy, firm breasts and all their hair!

Building Up Your Sagging Self-Esteem

Do you feel unable to use the previous bits of advice on how to get started socializing because you don't feel very good about yourself? If you perceive that you are really different from most people at school and that you can't possibly compete successfully with the youngsters for your share of social opportunities or dates, it can be discouraging, to say the least. If all you allow yourself to see are the people who have desirable attributes that you think you don't, your self-esteem can sink lower and lower. A campus is an ideal place to compare yourself (either favorably or unfavorably) with other people because there are so many of them, and the atmosphere is competitive in all sorts of ways. Beware of the surface comparisons.

I strongly advise, first, that you look, dress, talk, and act your age. If you try to compete with the youngsters (except academically), you'll just end up looking out of place and actually turn most people off instead of on. Parts of your body and soul have gone through the mill; this knowledge can make you feel discouraged or inadequate and make you act silly, unless you are aware of what might happen and prevent those feelings from turning into unreasonable behavior.

What can you do to avoid the awful comparisons? Just try to look as good as you can with the raw material you've got. Wear comfortable, easy-to-move-in clothes in colors and styles that look flattering. Pay attention when someone pays you a compliment on how you look, believe them, and say a gracious "thank you." Get a haircut that fits your face and features, and (if you're a woman) go easy on the makeup if you wear it at all, and only use enough to enhance your natural good looks. If you need to lose (or gain) some weight so you'll be healthier and feel better about yourself, get some sound advice from your physician or other health care person, and work on it slowly. Work on your posture, too—stand up and sit up as straight as your creaky joints will allow. Walk with a pride that comes from surviving this tough world, and from knowing you are a unique, likeable person.

Pay attention to the myriad older students on your campus, and less attention (of a comparing nature) to the young students. If you must compare yourself with anyone, at least do it with those who are your own age, but force yourself to look beyond the surface level of people—let yourself appreciate and admire all sorts of nonobvious qualities in others. If you learn to do that, you are more likely to be able to look at yourself in the same way, and doing so will really help you feel better about yourself. Seeing only people's surface qualities is like going to look at houses or cars for sale and only looking at the outside of them, never stepping foot inside or trying out the engine!

Often, single parents and other mature students end up making friends with professors, graduate students, and other "seasoned" folks on campuses. Interacting with these mature peers is comfortable and reasonable. If you can mostly ignore younger students' enviable sexual and physical attributes at the same time and treat them just as people, not as persons with whom you think you compare unfavorably, you'll feel much better about yourself.

> *Try to have a lot of self-confidence. College is very competitive—especially when it comes to grades. You need to believe in yourself and to be determined to finish. College is a wonderful experience. It's not just getting a degree in order to get a good job, but it's a learning, growing experience. There's a lot to learn about yourself and the world around you. Try to stay away from people who'll discourage you, and have people to encourage you—friends, family, or support groups. You'll be a much better, well-rounded person and you'll gain a new perception on life.*

Some of the best ways to feel better about yourself are to do things that you value well, treat others (especially your children) with respect and kindness, enhance your capacities and capabilities, and show concern for and acceptance of other people. Allow your values to evolve so that you can come to appreciate most the qualities people have on the inside. Just because you are an older student newly in college doesn't mean you have to regress to a more immature level of thinking about attractiveness. You probably want to get to know people who focus on the inner workings of people, too. If you do this yourself, you'll naturally migrate toward them.

I never found the perfect answer to loneliness and finding somebody just to hug (or more) when I was a student. I don't think anyone ever does. A college student population is one very much in transition—most folks are going to move on, probably to different states for jobs or graduate school. It's difficult, to say the least, to find someone to spend time with and invest emotional energy in when everyone's lives are so in flux.

It's not impossible, though! My single parent friends and I managed to make and keep friends and lovers and still be respectably good parents and students and workers. It does take some effort to find and maintain friendship contacts and romantic relationships while you're in school, but you'll get better at it as you go along. Just remember that you won't get phone calls, or knocks on your door, or invitations to do things unless you are willing to take a few risks and make the time to socialize.

SPOTLIGHT ON COLLEGE PROGRAMS
Saint Mary College, Leavenworth, Kansas

Saint Mary College cooperates closely with Kansas Social Rehabilitation Services (SRS) to help single parents earn college degrees. All referrals of single parents to Saint Mary College come from SRS. Single parents are tested, and if they are not quite prepared for college work, are assisted in obtaining a GED or tutoring.

During the first semester of college work at Saint Mary, single parents take a course called "Becoming a Master Student" which covers areas critically important to the students' success, such as study skills and time management. These classes are small, and students receive individualized help. Career counselors, a psychologist, a student services office, and the financial aid office are all available to help a single parent student with his or her unique needs, concerns, and problems. Financial aid for single parents is fully covered by Pell Grants, Kansas Tuition Grants, and St. Mary College grants.

An original story written for Leavenworth's local newspapers by Peggy Mayhugh, Saint Mary Public Information Officer, further illustrates their program for single parents:

Unique Program Helps Needy Single Parents Invest in Hope
January 11, 1990

A light flushes orange as a young woman leans against her bedpost trying to read. While the television blares in the next room, her children scurry in and out of the bedroom to inquire what she is doing. Gradually, the children begin bringing in their own books to help mom study. Soon the television is quiet and the younger learners, too, are curled up on the bed. It is night and the light still glows.

It is impossible to measure the worth of a child who has uncovered a desire for knowledge. That greatness abounds when the trait is learned from a parent working to better himself or herself—like the Saint Mary College student in the story above. For a number of single parents in Leavenworth County, the opportunity to pursue a college degree has been deemed a forgotten dream. However, Saint Mary College and Kansas Social Rehabilitation Services have created a reason for them to invest in hope.

Every day social worker Carol Gustafson at SRS sees people in need. She visits with men and women who desire to be self-supporting, who want to better provide for their children.

"They have found that the low-paying jobs for which they are qualified are not getting them anywhere," said Gustafson, who assists with job preparation. "The answer then is education."

In a joint effort, Saint Mary and SRS implemented the Single Parent Program to support capable, interested persons in acquiring an Associate of Arts or a Bachelor's degree. Marking its second anniversary this month, the program has proven unique in several ways.

Both Gustafson and John Estes, the program's brainstormer, agreed that to the best of their knowledge this single parent education effort is the first four-year degree program in the state to work so closely with SRS. Estes directs Saint Mary's Educational Training Services.

"The Single Parent Program is a wonderful example of state, federal, and local dollars at work," said Gustafson. "Nowadays more welfare dollars are being spent to elevate and educate people into the workforce. SRS pays for books, child care expenses, and a transportation allowance. Students are eligible for the Kansas Tuition Grant, federal Pell Grant, and grants-in-aid from Saint Mary. The college underwrites a lot of the education cost. It's something people who contribute to Saint Mary should feel really good about."

Many of the students' first personal contact with Saint Mary is through Sister Margaret Petty, coordinator of the Single Parent Program, who does academic advising and assists with admissions. Part of Sister Margaret's job is to teach the required introductory lessons of such topics as time management, nutrition, and parenting. The skills development courses are offered to help students cope with so many of the economic variables against them—no transportation, continuing family disturbances, two or more dependent children, no sitter, no regular job.

"It takes a lot of courage for them to step out," Estes said. "The lessons on skills development help build a social matrix and a realistic perception."

In May, the first of the program's dozen students will be awarded degrees. One woman, who will receive degrees in business administration and accounting this December, said it has taken a lot of work and commitment to further her education after family problems caused her to face raising two young sons alone. She now has confidence in knowing that she will be able to better support her children.

This single mother shares part of her increased self-esteem by serving as a mentor for the program. Students who have proven themselves to be good role models were asked to assist their classmates by tutoring and providing encouragement. Sister Margaret explained that the mentoring feature was implemented last fall and is being viewed as a very successful component of the Single Parent Program.

Estes, who has seen the program through its infant stages, considers the new mentor feature necessary. "The idea of students helping students is quite a resource. Personal testimony is a powerful tool—to say 'I did it, you can do it, too.'"

The idea behind the Single Parent Program and Saint Mary's involvement was triggered by Estes' discovery of the high percentage of single parents in Leavenworth and Wyandotte counties. He elected to help this select group have the advantage of a higher education. Since SRS was most readily in contact with the single parents in need, he channelled his efforts through the state welfare office.

SRS now screens persons who have demonstrated an avid interest in a college education. The focus is to identify people who are capable of going to college and who would benefit by it. These people are then assessed and a career exploration is conducted. Program participants may choose any field of study offered through the college. Currently the most popular areas are accounting, education, and human services.

"It is not a big program," Estes concluded, "but an important one, with great impact on lives."

For more information, contact:

Single Parent Program Director
Saint Mary College
Leavenworth, Kansas 66048-5082
(913) 682-5151

10

JUST STRESS, I GUESS

The amount of daily stress that a single parent student experiences can be staggering. The essence of stress is change that you must deal with, and the essence of life is change. The more you try to do in your life, the more changes you will have. But then again, if you never had any changes in your life, life would be incredibly *boring*.

If you're already in school, I don't need to tell you how stressful it is. If you aren't in school yet, be prepared for it. Let's just say that when you go to school as a single parent, you will never, ever be bored!

Once you're a student, you'll have all the stresses other people have, and more. First the not-so-good news, then the better news. The not-so-good news is that life will be difficult much of the time, and you'll probably feel, as one single parent student put it, frazzled! The better news is that you have the brains and will power to deal with all the stresses. In addition, stress can have major positive effects in your life, like helping build your self-esteem, increasing your self-confidence, strengthening your resolve, fine-tuning your coping skills, and much more. You just want to avoid the negative effects of stress: illness, depression, anxiety.

> *I've been depressed and/or angry regarding my ex-spouse almost all semester and that has affected my grades, studying capacity, and motivation. Now that final exams are rolling around, I can spend less time with my son and that's hard because I miss him.*

Good Stress, Bad Stress

A useful definition of "bad" stress is events or circumstances which you have little control over, and which are harmful, threatening, or otherwise crummy. Examples of bad stress may be you or your child becoming ill, standing in long lines to get registered for classes or pay tuition (when you have at least ten million other things to do), conflict with an ex-spouse, your car breaking down, late buses, child behavior problems, the end of any close relationship, breathing cruddy polluted air, not getting your child support on time, and on and on. You know what bad stress is, you've been through enough already!

"Good" stress, on the other hand, may be things that you do have some control over, and which are only a little awful or even mostly good, but which force you to use your mind and skills to deal with it. Although most of us don't think of good stress as being stressful, it can have some of the same negative effects on you that bad stress can, if you don't handle it very well. Some good stress may include beginning college, taking a test you are prepared for, receiving a scholarship, moving to a better place, dating someone new, or helping your child with a tough assignment or problem of his or her own.

Relax, Think, Act

No matter what kind of stress you are experiencing at the moment, the way in which you handle that stress will determine, in large part, the effects of that stress on your body and mind. Because you are an intelligent human being, there are three things you can do whenever you are confronted with any stressful situation:

- Relax
- Think
- Act

To help yourself relax, you can do some of the following things: consciously un-tense your muscles, breathe slowly and regularly, sit down or lay down, walk around briskly for about five minutes, take a warm bath, listen to some quiet music, ask a friend or one of your children to give you a massage, and so on.

Now that you are more relaxed, you can think more clearly, and you can: prioritize your concerns, determine whether you need to deal right away with a problem, remember what strategies worked well in the past to solve a problem, develop alternative solutions to a problem, decide how you will deal with a problem, and keep facts clear in your mind.

After you have relaxed and given a problem some clear thought, you can act by: putting a solution into effect, talking with someone about the problem, avoiding the problem, and taking steps to avoid a similar problem in the future.

No matter what kind of stressful situation you find yourself in, you can use the RTA (Relax, Think, Act) strategy. If your children are old enough to understand what to do, you can teach it to them, too. Their lives will be stressful while you are in college, too. Anything you can do to help yourself and them manage the stresses that occur will make your lives much easier and your time in school much more rewarding.

> *I get very depressed at times and have to take time off in order to recuperate, only this compounds the problem to some extent. I haven't (yet) failed a course, and I've only once dropped a course because of ill health. My biggest problem is always money. I never have enough to even keep decent food in the fridge and the utilities, phone, cable tv, etc., are constantly threatened to be cut off. My debts pile up and I have to juggle everything just to get by. I spend so much time trying to run around and get money that I don't have time to study as I should. The boys keep me so busy that I have no energy for studying at the end of the day, and the floors always need to be scrubbed and laundry folded. When I do find a babysitter for a night, I need to get away, not just go to the library! I hate feeling totally responsible for everything!*

Stress Relievers

What could that stressed-out person describing life in the last box do to alleviate some stress and distress? He or she, and you, can try each of the following suggestions to help you relax, think, and act:

• Eat only good, wholesome, packed-with-nutrition food. Don't waste your money or your health on junk food. Take a course in nutrition in college.

• Get enough sleep; you know how much you need to feel well.

• Talk to people about your problems: friends, family, other students, counselors, professionals—anybody who can offer some good listening and maybe suggest some as yet untried solutions.

• Work very hard at beginning or maintaining an even-keel, honest, friendly relationship with an ex-spouse if you have one. Unless he or she is an axe murderer, spouse or child abuser, drunk, or something equally awful, try very hard to put old wars out of your mind and try to get along now. This will help immensely.

• Take at least fifteen minutes to a half hour each day to just relax. This means really relax. Get a relaxation skills audiotape from the counseling center at your school, another mental health professional, or a library. Then use it. You can also check out books on progressive relaxation from your library. After you've learned the skills, teach them to your children.

• Expect reasonable competence and performance from yourself, not perfection. Don't expect perfection from anyone else, either.

• Keep a small smile on your face—not a silly clown one, just one like the Mona Lisa. This will help improve your mood (confirmed by psychological studies).

• Ask your children to give you a shoulder rub, and do the same for them when they're stressed and tense. Even little hands can help you feel better.

• Use a heating pad or hot water bottle to place on sore muscles to help them relax. I discovered a neat trick one day. You can use an electric heating pad on sore shoulders while you study. Just sit near an outlet, attach the heating pad to your clothes at the shoulders *using wooden clothespins* (never metal safety pins) and turn it on. This really helps relax tired and sore muscles, and helps you feel better so you can concentrate more. Just be sure you don't turn it on too high, or you might fall asleep over your books!

> *I have been sick about one week at least every month. I have had trouble socializing at school mostly due to the time factor. I have had to accept, due to the lack of time and extra stress plus learning a new system (I'm a visiting student), that I won't get the grades I'm used to getting, and that has been a major disappoinment for me.*

• Practice keeping your muscles as relaxed as possible throughout your busy day. Drop your jaw (lips closed). Drop your shoulders. Un-tense every muscle that is tense. Practice this when you aren't faced with a problem, so you can relax more easily when you have one.

• If a problem comes up, deal with it fast. Don't let it degenerate into a larger one later on. Try to stay on top of things instead of letting things pile up on you.

• Read something that's just for fun once in a while. Try a few Agatha Christie mysteries, P.G. Wodehouse's hilarious satires, "Mrs. Pollifax" books, Elizabeth Bowen novels, or Helen MacInnes spy thrillers. Ask your local librarian for some more escape reading suggestions.

> *Allow the first semester to be one for adjusting to the institution and the routine of being in school. Don't take a load that you can't handle; too many courses, etc. Make sure there is not stress from other areas in your life regarding an ex-spouse, etc., to distract you from school.*

• Don't accept unreasonable pressure from other people. Spend time with people only when you can and want.

• Don't hold all your frustration and other negative emotions in all the time, and pretend they aren't there. (This doesn't mean that you let your emotions fly all over the place.) You can explain to your children, in terms they can understand, why you don't feel particularly happy at the moment. Sometimes we try to put on a brave front when we shouldn't.

• Make big "smiley" and "frowney" buttons out of paper that you can pin to your shirt and wear around the house. Even small children can be made to understand that if you're wearing a "frowney" button, that means they need to be extra nice to you and stay on their best behavior, if they want to stay in your good graces. Let them wear similar buttons, too, to alert you to their moods without having to explain a lot.

> *Set up a schedule and follow it for chores, errands, and laundry. Include your child(ren) if they are old enough. Set aside time for you alone, no schoolwork, no housework, no kids. Set aside time for just you and your child, whether it be reading together, walking together, or talking together.*

• Put "Please Do Not Disturb" signs on your door and unplug your phone when you need to be left alone by the rest of the world.

• If at all possible, form a child care cooperative with other parent students in your area, single or not. Then use each other to help out when the stress gets too high.

• Find out if there is a children's shelter that you can use if you feel you are in danger of losing your cool and hurting your child. Find this out in advance of a crisis. Then use it if you need it.

• Breathe from your diaphragm instead of your chest. Pretend your lungs are where your stomach is, and use those muscles to pull the air in. Drop your shoulders, breathe in and out (normally, not in an exaggerated manner) pulling the air way down. Don't continue this deep breathing for more than a minute or two—just enough to really get some oxygen in and carbon dioxide out. You don't want to hyperventilate. Then just breathe normally again but use the right muscles.

• Make it an absolute household rule that there will be no running, no yelling, no slamming of doors, and no loud music, television, games, or roughhousing—at any time. Children can be expected to help keep your household noise level down, and you can use an effective discipline procedure to enforce this (see "Keeping the Peace"). The quieter and calmer your home is, the better you'll feel.

• If you're a woman, and recognize symptoms of premenstrual syndrome in yourself, be extra kind to yourself during the ten or so days before your period. Get more sleep, eat particularly well, watch your salt intake carefully, drink lots of water, and take a vitamin or mineral supplement if you've been advised to at that time. Stay away particularly from sugar and refined food. One of the best ways to deal with this problem, though, is to just recognize that you have it, and realize that there will be about a week out of the month when you're particularly susceptible to becoming angry, depressed, or feeling hopeless and too pressured. Once you realize that you are not going crazy, you're not going to feel out of control forever, and you're just responding to normal hormonal shifts, you will feel much better. You should consult a doctor or women's clinic if your symptoms seem to be major or really bothersome.

• Walk, walk, walk. Most of us have real trouble sticking to an exercise schedule, and walking is one of the best exercises you can do. I recommend that you walk with someone else, particularly if you're a woman. It gives you someone to talk to, as well as increases your safety. Even walking around campus helps, and a good brisk walk in the evening (it doesn't have to be long) will help you relax and sleep better.

> *Money—it's so hard with so little money. You never have enough food, clothes. It's a big deal to get the basics. I hate that pressure. Gas costs, etc. I get migraines bad and serious side effects. I hate always being sick. A lot is due to stress from everything. I want to go to graduate school, but don't know if I could handle it.*

• Take, if possible, an assertiveness training course at your school. A lot of our stress comes from not being able to deal effectively with other people and our environment, and a well-taught course on how to become positively assertive will help you gain some skills that will decrease your stress level. Here is the content of a handout on assertiveness I obtained from a course offered by my college's counseling center:

> Occasionally we feel guilty when we stand up for ourselves or think we don't have a right to our own opinions; however, every human being has certain rights in interpersonal situations. The following list gives a brief account of some of them:
> 1. The right to refuse requests from others without feeling guilty or selfish
> 2. The right to feel and express anger and other emotions
> 3. The right to feel healthy competitiveness
> 4. The right to use your judgment in deciding your own needs
> 5. The right to make mistakes
> 6. The right to have your opinions and ideas given the same respect and consideration other's have
> 7. The right to ask for consideration, help, and/or affection from others
> 8. The right to tell others what your needs are
> 9. The right to ask others to change their behavior
> 10. The right to be treated as a capable adult and not be patronized
> 11. The right to be treated with consideration
> 12. The right to have opinions different from others and not assume you're wrong
> 13. The right not to have others impose their values on you
> 14. The right to take the time you need to be able to sort out your reactions—to use your own time and space
> 15. The right to get the information you need
> 16. The right to choose not to assert yourself

Now, you probably have a few stress relievers of your own that you remember to use from time to time. To help you remember about them when you're really stressed-out, write your ideas down on a piece of paper, and keep it handy to refer to them when you need to. When we're really stressed-out, we often forget about the simple things we can do that will help.

Courses on Stress Management

Most colleges and universities offer classes on stress management for students. Call the counseling center or resource center to find out if and when one will be offered, then go. It will be well worth your while. If you can't find such a course on your campus, call your local county mental health clinic or a local medical center or hospital and ask if they offer one. Even if you have to spend one evening a week away at such a class for a few weeks, it will help you all the way through school. If the course is only taught in the evening, you could make a deal with another single parent to swap child care while you attend; then tend his or her kids when your helper takes the course the next time it is offered.

> *Toward the end of my degree program I began to feel more stress and often took it out on my child—yelling and spanking. I was adjusting to the end of the semester, entering the work force and dealing with a five-year-old's development problems.*

Professional Help

Whenever you feel out of control, too stressed, unable to cope, or if you're taking your stress out on your kids (or if they're taking their stress out on you!), seek professional help immediately. You will know when your normally high level of stress is getting out of hand, and the smart thing to do is to get help fast, before a real crisis occurs—especially before you hurt your child or yourself.

If you seek professional help for stress or another problem, be advised that the following things will probably happen first. The first time you go in for help, the counselor, staff person, or secretary will have you fill out forms and will go over payment plans and some other administrative stuff. This might not leave you a lot of time to talk about your real problems with the professional that day. You will be able to describe, briefly, your major concerns, and the professional might be able to give you an idea of his or her areas of expertise and philosophy. *Go back to the professional for your second appointment!*

The second time you go in the professional will "get down to business" and start to really help you with your problem. It is unfortunate that a good many people don't go back to their second appointment because they are so disappointed in the first one! It's just the way things are usually done when you first go in.

If you are in real crisis the first time you call or go in, however, an effort will be made to get you through that week, at least. You may be offered some mild medication for depression or anxiety, or be given crisis counseling to help you until your next appointment.

If after three or four or five sessions with any professional you don't seem to be getting any real help, you may certainly try again with someone else. Don't get discouraged; it sometimes takes a couple of tries for you to find a good "fit" between you and a helping professional. Most professional mental health people are competent, caring, and helpful. A few aren't, and if you're unlucky enough to run into one of them the first time you go, it's just bad luck. Find another one.

It helps if you ask the counseling center if there is someone on staff who is sensitive to and aware of the needs and concerns of single parents. You may also ask to see an older, more experienced counselor or therapist. You may request that you see a male or a female therapist, a single or married therapist, depending on your needs and wishes. Ask your friends if they know of someone good, or ask your family doctor or your social services caseworker.

Many single parent students have counselors they see all through college to help them with various problems as they come up. You may certainly do this, too, if you can find someone you can afford for a long time—if the professional has a sliding fee scale or only charges students a little bit, or if social services will help with the cost (social services only pays for a certain number of counseling sessions; make sure you find out how many, so you don't get stuck with a large bill!).

Sometimes professional counselors take the place of friends and family. This is certainly okay for a while. You just want to be careful, however, that you don't become too dependent on a professional so that you never seek out other friends and family members to talk with. They are important, too.

SPOTLIGHT ON COLLEGE PROGRAMS
Andrews University, Berrien Springs, Michigan

The Single Parent Program at Andrews University in Michigan is designed to help single parents achieve self-sufficiency. The program prepares parents for careers in the areas of their choice, with the ultimate goal of assisting them complete their college education and find meaningful employment to support their families. Andrews has more than one hundred undergraduate programs, and dozens of graduate specialties that are offered through the five schools of the university.

The Single Parent Program offers the following: realistic financial aid packaging; convenient housing in on-campus apartments; free professional counseling aimed at the specific needs of single parents; inexpensive, on-campus child care for children ages 2½ to 13; social and recreational programming designed especially for single parents; the supportive spiritual environment of an active Christian community.

With the assistance of a carefully monitored program coordinated by Andrews University and state and local agencies in Michigan, single parent students may obtain and retain public assistance benefits throughout a complete four-year baccalaureate (bachelor) degree program.

For more information about this program, write:

Elizabeth Watson, Director
Single Parent Program
Office of Social Work
Andrews University
Berrien Springs, Michigan 49104
(616) 471-9896

11

CRISES AND CREATIVE PROBLEM SOLVING

When you become a student you will be faced with at least one problem, and most of the time several problems, to solve each day. You can get bogged down with the load and use "band-aid" strategies. Or, you can strive to keep your sense of humor and use a few creative problem solving techniques. This will help both you and your family through these tough years.

Creative Problem Solving Steps

There are four main steps in creative problem solving: 1. Decide exactly what the problem is and get agreement on the definition of the problem by all persons directly involved. 2. Come up with as many solutions to try as you can. 3. Use what seems to be the best solution to try to solve the problem. 4. Evaluate how well the solution attempt worked.

Step One

The first step in creative problem solving is deciding just what the problem is. You might think that sounds peculiar, since problems seem to be obvious most of the time. However, sometimes we get sidetracked, tricked, or manipulated into thinking that one problem is really another. So, first decide and write down exactly what you think the problem is. Then, if the problem belongs to other people as well, perhaps your children, ask them what they think the problem is. It's sometimes surprising to find that people may have different definitions of the "same" problem. Other people may even have different goals in the problem's solution. You'll need to try to get agreement on the definition of the problem. (If you can't agree, then that becomes a problem, too!) Once all the people involved agree on what exactly the problem is, you can go on to the next step.

Step Two

Write down as many possible solutions to your now-defined problem as you can. Put them in order of practicality and feasability. Then examine what the consequences of putting each of these solutions into action are. You may do this part alone or with help from others. You might be able to stop the thinking part of this process at this point, and put your plan into action. Or, you may not be able to stop here, especially if other people involved in the problem indicate they won't cooperate with the plan.

Therefore, you may have to come up with some different and creative solution attempts, ones which may seem "off the wall" or weird or silly. One of the best ways to come up with these innovative solutions is to talk out loud to yourself or to other people. Getting ideas from other folks is useful here—children, extended family, friends, teachers or other professionals, or anybody you feel comfortable confiding in about the problem.

Step Three

Once you have accepted a routine possible solution to try, or even an unusual one, then put it into effect. Give the solution attempt a good try for however long you think you need to implement it to get the result you need. Most solution attempts to major problems need at least two weeks to a month to start to work.

Step Four

Finally, evaluate how well your solution attempt worked. This is very important, but the evaluation phase is something that most people forget in the problem solving process. Sometimes other problems come up and divert our attention away from the problem we were trying to solve. Then our attempted solution just fizzles out and the problem remains or recurs. Sometimes our solution just doesn't work, and the problem may escalate into a crisis that seems unmanageable and too stressful to even think about. It is, however, very important to evaluate each attempted solution to a problem. That way, you won't keep on trying ineffective solutions over and over, and you'll learn which kind of solutions really do work.

Minimizing/Maximizing

Most people use a "mini-max" strategy when dealing with problems and attempted solutions. They try to *minimize* their pain, effort, and risks, and *maximize* their comfort, security, and benefits. This is normal. Sometimes, though, especially with long-term or recurring problems, this strategy is only partially successful, because we get stuck in patterns of using the same old solutions to problems again and again. These solutions may only work as well as band-aids would on major wounds. Sometimes solutions will work for a brief while, just long enough for us to catch our breath, and then the problem comes up again or gets worse. Sometimes we use unworkable solutions because we've been taught to use them, perhaps indirectly, by our parents, society, or other people. Sometimes we really just don't know any better, and are so stuck in the problem that we simply can't see our way out.

Let's take one example. If you have a "problem" child who disobeys you quite a lot, you may use the strategy of yelling and screaming and physically punishing the child when you reach your limit and lose your temper. You can usually manage to terrify your child long enough for him or her to quit doing whatever was bothering you. This gives you some peace, for a little while. This solution attempt only "works" for a short time, but it manages to reinforce your methods because it does work, at least a little. It does send a pretty awful message to your child, however.

What might happen if you were to try to use a creative solution attempt, something you hadn't tried before? What are some alternative solutions to the problem described above? Some suggestions follow. You can also come up with some of your own using the creative problem solving steps described above.

How about using "time-out" with your young child? How about trying to discover the trigger of the bad behavior and stopping it before it starts? (Does your child act awful when hungry or tired?) How about making a date to spend a little extra time this week with your monster child, to help him or her feel more important and cared about? How about talking with your child about how the behavior affects you, in "I feel . . ." language, *not* "you are awful" words. How about providing yourself with some more time away from your children, so you don't feel so pushed all the time? How about professional consultation for a child who seems really out of control?

All of these potential solutions take various amounts of your time, energy, and resources. You will discover that most single parent students try to minimize the amount of time and energy they spend dealing with problems simply because there are so many to deal with all the time, and because they feel so alone. We find to our dismay, however, that this strategy is often unworkable and makes some problems worse in the long run.

> *Social services create a plethora of problems that I must deal with as they arise or we face being cut off. I sometimes am not in a position (time-wise) to deal with the current situation, yet there is no choice but to deal with it.*

What is a workable and useful solution worth to you? What is using a good solution to a chronic or major problem worth in terms of your time and effort? You are the only one who can decide this. When you use a creative problem solving technique, you're more likely to come up with a solution that will work, one that will be acceptable to all or most people involved in the problem, and one that will bring you much more peace and much less stress in the long run.

Another Problem Solving Example

For more practice with creative problem solving, let's handle a different chronic problem: You never have enough time to study to get the kind of grades you want and need. Let's go through some problem-solving steps and see what happens:

1. What is the problem? The problem is I never have enough time to study. Is this really the problem? Well, I might not manage my time very well, and I feel too tired all the time. Or, I may be trying to take too many classes this quarter. Or, the problem might be that I can't keep the kids quiet while I try to study, or there seems to be too many other things that I do instead of studying.

What is the problem now? I've decided that my real problem is that I don't manage my time well enough to be able to study enough to earn the kind of grades I want and need.

2. Okay. Now, what are some of the usual solutions? Well, I holler at the kids to be quiet so I can study. I let the dishes and laundry pile up and study instead. I get mad at my professors and feel that they're unfair and don't understand my situation and just feel angry and frustrated and choose not to study, just to prove a point! I stay up real late at night studying and then I'm too tired and irritable the next day. I cram before tests.

How well does each of these "solutions" work? Not very well!

What are some more creative solutions to this problem, or ones I haven't thought of before? Well, I could go to bed when my children do and then get up at 3:00 or 4:00 A.M. to study when it's quiet and I don't have any interruptions. I could keep up better with my reading and writing, doing a little every day early in the morning, so I don't have to cram. I could try to swap child care with someone else in my situation who has to study, too, and get a few hours to myself once a week. I could try very hard to not let a messy house bother me so much, and learn to live with the clutter, instead of cleaning house when I need to study. I could ease up a bit and take fewer classes (if financial aid constraints will allow) so my workload is lessened.

3. Which one of these solutions do I want to try for a while? Well, I can't change my course schedule right now, or drop any classes. I think I'll try going to bed with the kids and get up at 4:00 A.M. to study. We'll see how that works for two weeks, and I'll evaluate the solution at the end of that time. I'll write it down on my calendar so I don't forget.

4. Okay, I tried that solution for two weeks. I seem to be keeping up

with studying better, and I'm still getting enough sleep. I think I'll use this solution as long as it keeps on working.

Your creative thoughts may not exactly follow the same paths, but you get the idea. Can you come up with even more creative solutions to that problem, one you will certainly face in college? Take a few minutes and think about it.

> *Have you established a good support system, so if you need a night off or a weekend away there is someone to help out? My kids feel better when I have time for myself because it gives my energy and tolerance level a boost.*

Use the Same Problem Solving Steps for All Problems

When you have any problem with your children, with school, with work, or with administrators, practice using the problem solving steps (problem definition, creative solution finding, solution trying, and solution evaluation). If you consistently use this rational approach, you'll find that you'll feel much more in control, much less overwhelmed by it all, and much more able to really solve your problems. Your self-esteem will rise, and you will be more respected by the professionals you will deal with while in school. You will practice valuable strategies that will help you in your career.

Thinking Clearly

Because creative problem solving is a rational approach, you'll need to control any strong feelings you have about the problem in order to think as clearly as you can. First, relax, using some of the suggestions in the previous chapter or that you've learned from a stress management course or book. If you find you're really upset about something, go through the first three creative problem solving steps above on one day. Then, after a good night's sleep, go through the same steps again the next day.

Since many problems don't have to be solved immediately, give yourself enough time to come up with a good plan of action, one that is based on logic and reason. That's easier said than done, but work on it. It will get easier with practice. You may want to start using the steps outlined above on small problems, to practice for big crises.

Crisis Management

You can certainly use the problem solving steps outlined above in a crisis. What is a crisis? A crisis is just a large problem that needs to be solved right away, so you'll need to go through the steps relatively quickly. If you've practiced the steps for problem solving along the way, you'll get better at using them quickly and be able to use them effectively in a crisis situation. The next thing to do in a crisis is ask someone for help.

> *Illness of my daughter is a difficulty because I either must miss classes or hire a babysitter at rates which I cannot hope to budget for. It would be nice if there was a solution, but I am not currently aware of anything in this area.*

Asking for Help is Sometimes Hard to Do

Single parents are notorious for being independent, strong willed, tough as nails (on the outside at least), and are sometimes reluctant to ask others, even professionals, for help. Those qualities can work for you, but can also work against you. There will be times when you need to ask others for help.

If you almost never ask anyone for a favor or a helping hand, it's much harder to ask someone for help when you really are desperate. Practice asking folks for some assistance when you could use it but when you would manage, with some difficulty, on your own. You can practice asking for small favors. For example, if you know your neighbor is on the way to the grocery store and you are running out of cereal, ask your neighbor if he or she would pick up a box of cereal for you—you'll provide a couple of dollars, of course. This probably won't be a big deal for your neighbor, but it will save you a trip and valuable time, since all you need is cereal. Or, if the student sitting next to you in class mentions that his or her next stop is the library, and you need to return a book before it becomes overdue, ask the person to drop it in the book return for you. This is also not a big deal for your classmate, but will give you practice asking and save you some time. Start small, and work your way up. Ask for small favors, and when you discover how helpful people really are, it will become easier to ask for larger ones. When you can reciprocate and help other folks out, by all means do so.

You might be afraid you will get to be a pest and not be able to help others in return. Or you might be afraid of being taken advantage of, especially when you first start school. This may be because you may have trouble saying "no"—you might be afraid that if you ask someone for something, he or she would turn around the next day and ask you to do something even more, something that you really couldn't handle without dropping your own important tasks. You'll probably find out that your fears are groundless. Most people are both considerate and reasonable. If you do get "burned," just don't deal with that unreasonable person twice!

You may feel that there just isn't anyone whom you *could* ask to help you. That isn't an unusual feeling. We live in an time when it's much harder for people to depend on each other for assistance. Families are much more isolated. Everybody keeps moving around. You get new neighbors all the time, and your family members are probably spread out all over the country, if not the world. It used to be that extended families (parents, aunts and uncles, grandparents, brothers and sisters) at least lived in the same town. When a problem came up there was always someone to call on. Now most people live pretty far away from their families of origin and relatives of all sorts. They are forced to ask neighbors or friends for help. This is a lot harder for most people than asking family for help. Families naturally want to help each other out. They are invested in the successes and well-being of their family members. Most of us don't feel as funny asking family for help.

Forming Your Own Support System

You might find yourself feeling very much alone. If you do, one thing you can try if you live far away from your natural family is to adopt yourself and your children into another family. Each group can "adopt" the other. This can work between any number of people, and between single parent families and other kinds. You might find a compatible family through your church, college, your children's school, or any other organization you belong to. You could, if you're brave enough, put up a poster in a student center. You could advertise with flyers or in newsletters or the school paper.

Describe yourself and your family's needs briefly, add what you have to offer, and ask if some other family would be willing to "adopt" yours and have you "adopt" theirs, with the aim of helping each other out in crises. Don't include your telephone number or specific address in ads, though; you'd be asking for trouble. Indicate that anyone who wants to contact you can do so through the school paper or an office on campus or by mail to another address (it's best if you can have something sent to you, for instance, in care of the women's resource center in your college).

> *I would not be able to do any of what I do without the help from family, friends, A.A. people, social workers, etc. Just knowing they're there makes all the difference.*

This informal "co-adoption" usually works out well between single parent families, and you can find many on your campus, with a little work. You don't have to go through a big formal procedure, though. You might just meet someone who would like to become your "brother" or "sister" or "cousin," and who would like to be able to ask you for help on occasion, too. You might meet another such parent at the day-care center, in class, or in the school cafeteria.

If you can't bring yourself to ask friends, neighbors, or other people around you for assistance, you can try contacting a professional or paraprofessional for help. People such as psychologists, social workers, county extension workers, medical center volunteers, community mental health crisis workers, volunteer homemakers, crisis child care center workers, legal service society members, women's center personnel, and others are there to do a job: help people who need it. You might feel more comfortable asking one of these people for help, since they are professionals and won't be asking you for help in return. There may or may not be a charge for their services. Some kinds of assistance may be covered under Medicaid or your own private health insurance; you may be billed for others on a sliding scale according to your income level.

> *It's hard to stay "up" when you're stressed out, exhausted, living in crummy housing, and it seems every time you turn around something else goes wrong. My best way of coping has been to join a support group for divorced people in the community. It helps to be with people who are struggling with divorce, poverty, and rebuilding their lives. Also, I went to a counselor for a few months—she was very helpful in sorting out my feelings and keeping me focused on my goals.*

Sometimes the best place to call for help or a referral is your local family services office. If you have a runaway child, trouble with an ex-spouse, trouble with a landlord, or you're running out of patience with your children, this office can either help you directly or suggest another agency or person to call. They are less likely to be able to help you directly with a broken-down car, a health problem, or other things that aren't "people interaction" problems, but they will probably be able to direct you to someone who can offer assistance.

> *I am in touch with the Women Students' Office on campus. I have taken every course available in how to cope with returning to school, assertiveness training, creative techniques to deal with stress and anxiety, women and self-confidence, and women and careers in a changing world. These have all proven to strengthen me. I do a lot of reading of psychological self-help books. Also, what I study helps me to gain insight into myself. I am constantly trying to improve myself and am willing to take risks and make necessary changes. I now have faith in myself, whereas before I didn't. I have never been happier, even if I feel the pressure of having too much to do, not enough money, no break from my daughters, and so on. I also set high standards for myself, but I am feeling the rewards of all this!*

One single parent student mother made the following astute comment: "People are always giving parents, especially single parents, lots of *advice,* but what we really need is some *help*." Even this book has a lot of advice in it, but cannot really help you if you don't put some of the advice to work. I can't come to your house to babysit your children, I can't tutor you in English, and I can't go to the financial aid office with you to help you fill out the forms. I'm sure the woman who made the above comment realizes that if single parents want and need real help, they must actively seek it—it won't come calling on it's own! The old adage, "An ounce of prevention is worth a pound of cure," should be a guiding rule for every single parent student. Of course, the best way to deal with a crisis is to try to prevent it in the first place. When you can't prevent it, for heaven's sake ask for help!

SPOTLIGHT ON COLLEGE PROGRAMS
Texas Woman's University, Denton/Dallas/Houston, Texas

Special programs and assistance that single parents can receive from Texas Woman's University are:

1. **Family Housing.** Apartments are available on campus for students with families. Approximately 80 percent of the students residing on campus are single parents with young children.

2. **Child Development Center.** The university operates an accredited child care, nursery school, and kindergarten program for children (eighteen months to five years) of TWU students, faculty, staff, and alumnae. The kindergarten and nursery school programs are also open to the community when space is available. Students are charged a lower rate than faculty, staff, alumnae, or the community.

3. **The Clubhouse.** The Department of University Housing operates an afterschool and day-long summer recreation program for children of TWU students (ages five to twelve). Priority is given to TWU families living on campus. A large number of commuter students' children also participate in the program, however, particularly during the summer months.

4. **Financial Aid.** The university has received a Roddy Foundation Grant to provide financial assistance to single parents in the health science field. Additional funding for single parents is being pursued on an ongoing basis. Students inquiring about the Roddy grants or other financial aid should contact the University Financial Aid Office at (817) 898-3050.

5. **Marriage and Family Therapy Clinic.** The department of Family and Consumer Studies operates this clinic providing services for students and their children as well as the community.

6. **Other University Clinics.** There are several other clinics on campus that provide low-cost services for students. They are: Dental Hygiene, Occupational Therapy, Physical Therapy, and Speech and Hearing.

7. Other key departments that provide specific services for single parents, as well as other students, are the Counseling Center and the Department of Commuter Services and Campus Organizations. There is also a special orientation course offered by the university (University 1000). Although open to all students, this course has been most helpful as a support group for nontraditional students who are primarily single parents.

A number of the single parents living on campus and off campus receive funding for their housing through the Denton Housing Authority. There is a waiting list, so students are encouraged to apply early because there can be as much as a six- to twelve-month wait.

For more information, contact:

Office of Student Life
206 Student Center
Texas Woman's University
Denton, Texas 76204
(817) 898-3601

12

BE KIND TO YOUR BODY

Perhaps you have your own set of health concerns or problems, and are dealing with them well. Or maybe you're disgustingly healthy right now. Maybe you are following a diet and exercise regimen that is good for you already. But, if you're usually a junk food junkie who doesn't get much exercise, hasn't seen a physician for a checkup for a long time, but who takes reasonably good health for granted, read on. Most of what follows is just common sense, really. The trouble is that you know the guidelines, but may not follow them. Start treating your body better *now*. The rewards are infinite.

Before you start school, get thorough physical and dental checkups for yourself and your children. If you're already in school, get checkups as soon as possible. This will help spot small problems before they become major ones when you and your children are under more stress. Contact your physician or a nutritionist for advice on an inexpensive but wholesome and good diet you can follow while you're in school. Such a diet will optimize the good health of you and your children. Follow an exercise plan tailored to you, suggested by a health care expert who is acquainted with your physiology, abilities, and needs.

> *Maintain an exercise program three times a week to give you energy.*

Now I'll offer some advice that you must not substitute for professional advice, but which may be helpful to you.

Don't drink coffee. It's the norm for college students of all kinds to keep themselves going on it, but it's a bad idea in the long run. Did you know that ingesting high levels of caffeine can contribute to fibrocystic breast disease, osteoporosis, and cardiac irregularities? If you smoke, quit before you even begin school, if at all possible. It will be that much harder to quit once you're in. Get enough sleep every night (6 to 9 hours). Avoid refined sugar as much as possible—be aware that it is in a lot of things, and you don't have to sprinkle it on to get it. Don't eat the junk food out of the machines on campus.

Eat a diet of whole grains, lean meat, lots of vegetables and fruits, non-fat dairy foods, and drink lots of water. Don't drink soda pop, with or without caffeine. Most colleges offer courses in nutrition. Fit one into your schedule.

Walk around as much as you can for some exercise. Swing your arms and walk fairly fast—ignore any self-conscious feelings.

Don't take any drugs that aren't absolutely essential or that aren't prescribed for your good health or to correct a problem. Try nondrug treatments first for such minor ailments as sore feet and shoulders, or headaches. Try using a heating pad or hot water bottle like grandma did, or lying down in a darkened room with a cold cloth on your head. You say your kids won't let you do that? Try a discipline strategy discussed earlier. Don't pop a pill for every minor thing. For your sake and your children's, stay away from illegal drugs.

Do take prescribed drugs at prescribed times for major ailments, such as high blood pressure medication or insulin for diabetes. Don't let your busy schedule interrupt or make you forget these important things. Eat something wholesome and nutritious every two or three hours to keep your energy level up and your blood sugar level stable. Again, try not to rely on coffee or other artificial stimulants to keep you going. Stay away from off-campus fast-food places. Find a place on campus with a refrigerator to store your brown-bag lunch (ask a graduate student or professor for locations). Take a vitamin supplement if your doctor or nutritionist says your diet is inadequate and you need one; otherwise don't waste your money. Teach yourself how to relax, even if you're not very good at it at first. Take a stress reduction course at school, or at least check out a good book on the subject from your library. There are also cassette tapes and videos available now on relaxation and stress reduction. Your local mental health center or community hospital might lend these out to the public for free or a minimal charge. Hug your children a lot, and do a lot of touching with people you love. Gentle touching and being touched is good for your body and mind.

> *I felt I was definitely handicapped by not being able to stay up to late hours, and get up very early as other students did—if I tried to do such things (and sometimes I had to) I inevitably got very sick very quickly, resulting in missing two or three days of classes and thus getting myself into even worse trouble!*

If you're sexually active, or plan to be, use a highly reliable form of birth control, and protect yourself as much as you can against all kinds of venereal disease. Even if you use another type of birth control, you and your partner could use a condom and a diaphragm at the same time. Oral contraceptives (birth control pills) also help discourage some kinds of sexually transmitted diseases, because they increase the thickness of cervical mucous to provide a physical barrier against germs. Contraceptive jellies and foams also provide some germ-killing protection.

There may be a free or low-cost health clinic on campus to help you with birth control and disease prevention if you're uneasy about consulting your regular doctor. Or try your local Planned Parenthood office. There's nothing like a pregnancy scare or a fear that you've contracted a disease to make your whole life miserable; and you'll need to prevent these situations from ever happening.

Be aware that if you do get sick and you go to a doctor and explain your symptoms and your lifestyle, he or she might tell you that whatever is wrong with you is just stress (this happens a lot in on-campus student health centers). Don't take this sitting down! Demand that a reasonable diagnosis be made so that your symptoms can at least be treated or, better yet, prevented in the future. You're not likely to quit school or quit being a parent just because those activities make you more susceptible to illness!

Make keeping your good health and the health of your children a high priority. Make it even higher than studying or working or going out with friends. With good health, you can take care of other things; without it you can't do much. You're the only one who can keep you healthy, and you are probably the major person responsible for your children's health, too. I guarantee that if you live as healthy a lifestyle as possible it will help you get through college much easier. You and your children will become sick a lot less often, and you'll all learn more and feel less stressed. If you have good food, good rest, good exercise, and good energy (you can remember this by the acronym FREE) you and your kids will do fine.

SPOTLIGHT ON COLLEGE PROGRAMS
Eastern Washington University

The goal of the Single Parent Project is to assist single parents who are receiving AFDC benefits and enrolled in Washington's Family Independence Program (FIP) to achieve self-sufficiency by obtaining a college education. The project features a myriad of supports, assisting single parent students in meeting the needs of their families, as well as the tough demands of being a full-time student.

The project coordinator is an experienced therapist, offering personal, child, and family counseling to project participants. Student support groups protect the single parent student from the isolation felt by the nontraditional student on many college campuses. Networking with one another, project participants can solve many of their problems without having to utilize the more "public" community services; i.e., a project-coordinated clothing bank and an emergency child care network. Coordinated family activities and social events enhance the concept that a nonisolated student is better able to function in her or his dual role as a single parent and university student.

A key component of the Single Parent Project is academic excellence. Among the best students on campus, the single parent is highly motivated. Academic workshops are designed to offer specific advice on improving study skills, developing study partners, and pursuing excellence as a student at the university. In addition, the project offers various workshops pertinent to the single parent student; e.g., parenting, self esteem, time management, and others.

In recognition of the special needs and concerns of single parent students, Eastern Washington University obtained a Fund for the Improvement of Post Secondary Education (FIPSE) grant to cover the major costs of the project, and committed both staff and faculty to assist in the project's implementation. For more information, contact:

Sandy Kleven, MSW, Director
Single Parent Project
MS 11
69-71 Louise Anderson Hall
Eastern Washington University
Cheney, WA 99004
(509) 359-7373

EWU's H.O.M.E. Program

H.O.M.E. (Helping Ourselves Means Education) is a voice of advocacy for nontraditional students and their concerns on campus. We network with Eastern's administration in the areas of financial aid, student services, registration, admissions, academic affairs, and academic advising. This year we are also building relationships with the Associated Students of EWU, the Student Council, and the Activities Programming Board, with an eye toward affecting campus issues and activities controlled by other students.

We are formally recognized as a campus organization, which requires us to fulfill certain obligations with regard to the EWU Clubs and Organization Board. Our yearly budget of $500 is allocated through them. Our office space and some of our supplies are provided as in-kind services from the Women's Studies Center. Positions as program coordinators are funded through work study grants. We keep client contact sheets in order to track and document contacts with our clients and students. H.O.M.E. tracks its students through a computer program managed by Financial Aid and the Registrar's Office, keeping quarterly figures on our students' GPAs, class standings, program majors, and family status. These figures have shown that nearly 55 percent of Eastern's student body is nontraditional; our students' compiled GPA currently stands at 3.1, and H.O.M.E. students have a greater overall retention rate than the general student body.

We engage in a tremendous amount of networking and referral, both on campus and within the communities of Cheney and Spokane on behalf of H.O.M.E. students. We deal with issues of housing, child care, financial aid, medical benefits, food, public assistance, transportation, employment, physical/emotional/mental disabilities, study problems, family dysfunctions, legal aid, crisis intervention, and the need for support and inexpensive local entertainment to offset the rigors of attending school and raising a family.

H.O.M.E. sponsors speakers and presentations of interest to the nontraditional student, facilitates weekly support groups, and mails out a quarterly newsletter with a list of scheduled presentations and items of interest to our clients. We maintain a Revolving Loan Fund, which is administered by the Student Activities Office, providing short-term loans of $20 to students in need, and a Child Care Scholarship Fund through which we awarded four child care scholarships of $500 each to very deserving nontraditional students this fall.

We have several programs which tap the resources of Eastern's academic community with regard to raising funds for the accounts of the H.O.M.E. program. Each year we print a Child Care Scholarship Fundraising Letter which goes out to all faculty and staff on campus, familiarizing them with the H.O.M.E. program, explaining our needs and procedures available for donating funds, such as automatic withdrawal from a paycheck. This has worked well for us, building our scholarship fund from $800 to almost $2000 in two years, and the fund continues to grow and will allow H.O.M.E. to award more scholarships in the future.

We also work with other campus clubs and organizations in sponsoring yearly events, such as the 1990 Spring Bike Ride. The entry cost is $15, and we provide silk-screened t-shirts with a different print each year, along with food and beverages at the check points. Two courses are offered: a fifteen-mile course, and a thirty-mile course. The Ride is not a race, and family participation is encouraged. H.O.M.E. held the first Ride last year and it was tremendously fun and successful. Proceeds were divided with Psi Chi.

Another opportunity to raise funds presents itself each winter with the annual Child Care Scholarship Luncheon. Each year we tap the community for a gourmet cook who will donate time and whip up a fabulous culinary luncheon delight. This year we will hold two luncheons. We purchase the comestibles at Costco, and help prepare and serve, making use of the excellent campus kitchen facilities in EWU's Diet and Nutrition Department. H.O.M.E. earns approximately $150 per luncheon. We charge $5 per plate, and take reservations in advance for 55 individuals.

Last year H.O.M.E. sponsored Children's Day at EWU with a parade of students' children across the campus, and activities for the children such as a puppet show and a brown bag lunch. We encouraged our students to bring their children to classes, in an effort to illustrate the need for campus child care and build support for the idea. (During the summer of 1991, the EWU administration effected a new child care program, and we now have campus child care available to meet the needs of our students.) EWU Children's Day was so successful that we decided to make it an annual event. This year we will focus on the disparity between the Public School calendar in our district and EWU's quarterly calendar, which causes a great deal of trouble for our students who must arrange child care. We are also considering sponsoring a rally day to focus administrative and faculty attention on nontraditional student needs, and bring out an awareness of this group as a majority whose voice should be taken seriously in the years to come.

This fall, for the first time, a Nontraditional Student/Single Parent academic scholarship of $1000 was awarded and funded by the EWU Scholarship Committee and the EWU Alumni Association. The support of the Scholarship Committee and the administration at EWU is directly attributed to the efforts of the H.O.M.E. Program and The Women's Studies Center. Both organizations have been extremely successful in focusing attention on the needs of the nontraditional students.

H.O.M.E. is a lively, vital link in the campus support system, and we are fortunate in enjoying a respectful, reciprocal relationship with EWU administration and faculty, as well as the community of Cheney and its mayor. We view building these connections as vital to our successful function.

For more information, contact:

H.O.M.E. Program
Women's Studies Center
Eastern Washington University
Monroe 114, MS-166
Cheney, WA 99004
(509) 235-4237

13

OVERCOMING COMPUTER PHOBIA

You would be wise to try to learn how to use a computer very early on in your college career. Anything you can do to learn how to use these wonderful, awful machines is worth it.

Wonderful and awful? Yes, that's still how I view computers, leaning more toward wonderful the more I learn about them. They are wonderful when you know the steps to get them to do things and you know how to fix the glitches. But they're awful and intimidating when you're just learning and you're sure that you'll destroy the whole setup, not to mention lose all the data or files in the system. I still shudder when my computer does something I don't understand. But I've learned that I'm not smart enough to really muck up the works!

I suffered from computer phobia for years. It wasn't until my third work-study job in my third year in college that I was encouraged to do some simple data entry on an IBM PC (PC means personal computer) as a supplement to my regular duties when I had some free time. Now I'm glad that I was able to learn how. I did suffer from massive anxiety attacks every time I sat down in front of the keys at first, however, and was afraid to let my trainer leave my side even to go to the bathroom.

But it only took me a little while to learn how to turn the computer on, put in the disks, "boot up" the system, enter the data, save it, and get out of the system without a hitch. Now when I look back at all the time I spent in typing term papers and research reports (on second-hand manual and electric typewriters), correcting my mistakes with that awful white liquid or that flaky correcting paper, typing pages with major changes over and over and over and over . . . well, I just shake my head in shame that I didn't force myself to learn how to use a word processing program on a computer sooner.

Reassuring Words About Using Computers

There are a few things you might like to know about computers and about using them that might help set your mind at ease. If you hit the wrong key, and something weird happens, there is usually another key that will cancel what you just hit. Most steps to using a computer are just that, steps. You can write them down and follow them just like any other instructions. You don't have to be brilliant or even above average in intelligence to use a computer. Most word processing programs will ask you if the key you pressed for a function is what you really want to do.

For example, if I press the "delete" key, the software program I'm using will ask me, before it deletes anything, if I really want to do that. If I decide that I pushed the delete key by mistake, I can just say "no" and the machine will set everything back to where it was before I pushed "delete." This is very comforting, and saves a lot of worry. You can let your fingers fly over the keys and rest assured that if you push something you shouldn't, you have a chance to correct your error before anything drastic happens. There are all sorts of safeguards built into systems and programs that will save you pain and strain.

How to Learn How

Take a course in using computers, or become familiar with them in other ways, such as on-the-job training in a work-study position. A cautionary note, though, about taking computer classes, especially to learn how to program computers. If you are not majoring in computer programming, and don't have all the time in the world to practice on the computers at school (and you must practice), it might be difficult. Most schools just don't have enough computers to make it possible for every student to have enough time on them to really learn what to do, and it's even tough to complete the course requirements. It's not unusual for college computer centers to be open twenty-four hours a day, but then again, you don't have twenty-four hours a day to work with in trying to get time on a machine. It's not unusual, either, for regular students to have to schedule time very late at night and well into the wee hours of the morning in order to get their program to work right. Since you're not footloose and fancy free, and have children to be with at night, you may not be able to handle this. Just be sure you check all these things out before you sign up for a computer programming class.

An alternative to a course might be for you to try to get a part-time job, preferably work-study, in which you could be trained to use a word processing or data entry program. There are several popular programs on the market: WordPerfect, Microsoft Word, Excel, Word Star, Clarion, PC Write, New Word, Lotus, and so on. Each has its own peculiarities and capabilities, and each place you work might use its own favorite. And, each office has its own kind of computer, such as Epson, Macintosh, Apple, IBM, Tandy, Commodore, or Hewlett Packard. If you can find a part-time job on campus, you're more likely to be able to use one of the better computers and better word processing or data entry programs, since large institutions often get a good deal on buying multiple units.

In short, the only way to get over your fear of the computer is to learn how to use one. Don't let the specialized computer jargon scare you away—megabytes, floppy disks, modems, defaults, hard disk drives, on-line, computer files, disk formats, backups, downloading, uploading, and so on. These are just words, not magic incantations or curses! You may find yourself cursed, instead, if you don't learn how to use a computer! And remember that computers aren't magic, either, but are very useful machines that can help you do things much better and faster. Almost *any* career you have after graduation will require that you know how to use a word processing program, at least, if not spreadsheets and databases. Learn *now*, and you'll be ahead of the game.

SPOTLIGHT ON COLLEGE PROGRAMS
Community College of Philadelphia

STEP-UP is a unique program designed to enable single parent AFDC clients to achieve self-sufficiency. The program is a five-year project that represents a partnership between the Community College of Philadelphia and the Pennsylvania Department of Public Welfare. STEP-UP's goal is to graduate six hundred participants with an Associate Degree who then take employment and exit from welfare.

STEP-UP is based on a number of important assumptions: in light of education and training experiences over the past decade, we know what works, but we have not utilized this knowledge in "welfare reform" programs; short-term solutions are ineffectual; in a time of scarce resources, integrating what resources are available promises a higher degree of success than more piecemeal approaches; a successful program must be voluntary in nature to the greatest extent possible; major public institutions need to act in concert to have a major positive impact on the problem of dependency; mainstreaming welfare clients is preferable to special classes or training sessions; an earned college degree has substantially more potential for enabling single parents to move into a career path that can earn them a respectable livelihood; and participating public institutions need to make major public policy evaluations and modifications.

The college has received a five-year grant to serve one thousand clients so that upon graduation they will obtain employment with income adequate enough to exit welfare and to leap-frog "working poor" status. Since

July of 1988, STEP-UP has enrolled 1,900 single parent clients because of its popularity with welfare department staff and clients. A small amount of funding has been received from the Pennsylvania Department of Education, and a "Job Placement Specialist" is funded with JTPA funds. STEP-UP is seeking additional funds to maintain services and enhance the program for additional clients.

The potential implications of the STEP-UP program are enormous. It is hoped that the program will preclude the possibility of intergenerational dependency on welfare. If successful, STEP-UP can be a model for other welfare programs around the nation. There is a potential for large taxpayer savings. Clients, because of respectable incomes, will become taxpayers. This program also holds the promise of placing skilled workers into jobs and careers where there are substantial needs. The most important aspect of the STEP-UP program is that large numbers of clients can substantially improve the quality of their lives.

For more information, contact:

Ronald Feinstein, Ph.D., ACSW, Director
STEP-UP
Room MI-20, 1700 Spring Garden Street
Community College of Philadelphia
Philadelphia, Pennsylvania 19130
(215) 751-8835 or 751-8195

14

PROFESSORS ARE HUMAN

One of the most pleasant surprises you will have in college is that most of your professors and instructors are willing and able to help you get through college academically and survive the rough times. Most of them are considerate, helpful, and genuinely concerned. This isn't always self-evident, though, since professors can appear very preoccupied and unconcerned a good deal of the time. I'll try to explain why they may appear to be that way, especially when you first start school. During your years in college you may be able to foster some lasting friendships and intellectual partnerships with a few of these folks. Here are some of the things you might need to know about them that I learned by getting to know them as people. What I have to say applies to professors and instructors in two- and four-year colleges and universities, not to those in technical or vocational schools. Those schools are considerably different, and may have other priorities.

What Makes Them Tick?

Professors—tenured or not, in big and small colleges and universities— are always under tremendous pressure to *produce*. Producing means doing original research and study and then writing it up and getting it published. These activities are of paramount importance in most post-secondary academic institutions, because the salaries professors receive and their qualifications to gain and retain tenured status (or move to a better position elsewhere) depend very heavily on those accomplishments. Teaching becomes a secondary pursuit in all institutions that aren't primarily teaching colleges or universities. This fact isn't usually by professors' own design, but by institutional necessity. Competition is very fierce.

While the quality of a person's teaching does enter into their department's overall assessment of him or her as a faculty member, teaching ability and enthusiasm receive less weight in general. Teaching skill and enthusiasm for interaction with undergraduate students are not usually of primary concern when a professor is evaluated by his or her peers, department chair, dean of the college, and departments to which the professor may apply for a position elsewhere.

I tell you this because you'll need to understand that you will probably find yourself in a post-secondary institution that exists primarily to support research, writing, and publishing of that research, and secondarily to support teaching and learning of students (vocational/technical schools are the exception). The larger the college or university you attend, the more likely this will be. When you come to terms with the fact that your college or university may not exist primarily to teach students, you'll be able to understand some of the seemingly strange and conflicting priorities that become clear after you've been in school a while.

Professors' Responsibilities

Most faculty members, and particularly junior faculty members, have tremendous and varied and sometimes incongruous responsibilities. They are engaged in original research and writing, course preparation, teaching, grading and student supervision, supervising labs and other's research, committee work, library work, reading masses of information, collaboration and competition with their peers, and more. If you get the feeling that most of your instructors or professors aren't primarily concerned with you as an individual, how much you are learning, or your own set of problems and pressures, your perception is probably correct. But most of these folks are people who, underneath it all, care about their students and want them to learn as much as possible and become educated people. This only becomes apparent, though, if you can get some one-on-one or small group interaction with your professors either in or out of class. Underneath that preoccupied, very busy person is someone who probably genuinely wants to be a good teacher and be a positive influence in students' lives. Most of them need to receive good, positive course evaluations at the end of each quarter or semester, too, for their own self-esteem and self-confidence. Oh, there are some hard-core curmudgeons, but it's a rare professor who doesn't care at all.

Cultivate relationships with professors who are supportive, can act as mentors, and who can give you essential references for employment or graduate school.

You can discover this by taking advantage of professors' "available-for-students" office hours. You can go in and ask questions about course material, argue a point, discuss an idea you have for your own research project, get advice on a course of study and so on. Don't go to just socialize, however. These people can spot "apple polishers" a mile away. If you are unable to approach your professor during the office hours that have been set aside for such interactions, don't hesitate to ask him or her if you could come to the office at another time that is convenient for both of you. Finding another time that fits both your schedules is usually not a big problem, and most of them will be more than happy to accomodate you.

Asking for Help

When you are in a large class it's very easy to feel like you, the single parent student, aren't very important. You can continue to feel that way if you don't take advantage of the opportunities for interaction with your professors, course instructors, teaching assistants, and other students in your class. Now, most students just aren't very comfortable asking for help or clarification of a problem, so they don't approach their instructors at all. They're afraid of looking stupid or of taking up an instructor's valuable time. You know what? Most professors and instructors despair because nobody in their classes shows much interest in the subject, at least not enough interest to want to discuss some material with them during office hours. It often seems that few students can muster up the courage to ask questions during class and allow themselves to feel a little vulnerable for a while.

Most professors I've been acquainted with would love for their bright, motivated students (you fall into this category) to come and talk with them about elements of what they are trying to communicate in class, or surrounding issues and ideas. They feel ineffective when it seems like no one in their classes cares much about the course material, or when students don't ask questions or try to understand the subject matter a little more deeply than what might be required for the test. Most professors and instructors do put a lot of effort into their courses, trying to make them interesting and informative, and really want to do well, just like you do.

If you're a shy person, and find it hard to approach a professor during office hours or ask a question in class, ask yourself what is the worst that could happen if you did so. Are you afraid people will think you are stupid? Are you afraid of being laughed at? Are you afraid of rejection or being ignored? I can tell you that in my five years of college, when I gradually built up my self-confidence to be able to ask questions or make comments, I never once was laughed at, ignored, or made to feel stupid in class or at any other time by one of my professors or classmates. And that wasn't because I asked particularly brilliant or insightful questions or made wonderful comments! Most of them were downright dull and showed my real ignorance.

In addition, I never sat in a class where another student was treated badly, either. The classroom isn't a hostile environment—it just gives that false appearance sometimes, and that's too bad. Another hot tip: Don't ask questions about what will be on the test, or what your paper should be about. Most of the questions professors get asked are about what will be on a test, what will be covered, what the professor expects the students to know. Can you imagine how tiring, boring, and frustrating that gets for them?

About the Lemons

Okay, there are a few who really don't like to teach, and there are some who just aren't very interesting or very good at it. It's too bad that people can become college faculty members without having had much (or any) training in classroom skills, communication skills, or even rudimentary "people" skills. You just have to suffer through some of those classes and try to avoid the same instructors in the future. Or, you can try to discover if the classes seem dull because no one is interacting or asking questions, and the professors are standing up there struggling to get some interaction going. The worse it seems to go for them, the less effective they are.

Put yourself in his or her shoes. How would it be for you to get up in front of thirty, fifty, or one hundred people or more and try to teach something for an hour or more, day after day? How would it feel if most of the class members seemed to be mostly asleep, or bored, or semiconscious during that hour? This is what most professors face all the time! And as a result they unfortunately sometimes develop uncomplimentary opinions of their undergraduate students.

So, give them a break and ask a question or two that isn't about an upcoming test. You can be sure that some other folks in the class who aren't asleep are asking the same thing in their minds but don't have the gumption to ask out loud. You might find it easier to sit in the front of the class, then when you want to ask a question you don't have to shout, and the instructor will usually repeat the question for the rest of the class if they don't hear it. Take a deep breath, formulate the question or comment in your mind, or better yet write it down in your notebook if you have time, then raise your hand and go for it. After you do this a few times, you'll find out that nothing awful happens at all. If you're the first one to speak up during a class time, you may find that you've now made others feel more comfortable about doing the same thing. The class will become much more interesting because people will start to participate.

Real People, with Real Lives

What else about professors and graduate student teachers? They are real people with their own real problems and unique lifestyles. Many of the older ones have or have had families, and they know what it is like for you, they know what responsibility for other people is like. Most of them can understand, at least on an intellectual level, what kinds of pressures and demands you have all the time. These people are, nine times out of ten, more than happy to be of assistance if you go to them early on in the semester for help. They know what it is like to be in college, since they all went through, or are going through, themselves. Most of them also know what it is to be poor and to struggle for independence in their own way. Some of them may be single parents, too, and can understand more fully what it is like for you.

In short, they are people, not gods, not computers, not walking, talking robots, not perfect intellectual beings! When you run into the few who seem inhuman, give them a real chance, then judge. If they still seem unreachable or incompetent, go on with their classes anyway. Study and learn as best you can, ask other students or teaching assistants for help, and sign up for someone else's class next time.

> *I'm attending a Catholic college. The older priests do not think very highly of single parents, no matter what the circumstances. To get past this attitude, I just stay out of their classes. The college is actually very helpful and understanding of single parents. The only problems are in two areas: no day care on campus, and the five older priests.*

Beware the Excuses

When dealing with your professors and others, you can point to all sorts of reasons why you might not do very well in school some of the time. You lack time, you lack energy, you lack space, you lack money, you lack peace and quiet, you lack support. All these are valid reasons why your grade point average (GPA) isn't as high as you'd like, or why you don't do very well on a particular test or paper or during an entire quarter or semester. These reasons are real—you deal with them.

The danger of having these perfectly valid reasons close at hand is that you can come to use them as excuses; and there is a clear distinction between a reason and an excuse. This distinction makes a big difference in how you get through life, and in how well you deal with your professors and instructors throughout school. A reason is something that exists, that has a definite impact on your life, and is something you either can or can't do anything about. An excuse, on the other hand, is something in your head, something that may or may not be true at a particular point in time, and something that is sometimes used to rationalize away poor performance. Excuses also *always* come after the fact, when a problem is much less likely to be solvable.

It Is His, Her, Their Fault!

Excuses often go hand in hand with blaming, and blaming gets you absolutely nowhere. You can blame your children for your not having enough time to study. You can blame the social service system for being unfair. You can blame an insensitive professor for not allowing you a little more time on a paper when you or your kids were sick a lot during the course of the

class and you couldn't keep up very well. You can blame anything on anyone or any institution. Blaming then becomes an extremely poor substitute
for action. Blaming is only an emotional reaction that keeps you from doing
something about a situation now. It prevents you from finding either creative solutions or some degree of grudging acceptance for the way things
are, if they really can't be changed.

You are warned against excuse-finding and blaming for a couple of reasons. First, doing so drains your energy and makes you focus only on the
negative aspects of your situation. Second, it doesn't help anything, but
simply helps you feel better in the short run. In the long run, excuses and
blaming leave you feeling depressed and angry. In addition, other people
don't respond positively to excuses, and most certainly don't respond well
to blaming.

Using Reasons in the Best Way

You may use reasons judiciously in dealing with other people in positions of power. By judiciously I mean using reasons in nonemotional, non-
blaming, and nonattacking ways. You also must not use them very often,
but only when absolutely necessary.

How should you use reasons? Let's say that your children come down
with the chicken pox one after another during a semester (that happened to
us) and you must stay home with them and miss several classes. So, simply
call, write a note, or see your teachers in person as soon as the situation
arises. Explain what is going on, calmly, matter-of-factly, and ask them for
possible solutions to your dilemma from their points of view. Tell them the
reason why you must miss some classes. You will find to your delight that
when you do this as soon as you are aware of a problem, 99 percent of the
people you approach will be willing to help you through a difficult time.

Your professors are likely to offer several ways you can get through their
courses without being penalized inappropriately. They may allow you some
extra time on a paper, or let you take an exam at a different time when you
can get a sitter to stay with your sick child. You can discuss ways to help
make the situation fair for you without making it unfair for the other students in the class. After you are thus relieved of your anxiety, you can tend
to your sick children, study while they sleep, suffer little or no anger or depression over the situation, and keep your grades up.

Now, let's take the same situation, using excuses and blaming instead of
reasons. The course is almost over, you have missed several classes because
your children were sick. You're struggling in vain to keep up with the reading, writing, and exams. Now you go to your professors in tears, giving excuses why you haven't been doing very well and why you've been missing
so many classes. You blame your failure on your children's illnesses. You ask
if there is anything you can do now to salvage your grade.

Well, now you've put your professors in a very awkward position. They are likely to tell you that there really isn't anything you can do to make it up, since time is so short. They may also say that you cannot receive special consideration since everyone in the class has trouble now and again. Your professors may say that you should have come to them when your trouble began, and that they may have been able to help you then (and they are absolutely right). You may be given the relatively poor, but only, choice of taking an "incomplete" in the course and retaking it later, but little else will probably be suggested. So, you walk away feeling mistreated and there are bad feelings all around. You may avoid that professor in your choice of future classes, thinking that he or she is an insensitive, callous nincompoop.

You're angry at yourself, angry at your children, angry at your professors, and angry at the whole thing. Then you get depressed as finals approach. You see the world in a pretty negative light, since nothing seems to be going right. Your perfectly good reason for missing classes and not keeping up is no longer valid, because the reason has become an excuse and has been complicated by blaming, and you've not been able to improve your situation at all.

You can see from the hypothetical situation above that you can use valid reasons in such a way as to get the maximum amount of help and consideration from others, and that excuses usually get you nowhere. One important thing as you use this strategy, though, is to realize that most of the time it will work very well, but a very small percentage of the time it will not. The trick is to not let those rare times discourage you from using reasons effectively. There is a very small chance that when you approach a professor with a good reason for a problem beyond your control and ask for a solution, that person will not be helpful, supportive, or understanding at all. Then, you just have to be tremendously creative by yourself, seek assistance elsewhere, or you have to live with the problem and go on. But don't let things degenerate after such an uncommon interaction so that you then end up using excuses and blaming.

When you do run into that small percentage of unhelpful people, you're probably dealing with folks who have a major problem of their own, so they can't or won't help you with yours. Most aren't out to get you or use their power inappropriately, they're probably just ignorant or lazy or stressed-out. Never blame on malice what can be explained by incompetence! Accept the reason for a bad situation, do the best you can, and take steps to try to avoid a similar problem in the future.

A final word about reasons. Part of using them judiciously lies in using them sparingly. You don't want to become known as a complainer or a whiner, and the best way to avoid this is to use reasons only when you must. Professors get so tired of the same students coming to them with crises time after time. Did you know, based on what students tell their teachers, that grandparents most often get sick or die during their grand-children's midterms and finals? In addition, all modes of transportation are late or break down, several students must leave town suddenly, and all major natural disasters occur more frequently during test-taking times. (Scientists should study these phenomena.)

So, don't let yourself become one of those constantly whining students (even though you may have a lot to whine about!). Stay calm, collected, use a matter-of-fact tone of voice, and solicit assistance only when you need it. In addition, if you find yourself often making excuses, you need to take a good hard look at your time management skills, your ability or lack of ability to ask others for help before things really go to pot, and your capacity to manage stress in effective ways. Making a lot of excuses all the time can be a warning symptom of overwhelming stress and pressure, and you'll need to take steps to learn how to deal with time and stress better, and perhaps even seek some professional help in dealing with it all.

As a single parent student you will have lots of perfectly valid reasons why you aren't a perfect anything. After you have been in school for a while, people you interact with a lot (professors, too) will get to know you for the bright, motivated person you are, and will be even more likely to support you in times of problems and crises. Give them a chance to do so, by using the advice above and avoiding excuses. You don't need them.

SPOTLIGHT ON COLLEGE PROGRAMS
University of Southern Colorado

The Single Parents Grant Program is designed to support the educational goals of single mothers with dependent children, thereby increasing their opportunities for becoming self-supporting, contributing members of society as well as raising their children's horizons regarding the merits of higher education.

Begun in 1987 and funded primarily through grants from private foundations, including the University of Southern Colorado Foundation, the grants, payable in spring and fall of each year, cover in-state tuition and fees.

To be considered for a single parent's grant, an applicant must:

1. Be head of a household.
2. Have completed at least one semester at the University of Southern Colorado.
3. Maintain a 2.5 GPA.
4. Be enrolled in at least nine credit hours of study at USC.
5. Complete an application form and financial statement (need will be considered).
6. Submit an official transcript.
7. Submit a one-page résumé.
8. Submit a letter stating goals and objectives along with a brief biography.
9. Submit two letters of reference.

Sixty-seven grants have been awarded and forty-four women have been assisted from spring 1987 to fall 1990.

For more information, contact:

Kathryn McHugh, Office Manager
University of Southern Colorado Foundation
2200 Bonforte Boulevard
Pueblo, Colorado 81001
(719) 549-2380

15

CHANGING COURSE MIDSTREAM

There's nothing inherently wrong with changing your mind about your major field of study or changing your professional goals. In fact, changing your mind once or twice might just be necessary in order for you to get through college and enter a career that you both want and are good at. You must be aware, however, that some people in agencies which are partially supporting you through school might think otherwise.

Career goals and work decisions aren't set in concrete, and people often change careers in midlife and other times. At this point in your life, if you're beholden to various government agencies for your livelihood, however, you'll probably be required to stay on a steady, progressive path. You'll probably also be required to choose and stay in a course of study which will lead to a specific career or a "recognized occupation." This is just because your government is making an investment in you, supporting you through a program that you have chosen, in order for you to become a financially independent and educated person. Social service agencies, in particular, will not support those who change their minds all the time, or who seem flighty and lacking direction in their efforts.

You should ask your social services caseworker before you enter college what their supporting agency requires of you regarding choosing and keeping a major course of study. They may or may not offer this information when you sign up for services. Knowing beforehand what they require will save you trouble later on. If you're one of the rare ones who knows exactly what you want to do and how you're going to go about it, and you've chosen an eligible course of study, then you'll be okay. If you're like most people, though, and want to go to college but aren't entirely sure what you want to be when you grow up, you're likely to encounter some reasonable and unreasonable demands from people in agencies and offices who are footing the bills. Just prepare yourself for this, and expect to have to fight sometimes for fairness and reasonableness. The system will seem fairly paternalistic in its treatment of you; that's just the way it is. You'll need to learn to deal with that quickly in order to get what *you* want out of college.

Check Out the Consequences

Before you anticipate changing your course, or in other words changing your major, you must find out what the consequences are (if any) from the financial aid office and the social services office if you get any aid from either place. You may not be allowed to change without suffering what will seem to you to be an unfair penalty. After all, sometimes you need to get into a subject and try it out before you can really decide whether or not it's what you want or even whether you are any good at it!

There is one way to avoid serious conflict if you use your head. When you start out in college, get your liberal education credits out of the way first. Get your general required classes done, and along the way explore some courses in majors you think you might be interested in if you haven't chosen your career goal and necessary courses for it already. This way you have a year or two to decide on a major, if this is allowed by your school. (Of course, this only applies if you're in a traditional four-year college.)

> *Avail yourself of every support service you can. Network and talk to people so you find out what you can do to "work" the system. I would say that it's vital to set specific career/educational goals, and to gain practical experience through the best use of internships and volunteer work.*

While you're getting your general classes out of the way, get as much information as you can from library books, professional people, and the academic advising center on campus about specific careers you might be interested in. If your school has a career placement office, they're likely to have a lot of information on just about any kind of career you might be interested in. Information would include salary levels, job duties, education requirements, special skills, risks, benefits, and so on. As mentioned earlier, it's best to contact this office before you even begin college, to get as much background information on several careers as you can. You might discover that a certain career you were interested in just doesn't pay enough to support a family, or that there is too much travel involved, or that it requires umpteen bizillion years of graduate school study.

So, if you find out that you must choose a major right away and plunge into study, get all the counseling you can about the fields you're interested in before you even start college. Then make an educated choice. This especially applies if you are going through a two-year college program. It's not enough to think you might like to be in a certain career—you must get some concrete ideas about what the career will be like before you invest your time and effort in school. It's just too hard to get through school to not investigate a career thoroughly before you start any program of study.

In short, just be aware that you might not be able to change your course of study once you start school. Therefore, it's imperative that you make an informed decision in the first place. If you run into a large road-block, and what you want to do isn't what "they" want you to do, you'll have some decisions to make.

If you rely on social services aid to help you and your family through college, you might have to take a second or third program choice in order to continue to receive aid. You might have to go through a program that is relatively short-term (two years or less) and gain concrete, employable skills. Or, you may wish to try to go without aid from social service agencies so you can freely choose to do what you wish, if you can afford it. Another alternative is that it may be possible for you to take *yourself* off any social service grants, letting them lend assistance to your children only; this might allow you the freedom to make your own educational choices. Ask your social services caseworker if this strategy is possible. You'll get less financial and other help, but you'll still get some.

If you ever run into an insurmountable hurdle thrown up in front of you by social services or any other organization regarding any aspect of your education, you can certainly fight back. Call your college paper's editor, every local newspaper, radio station, and television news office, and tell reporters your story. Call your local Legal Aid Society or Legal Services office and ask if they could help you. Call your local ACLU office, and tell them about your problem. Contact the women's center or nontraditional students' center at your college. There's no reason in the world why you can't fight to get the very best education and chance for long-term success as possible. Stick up for yourself, and find others who will stand by you!

SPOTLIGHT ON COLLEGE PROGRAMS
Champlain College, Burlington, Vermont

The Champlain College Single Parents Program offers training and educational opportunities to help low-income, single parents succeed financially and get off welfare permanently. It is partially funded by Carl Perkins monies obtained through the Vermont State Department of Education, and is run in conjunction with Vermont's Department of Employment and Training and Vermont's Department of Social Welfare. Even if they have no money to invest in school, single parents can attend college and continue to receive ANFC (AFDC), Medicaid, food stamps, fuel assistance, day care subsidies, and WIC. One hundred and ninety-four single parent students have attended classes at Champlain College during the history of the program.

The college offers a financial aid package to help needy students in whatever way possible. The remaining money may be obtained through

Vermont Student Assistance Corporation (VSAC) loans. A complete financial aid package generally includes some loans, in addition to grants and work-study. Students applying to Champlain College who are eligible for the Single Parents Program are accepted on a rolling-admissions basis. Their application fee is postponed until funding becomes available through financial aid sources.

Most incoming single parents lack the confidence that they can succeed in college, yet single parent students have done exceptionally well at Champlain. Their GPAs and retention rate have been higher than those for the whole school population.

Single parents are faced with a unique set of circumstances that can make education and training difficult to pursue. Champlain College has many support systems to address the needs of single parents. These include:

1. A services coordinator available to work directly with the single parents in order to assure that they receive the needed services.
2. A two-week summer orientation workshop to address academic skills such as studying, test-taking, reading comprehension, metacognition, writing, and researching. The workshop also addresses communication skills, time management, accessing services, stress reduction, career choices, and overcoming fear-generating circumstances.
3. An ongoing, weekly support group run by professional counselors.
4. Free tutoring to strengthen students' academic skills.
5. On-campus child care, for three- to five-year-olds, at the College's Child Development Center.
6. Career counselors to assist students in choosing majors, writing résumés, interviewing, and finding jobs.

Over 80 percent of the students who complete their studies at Champlain College enter employment within a few months. Sixteen percent of the remaining graduates transfer into four-year colleges. The average starting salary for graduates in the Chittenden County area is $12,000 to $26,000 a year, depending on the student's field of study.

Career choices at Champlain College include accounting, the business field, computer field, court reporting, engineering technology, respiratory therapy, radiography, human services, hotel-restaurant management, law enforcement, early childhood education, legal field, office administration and secretarial, studies in arts and sciences, or liberal studies.

For more information, contact:

Nancy Boldt, Program Director, Single Parents Program
Champlain College
P.O. Box 670
Burlington, Vermont 05402-0670
(802) 658-0800, ext. 2521

16

GOING ON WHEN
IT SEEMS IMPOSSIBLE

When No One Is Supportive

Sometimes while you are in school it may seem like no one cares what you are doing or how hard you are trying to be successful. No one stands up and cheers when you succeed, no one dries your tears when you are despairing of ever getting through. It may be, too, that not only are people in your life not being supportive, some might actually make it harder for you to get through.

An ex-husband or ex-wife may be vindictive and mean. Your parents or other family members might not hold the same value for education that you do and strongly suggest you do something else. The social services office may seem to be putting roadblocks constantly in your way. Some of your old friends may perceive what you are doing as threatening because they haven't been to college.

When you feel all alone and not supported by anyone, be good to yourself and listen to your own heart and head. You know that going to college is the best thing for you to do now, and if no one else sees that, well, to heck with them! You can remind yourself that it would be nice to have their support, but that their support is not necessary for you to go ahead and do really well.

It helps, also, to realize that most people are primarily interested in furthering their own lives and families and in doing what they value. You have the absolute right, and perhaps even the obligation, to go ahead and do what you value and to ignore or at least pay less emotional attention to those who would tell you otherwise.

How can you do this effectively, especially with people you care about? It's awfully hard to ignore family member's opinions and comments, and impossible to ignore what a "helping" agency does (mostly inadvertently) to make life harder. I suggest that if people around you that you care about or are dependent on are making life miserable, that you get some professional counseling about how best to deal with them. I can give you some advice, but each situation is just a little different, and it sometimes takes real diplomacy and tact to deal with unsupportive people who just end up making it all that much harder for you.

Reflective Listening

I suggest that you always keep uppermost in your mind that you know what is best for you, that no one else can tell you what is best for you, and that other people can only offer advice or opinions which you may or may not choose to accept. Sometimes the best way to keep this in mind (especially when you are having a conversation with someone who is not being very supportive) is to use what is called "reflective listening." Reflective listening is something most social workers, psychologists, and other mental health professionals learn in school and in internship training. You may already know how to do it, but just not know what it's called.

> *My family thinks I am draining the public purse and that I should just get a job.*

For example, if your mother comments to you, "It's really too bad that you can't just find a nice man to take care of you, instead of you going to college and spending so much time away from your children," it can set the stage for a nasty fight. You can reply, "Mom, it sounds like you feel that a mother should be home with her children." You aren't defending yourself (a mistake), you aren't arguing with her (another mistake), you aren't getting angry (biggest mistake) that your value systems are so different and she isn't helping you emotionally along the way. When you use reflective listening, remember to use a neutral tone of voice—watch out for the temptation to be sarcastic.

With reflective listening, you are paraphrasing and simply turning her comment back to her by use of a verbal mirror. You may get more comments like the first one when you reply in such a way. She might then say something like, "I'll say that mothers should be home with their children! Most problems kids have nowadays are because their mothers are out working or going to school and not taking good care of them."

What do you reply here? You can try, "I hear you saying that you think children would be better off if their mothers were home always to tend to their needs and wants, is that right?" You are again just reiterating what your mother is saying, and this can go on and on, as long as you keep your cool, and simply reflect back what the other person is saying to you. The number one rule here is don't let yourself be baited, don't get angry. It may be that the person you're talking with just needs you to understand his or her point of view, too, and wants to come to some understanding that you agree to disagree.

Reflective listening works pretty well in most cases. It may take people by surprise, though, the first time you use it with them, especially if they're accustomed to you getting upset and defending your point of view. The nice thing about using reflective listening when you are being challenged is that you aren't forced into a position of having to defend, argue, or otherwise engage in an unpleasant confrontation. You can keep your opinions and values in your head quite clearly, because you aren't trying to defend them with all your energy. You're just trying to understand what the other people are saying and you're getting them to clarify what they think. You're making them use some of their energy to explain their position to you, rather than the other way around! Counselors use this technique to get you to clarify your problems and issues that you bring into their offices.

When people feel understood they are less likely to fight with you. If you find that using reflective listening doesn't help in a particular instance, most of the time you can leave the situation and not interact with that person. You can separate yourself. You can say, "I'm sorry you feel that way, but since I don't want to get into a fight with you about it I am leaving now," and walk away.

> *No one in my family has ever gone to college, so they are very excited for me. And they are proud of me for my being able to provide for the kids and have a high grade point average.*

Build Your Own Support System

Another thing you can do when some people around you aren't very supportive is to try very hard to find other people who will be. This might take some work, and you'll need to put yourself in situations where you're likely to be able to get to know these supportive people. When you do find other supportive people, they will help you when others in your life aren't showing much enthusiasm for what you're doing.

> *I have a babysitting co-op with two other families. I receive tremendous support from all my family although they do not live near here. My four sisters have all been in school recently. Although only one of my sisters is a single parent, I receive an incredible amount of emotional support from them! My parents are the greatest!*

In your quest for supportive people, and in dealing with others who are not supportive, you might keep the following "human rights" in mind (they apply to you and other people):

The Bill of Assertive Human Rights

You have the right:
- To judge your own behavior, thoughts, and emotions, and to take responsibility for their initiation and consequences upon yourself.
- To offer no reasons or excuses for justifying your behavior.
- To judge if you are responsible for finding solutions to other people's problems.
- To change your mind.
- To be independent of the goodwill of others before coping with them.
- To be illogical in making decisions.
- To say, "I don't understand."
- To say, "I don't know."
- To say, "I don't care."
- To make mistakes . . . and be responsible for them.

(From the University of Utah Counseling Center)

When You Feel Like Quitting

There may come a time every quarter or semester (or maybe every day?) when you feel like quitting. You might ask yourself why the heck you're in school. You might think it was all just a big mistake. You may try to convince yourself that you would be better off elsewhere. You might tell yourself that you and your children would be happier if you weren't in school, if you were just working or staying home on welfare. Your good sense and basic intelligence tells you that those things are untrue, especially in the long run, but your feelings tell you differently. All the disadvantages and pressures and hardships loom before you and you can't see much good in what you are doing at all!

> *Sometimes I think that I'll be in school forever. I know that these few years are worth it, compared to a lifetime. But sometimes it feels like I've been in school forever, and I'll be in school forever. But I know what kind of jobs I've had before and I know I want better, so I just have to keep on trying.*

Something very peculiar can happen then, especially when we haven't allowed ourselves much enjoyment and relaxation. When the feelings of being pushed and controlled by everything but ourselves gets too overwhelming, sometimes we just spin our wheels and refuse to do anything! Not only do we not do anything enjoyable, we don't do anything we think we are supposed to do, either! We just unconsciously refuse to participate in life. We just stop.

I found that to be true of myself and most of my single parent friends when we pushed ourselves too hard. When everyone and every institution expects you to do what they want you to do, and when you find yourself trying to keep up with everyone else's "shoulds," sometimes in rebellion against that overwhelming feeling you just go on strike. What happens is that you stop doing what you and everyone else thinks you should be doing, but you feel too guilty to do something fun, so you do nothing. What a waste of precious time! Quitting altogether seems like a reasonable option because you feel so stuck.

A good example of this very thing happening is when your final exams come around, your house is a mess, your kids are cranky, and you're running out of money. At those times I often found myself feeling like I should do so many things at once that I couldn't do anything, and I just drifted from one activity to another without finishing or enjoying anything. You know, you go the bathroom to clean it, get halfway done and think you should really study a little. So, you leave the bathroom halfway done, and try to study (but you can't because you're thinking about everything else that isn't done), and you find you can't concentrate, so you go outside to check on the kids. Around and around you go, without getting a real sense of accomplishment for anything, feeling guiltier and guiltier for not getting done what you want to get done, and getting angry at the whole situation. And you've become a lousy parent to boot!

And Now For Something Completely Different

When circumstances get overwhelming like this, quitting school altogether can appear to be your only alternative. The pressures of it all can make your thinking really irrational. At those dangerous "I want to quit!" times, sometimes it's best to do something completely different just for a couple of hours or days. You don't have to quit school entirely, just give yourself a break. There are many ways you can do this. You should try to do something that is out of the ordinary, something that you don't normally do. Any unusual pleasant activity, either alone or shared, can help you escape the feeling of gloom and doom. For example, if you like to swim but haven't gone in years, rustle up a babysitter, trade or pay, and go to the local YWCA, college, or community pool and just swim for a couple of hours. Call around, and you might even find a pool at a community center which offers child care right there for a nominal fee. If you are sick of studying textbooks and would like to read something else for a change, check out something entirely different from your college or local public library—my "escape reading" was mostly Agatha Christie's mysteries or Helen MacInnes's spy thrillers. Or, if you're tired of telling your children, and they're tired of hearing, "No, we can't because . . . ," surprise them, and take them all down to the roller skating rink or a cheap matinee movie for an afternoon (don't take things to study—go skating!).

When you do something different, let yourself enjoy it by not thinking about what you think you should be doing. Only think about the enjoyable thing you are doing right that very moment. This will take practice and some self-control, and you will become better at being good to yourself without the guilt monster creeping up on you.

So, let almost everything go for a little while and do something fun, either with or without your children, depending on your needs. *The world will not end if you do this.* You will not flunk out of school if you take yourself and your kids on a picnic. Then come back to what you need to do and remember to divide things into small and manageable parts. Move from one small task to the other, in order of priorities, and completing each small task one step at a time.

Getting Back Control and Enjoying Life

There are a couple of things that will naturally happen when you occasionally just do something you want to do instead of always doing everything you think you must do or should do. First, you will get back some sense of control over your own life. That is very important for most of us, because being in school and particularly being dependent on social services can take away a lot of that sense of control. It starts to seem like everyone else controls your life, not you.

Second, you get a breather and you are reminded that there is more to life than drudgery and work and pressure. You allow yourself to be a human being, and you allow yourself some fun and relaxation instead of pushing yourself all the time.

You will come back from an unusual and enjoyable activity with more sense of control, some lessening of anxiety, and an increased ability to cope with everything that demands your time and energy. Try it. If several of these activities don't help, and you need a larger, longer break from school, read on.

Something's Got to Give!

You know when you've reached your limit. You know when you just don't have any more energy or enthusiasm left. At this time, you can approach a college counselor, dean, or other person who can help you get some real time off from school without penalty.

If you feel yourself slipping, and you know you need a break from school, don't assume that taking a long break is not possible until you try. You may be able to take a quarter or semester off and just work at your part-time job or do some light independent study without it affecting your financial aid or your academic standing. The most important thing here is to get the permission of someone in charge to take some time off, in writing, and get it approved by everyone who needs to approve it so that you don't lose anything. Start by approaching your academic advising center.

You may need a physician's verification that you're just exhausted and need a break for your health's sake. You may need to see a counselor and have him or her certify that you need a break for your mental health. In any case, don't just exit school for a while and hope no one notices! Even if people don't, the college computer will!

Most single parent students I knew (myself included) were so bound and determined to get through as quickly as possible that they didn't take needed breaks. Their grades showed it, their health showed it, their children showed it. I believe it's much better to take a short break and come back ready to go than it is to trudge on and on feeling more and more overwhelmed. I finally tried taking a real break once near the end of my schooling, and it helped a lot.

Again, be sure if you do this that you alert everybody else you need to. This includes the social services office, if you get aid from them. Get all the "Okay's" from your school and social services office that you need to (in writing!), then tell other helping agencies that you are taking an allowed break if you are receiving aid that is related to your attendance. Be sure you do all this before you take a leave of absence—that way you will head off any potential problems, and save yourself a major crisis.

SPOTLIGHT ON COLLEGE PROGRAMS
Emporia State University

The Emporia State University Single Parent Program was established to assess and respond to the needs of single parents attending Emporia State University in Kansas and to assist parents who are considering attending the university. With an enrollment of more than six thousand students, ESU is small enough to be comfortable, yet large enough to provide high quality, comprehensive programs. Emporia State University offers undergraduate and graduate degree programs through the School of Business, College of Liberal Arts and Sciences, School of Library and Information Management, and the Teachers College.

The Single Parent Program Office maintains current information on resources at Emporia State University and within the community, including financial aid, child care, housing, employment, and emergency resources. Need-based scholarships for child care have been made available through the Educational Opportunity Fund (monies from student fees) for parents attending Emporia State University. The money is paid directly to a licensed child care provider of the parent's choosing, and is subject to availability from year to year. On-campus child care is available for an affordable fee at the Child Development Center located in Butcher Children's School. Butcher School is a laboratory elementary school which accepts students by application. ESU also has family housing located within walking distance of the campus which is open to both married and single parent families.

The Single Parent Program Coordinator provides both personal and career counseling, vocational testing, and preliminary academic advising. If they wish, new students can be assigned a Single Parent Student "mentor," a friendly peer and resource person who has had the experience of adjusting to college life as a single parent. The coordinator also maintains contact with representatives of various community agencies in order to facilitate referrals and acts as an advocate for single parents on campus with faculty, administration, and student government.

The Single Parent Support Group provides a relaxed atmosphere to meet other single parents and share concerns and ideas. In addition, the program coordinator works closely with Nu Tau Sigma, the nontraditional student organization. Nu Tau Sigma sponsors social events for members and special activities for their families.

Various workshops and activities are available through the Single Parent Program, Neosho River Free School, Nu Tau Sigma, and other groups. Past topics include stress management, positive thinking, self-esteem, and assertion training.

For more information, contact:

Jaqueline L. Schmidt, M.S., C.R.C., Program Coordinator
Emporia State University
1200 Commercial, Campus Box 6
Emporia, Kansas 66801
(316) 343-5221

17

Expectations, Conflicts, and Courage

Expectations

Even if you haven't been to college before, you might have a fairly realistic idea about what it is like. Then again, you might not. I had some unrealistic expectations at first and they were quickly changed.

One of my expectations was that since it had been fairly easy for me to get good grades in high school years before, it would be equally easy for me to get them in college, too. Wrong. It took a lot more work! Nothing could have prepared me for the sheer amount of reading that had to be done for three or four courses a quarter. Assignments (all together) of 200-300 pages a week are not unusual. Add writing papers, library research, and studying for tests, and it's a tremendous workload. But if you expect this at first, it won't be such a shock.

The university wasn't always "user-friendly." I wasn't prepared for the long lines to pay tuition, buy books, see an academic advisor, or register for classes. Always expect everything to take at least twice as long as you think it will. Then if things take a normal amount of time you'll be pleasantly surprised.

There were many older faces on campus. I thought that the university would be entirely made up of eighteen- to twenty-year-olds with perfect bodies and minds. Wrong again. There were lots of folks like me—a little or a lot older, alone or not, with and without children, some part-timers and some full-timers. It just took a while to find them. I was pleasantly surprised to find students in my classes that I could relate to on a personal level as well as on an intellectual one. What surprised me the most was that it was these older students who often did the best in classes and in general while they were in school. They knew what they wanted, they went for it, and did remarkably well. In fact, because they were older, and had experience in the "real world," they actually did much better than many of the younger, unencumbered students.

Textbooks were sometimes tremendously expensive. Even medium-sized soft covered books could cost $30 or $40. One quarter I spent $150 on books, and was taking just a regular full load, four classes. Hardcover science books about two inches thick can cost from $50 to $75 or more.

My naive belief that professors were somehow elevated, superhuman beings was changed, too. I'm glad that I found out early how human and real they are. That made them a lot more approachable and easier to talk with and ask questions of. Just look at them as people, smart people, who can offer you a little of their knowledge about part of the world. Don't expect great wisdom or insight or perfection from any of them.

I didn't know that I couldn't always count on getting particular classes I wanted. Sometimes they were full or perhaps had been cancelled. I didn't know that it took sometimes two or three schedule changes (and a lot of time) before I managed to get a reasonable bunch of classes at reasonable times. I thought you just wrote down what you wanted and, "poof!" it happened. To get classes I wanted I had to register early, early, early, and sometimes just sit in on a particular class that I didn't get on my schedule, and ask the professor if I could be admitted. Every quarter was a scramble with add and drop cards. You'll find out what those are real quickly.

Sitting in classes for four or five hours straight can be decidedly hard on one's back, neck, and rear end. I learned after a couple of quarters to grab a seat in the back of the room and turn a desk in front of me around so that I could put my feet up for an hour. That felt a lot better. If there were any extra chairs in the class at all, no one cared when I did that, and some other students even caught on to my comfort strategy and did it too! No professor ever complained or asked me to sit up straight, not once. If I couldn't turn a desk around, I sometimes sat on the floor with my back against a wall and my knees bent up to sit my notebook on, near the back of the room. Nobody cared. At first I thought somebody would.

Every class at the university was not tremendously interesting, exciting, and informative. Some classes were just "Mickey Mouse" courses, but ones I had to get through with as much grace as possible. Others were mediocre, and one had to struggle to impart much excitement to the content or process. It was a rare course that lived up to my ideal of the college class, and most classes' coursework and lectures were ho-hum. When I found a professor or lecturer who was particularly good at bringing some amount of excitement, enthusiasm, good humor, and up-to-date information to a class of students, I always tried to take other courses from that person. On the other hand, I learned to avoid the teachers who were lackluster, uninteresting (and uninterested in us), dull beyond bearing, and who offered outdated lectures. A teacher or professor did not have to be entertaining or particularly witty for me to enjoy the class, he or she just had to have a certain spark that kept it going.

I wasn't expecting the positive support that other single parent students and I received from *individuals* at the university. This came most often from professors and certain people in administrative offices and was always tremendously welcome. Most people employed by the university in one capacity or another were somewhat in awe of us single parent students and really bent over backwards to help. I hadn't expected that! You might get tired, however, of hearing, "Gee, I could never do what you're doing! How do you do it?!" (Oh, please, don't ask me that anymore! It makes me think of how hard everything really is. Just smile and wish me luck, okay?)

Conflicts

So much for realistic and unrealistic expectations. The conflicts you will face now and later might surprise you as well.

A single parent student is reminded daily of the tremendous demands on time and energy made by children, school, and perhaps even work. It becomes very difficult for all single parents to constantly say to their children that time or energy or money is not available to do something or get something the child wants. When that same parent goes to school, the "No's" always increase. Children tend to be very egocentric, simply because they are children, and they make sometimes unreasonable demands. However, they also make very reasonable requests and have needs that only you can fulfill. Single parent students ask themselves often, "Am I doing the right thing? Is this all too unfair to my children? Am I making things too hard on them? Will all this have a long-term impact on my children?"

You are a single parent, and you want to go to college. One of the most powerful conflicts you will face is that on one hand you want to be able to provide well for your children in all sorts of ways; on the other hand, going to school will take a good deal of your time and other resources away from your children for a few years.

Hang in there—it's rough, but if I can do it for six years, anyone can. Apply for all kinds of aid right away to assure you possibly get it. A good roommate helps, but if it's too crowded, it just adds to the stress. Don't take too many credit hours—it's not worth pushing yourself. Try to remember your children are growing up as you go to school and they need you, too.

Part of the resolution of this conflict won't come from any books or advice. It has to come from your ability to put off immediate gains for long-term goals. In addition, since you are your children's major caretaker, you must make the decision for them to put off some of their wants for a long-term better life. You will also need to learn and use excellent time management skills and scheduling. You've discovered some skills in this book; experience and further exploration of techniques and resources will help you refine them.

Still, you'll want to communicate to your children, almost daily, what you are doing and why. A major, positive (and I believe necessary) thing to do to help all of you through these years is to set aside some special time each day (if possible) or at least each week with your kids, individually and together, just to show them that you really are still their parent and love them very much. These times should sometimes be spontaneous and sometimes be planned, according to the changing needs of you and your family.

Still other conflicts will come between you and government and school offices. If you rely on social services, they will want you to get off their "welfare" rolls as quickly as possible. Caseworkers (who might not even have a college education themselves) may not seem very supportive of you being in a long-term training program, and may hassle you about it and require all sorts of "proof" from you that you are succeeding. If you get financial aid from your college and the government, they will require you to take a certain number of credit hours per semester or quarter, and also will also require you to keep your grades reasonably high. If you work, your employer will want you to be on the ball and do a good job no matter what kinds of other pressures you are under. Each professor will expect you to do well in his or her class. You'll have all sorts of expectations for yourself, too.

So, you'll have potential conflicts with almost every person and every organization that you have contact with! You have your own set of goals and values, and they won't always be shared by your local caseworker, financial aid worker, professors and instructors, children, friends, and family. You must learn very quickly to stand your ground. You'll need to learn to not let others intimidate you—state very clearly what your goals and values are, and then stick to them. You'll also learn to do the best you can do under your very constrained circumstances, and accept your performance as such. The first step in becoming assertive about yourself and your lifestyle is to become comfortable with it yourself.

In the Long Run

Most of us will live sixty or seventy odd years, with luck. You're a parent now, and you'll always be one. That never stops, as your own parents can tell you! You'll be a college student for at least two, and probably four or more years. But think, you'll be a parent for probably thirty or forty or more years than you'll be a college student. And being a college student for just a few years can help you become better able to take care of yourself and your children for the rest of your life. This question was asked in the beginning of this book about your current lifestyle: "Do you want to go on living this way?" Your answer is probably "no", and that's why you are reading this book. *You, and you alone, however, must take the first step.*

Take Courage!

College or university life is what you make of it. You can learn as much or as little as you wish. You can participate in classes and activities, or not.

And special training or a degree is just the first step to independence and a better way of life for you and your family; a good deal of hard work and struggle comes after that. College is only one journey in a lifetime of journeys—for a person like you this particular one takes hard work, sacrifice, persistence, and problem solving every day. It is worth all of that, though, and it will afford you survival skills and employment skills that will greatly improve the remainder of your life and your children's lives. Once you're in school you probably won't be able to imagine doing anything better with your time and energy for a few years.

The more you and your children learn about almost anything, the better your lives will be. Please don't stop going to the library after you graduate from college; read as much as you can, all the time, throughout your life. Read for fun and read to learn. Watch public television. Attend free public lectures at the college and elsewhere. Talk to people about important issues. Volunteer (after you have some free time) to assist an organization that does things you value. Think about things; use your brain. Teach your children to do the same. You have probably heard the old saying, one that comes in many different forms from many different parts of the world, that goes something like this: *Give a person a fish, and that person will not be hungry for a day. Teach a person how to fish, and that person will never be hungry again.* This guidebook has attempted to teach you how to fish. Now you can teach your children, by your example, your words, and your commitment to a better future for yourself, for them, and maybe even for other people you don't even know.

You know, though, that sometimes people only see going to college as a way to get a better career, and that is unfortunate. You may even view this guidebook as being concerned only with helping you get through college and get into a good-paying career. That's an important part of it, but it's definitely not the only part. Becoming better educated means much more than preparing yourself for a career. It means becoming able to think about the world, yourself, other people, and issues in open-minded, rational ways. It means learning about history, and the ways in which the past, present, and future interact. It means learning how to find out about things, long after you've graduated. It means losing much of your preconceived ideas about people. It means developing a broader outlook on life, and means that you can look beyond your self and your immediate environment when you think about human problems and potential solutions.

So, when you leave college, please don't leave learning. But, for now, have courage! Take the first step! I'm smiling and wishing you luck.

Appendix A: Social Services

QUESTIONNAIRE

1. How many single parents attend colleges or universities and also utilize some form of social services assistance (financial, medical, day-care subsidy, food stamps) in your state?

2. a. Are single parent students (undergraduate) with low incomes or receiving AFDC eligible for state day-care subsidies? If no, will they be eligible in the near future? When?

    b. Is there a waiting list for such students for this kind of help? Average length of time to wait for assistance?

3. Are single parents on assistance (such as AFDC), encouraged or required by state social services to enter short-term (6 months to 2 years) training programs, rather than long-term (4+ years of college or university study) for state budgetary reasons or to meet Federal guidelines?

4. Is it possible for a single parent who has dependent children of any age and who receives social services aid (AFDC, food stamps, medicaid, etc.) to work out an individualized program with her or his caseworker that would allow the single parent to enter and attend college to earn at least a bachelor of arts or science degree in your state? If yes, how should a single parent approach the caseworker for assistance?

5. Are single parent college students, who are dependent on social services aid, required by state and/or Federal guidelines to work at least part time while they are in school in order to receive or continue to receive aid?

6. Have social services personnel discussed with college and university financial aid officers the financial barriers and constraints of single parent students trying to attend a college or university (i.e., one form of aid, perhaps student loans, decreasing another form, perhaps food stamps)? If no, are such discussions planned for the future?

7. Are state social services administration staff convinced that providing assistance to those single parents desiring to enter college and earn a post-secondary degree is cost-effective for the state? Does your state social services office have a way of tracking such single parent students to monitor their progress, drop-out rate, or post-graduation employment status? If no, do you plan this tracking for the future?

8. Please describe any specific state services, programs, or efforts directed toward single parents—specifically as they relate to college education and training to facilitate their long-term self sufficiency and lessened or discontinued dependence on state social services.

ALABAMA

1. Not available.

2. a. Yes. b. No.

3. Not necessarily. It depends on the individual and his/her career goals.

4. Yes. The individual should inform her case manager of her desire to attend college. The case manager would then provide whatever referrals or assistance is needed and/or available.

5. No.

6. These discussions are occurring on the local level with local task forces taking the initiative.

7. Information is unavailable at this time. We are developing an automated system that should be able to track this information.

8. Educational activities selected must be consistent with career goals. Supportive services such as child care may be provided to eligible individuals. Efforts will be made to assist the individual in locating sources of funds for educational costs such as tuition, books, and fees.

ALASKA

1. Documented figures are not currently available. Our estimate is 380 single parents statewide attend college/university and also utilize some form of public assistance.

2. a. Yes, single parents who are attending college are eligible to receive state day-care subsidies from the Alaska state day-care assistance program.

b. Depending on the availability of funding or licensed space—there may be a waiting list for all applicants needing day-care assistance, not just students. A waiting list usually occurs toward the end of a fiscal year when more funding is needed for delivery of services.

3. On 10/1/90, Alaska's Welfare Reform Task Force recommended that Alaska's JOBS program offer post-secondary education. Recommendation #14 of the final report of that task force states, "Alaska should include career training through post-secondary education." JOBS funding is limited, so the amount that JOBS may pay for an individual's education is limited, and an individual may receive JOBS payments for education for no more than 24 months. Single parents are encouraged to enter post-secondary education when vocational testing indicates this activity js appropriate. Individuals who choose to pay for their education themselves or who self-initiate training using other resources may receive JOBS child care and other supportive services.

4. Before 10/1/90, WIN caseworkers provided information and referral services to any WIN recipient. WIN participants who were able to obtain JTPA or Vocational Rehabilitation assistance to attend post-secondary education could get WIN child care. Those who had no children under the age of six may have been required to do a job search once a year when there was a substantial break in their educa-

tional activity. Since JOBS was implemented on 10/1/90, each individual in the program has a case manager who works with the individual and other agencies to develop a plan to help the individual to achieve their self-sufficiency goal. Again, JOBS funds will be limited as stated in #3, and although an individual may pursue a four-year degree, they must achieve a two-year degree or certificate first.

5.   Our current (1989) WIN/Employment Service Program places special emphasis on JOB Search for single parents whose children are over age 6. State guidelines require them to complete 4 weeks of JOB Search once per year. With the new JOBS program, Employment Search will continue to be a major component of JOBS; however, single parents will not be required to work while they are attending college. After a recommended two-year course of study in a higher educational setting, single parent recipients will be eligible to receive other types of supportive services through JOBS, i.e., transportation, etc., and can still receive AFDC.

6.   To date, federally-approved grants and educational loans will not affect a recipient's AFDC grant. Public Assistance and WIN local offices will begin building relationships with the post-secondary financial aid officers to make them aware of changes in public assistance policies relating to educational loans and grants. Case managers will also inform clients of the type of financial aid that may affect their public assistance.

7.   We currently do not have a way of tracking the progress of AF single parents attending college—we plan to build such a tracking system within our statewide JOBS program. Single parents who attend college through JOBS are required to have satisfactory progress in order to continue in school through JOBS. We believe that single parents who go to college will eventually become self-supporting Alaskans with marketable skills. We feel that an investment in education and training will mean long-term benefits for the individual families and Alaska as a whole. Although supporting a two-year educational program for single parents will be costly for the state, we feel this is an avenue that will help AFDC recipients get off the welfare rolls and into good quality jobs thereby reducing the long-term welfare dependency for those participants. In essence, we believe that the state's cost for taking care of these recipients will eventually be decreased.

8.   From Alaska's Welfare Reform Task Force:
Career Training Through Post Secondary Education
Component Guidelines
December 29, 1989

Goal: Participants in the Career Training Through Post Secondary Education component will be able to obtain gainful employment in the field related to their education or training within 30 months of component entry.

Priority for Component Entry: JOBS participants with the following characteristics will be given first priority for entry into the Career Training Through Post Secondary Education Component:

1.   Persons who do not have a degree. However, degreed persons who can no longer pursue employment in the field for which they are qualified by their degree because of disability, and who are accepted by the Division of Vocational Rehabilitation will be given priority for entering this component.

2. Persons who are not currently engaged in self-initiated training. The State would allow a parent or other caretaker relative or any dependent child in the family who is attending in good standing an institution of higher education (as defined in section 481 (a) of the Higher Education Act of 1965), or a school or other entity offering a course of vocational or technical training, at the time she or he would otherwise be required to commence participation in the JOBS program, to continue to attend.

3. Persons who had partially completed a secondary or post secondary program of vocational education or training and had the education or training interrupted for reasons such as marriage, or child care problems.

4. Persons who have a minimum of a high school diploma or general education diploma (GED).

5. Persons who have completed a course of training but need retraining for the current labor market.

Note: The above are not in any ranking order, but equally qualify as first priority applicants.

Guidelines for Participation:

1. Before JOBS funds could be applied for books, fees, supplies, and tuition expenses, participants would be required to exhaust all other resources including Adult Basic Education, Pell Grant, Vocational Rehabilitation, JTPA, and Vocational Education. Participants would not be required to incur indebtedness in order to access training and education through this component.

2. Education and training must be consistent with the person's employment goal, and the employment goal must be compatible with the job market.

3. A program of education or training must be completed within a period of 24 consecutive months.

4. In order to maximize successful completion of the courses of study, participants will be screened through testing and assessment of interest and ability before they can be approved for any program of education or training.

5. Only training located in Alaska will be approved for participants in this component unless such training is not found in-state. Supportive services may be provided outside the state of Alaska as resource availability allows. State agencies should develop any mechanisms that are currently lacking that would allow for provision of those services.

6. The maximum training cost (books, tuition, fees) payable by JOBS will be $2,000 per year.

Satisfactory Participation: After the first six months in the career training, component, individuals will be expected to attain and maintain full-time participation. Participants will be expected to maintain a "C" average or better in graded programs and "passing" status in pass/fail programs. the minimum requirement for successful performance is completion of 75 percent of the training objectives during each sequence of training.

Issue: Should the state pay the costs for AFDC clients to attend college? If so, should clients be allowed to enroll in two-year degree programs? Four-year programs?

FSA Requirement: The ACT (Family Support Act) leaves the option of offering post secondary education services entirely up to the state. The draft federal regulations state:

"We interpret the language of section 482(d)(1)(B) of the Act to mean that the offering of post secondary education is an entirely optional matter for the state welfare agency to address in its JOBS plan, except that we have limited such education to that which is directly related to the fulfillment of an individual's employment in a recognized occupation."

Rationale: Our discussion focused on the state's role in providing for the post-secondary education of AFDC recipients. If the state advocates for four-year degree programs, then are we essentially creating a four-year welfare recipient? Most of the state's AFDC families stay less than two years on the program.

Yet, we philosophically agree with educating Alakans so that they can participate in a meaningful way in the economy. Also, if the alternative to a four-year college involvement with a family is 14 to 16 years of public assistance involvement and perpetuation of poverty, then four years doesn't seem so expensive.

Cost: Costs for this recommendation above existing AFDC grants to these clients will be tuition, books, and supportive services costs paid during JOBS participation.

Benefits: The benefit to everyone will be more self-supporting Alaskans with marketable skills. We know that in order to break lifestyles of welfare, people must be able to support themselves over many years. A good example of how this component might work is the health care industry. The nation is currently experiencing a severe shortage of health care professionals, for which post-secondary training is necessary. The relatively short term investment into health career training could mean long term benefits both to the individual families and society as a whole.

ARIZONA

1. No information available.

2. a. Yes.
   b. No.

3. No.

4. No.

5. The only program which has a work requirement, which is a national requirement, is the Food Stamp Program.

6. No. No discussions have been held or are planned, as Federal law dictates what is or is not counted.

7. No opinion. No tracking is planned at this time.

8. No specific programs.

ARKANSAS

"As you will see from the responses, our welfare reform program—Project SUCCESS—provides varying employability services and support to AFDC and Food Stamp recipients. While our program does not specifically target single parents desiring post-secondary education, that group is included in the program."

1. Documented figures are not available. Estimate would not be appropriate.

2. a.   Parents receiving AFDC or Food Stamps generally participate in Arkansas' welfare reform program, "Project SUCCESS." When they do, day care is paid by the state for the time the participant is involved in Project SUCCESS activities (e.g., education/vocational training, etc.). Federal regulations provide for greater subsidies to AFDC recipients than to Food Stamp recipients. (This is true for most available services.)

   b.   No waiting period.

3. The initial steps in providing Project SUCCESS services to eligible participants include an assessment (employment history, family circumstances, supportive service needs, etc.) and an employability plan (barriers to be overcome, employment goals, etc.). Project SUCCESS policy does not attempt to encourage or channel participants into any general type or length of training/education; the paramount consideration in each case is the participant's realistic and attainable employability goal. (Federal regulations do not permit the payment of tuition, fees, books, etc., for Food Stamp recipients; however, support services, e.g., child care, transporation, etc., would be subsidized.)

4. While Project SUCCESS is not a panacea for all the social and educational challenges the state confronts, it does establish a basis upon which all welfare recipients can strive to attain their maximum potential, given their individual limitations, barriers, and the social setting in which they exist. It is possible for an eligible single parent whose employment goal includes the requirement for post-secondary education to achieve that objective. (Again, Food Stamp recipients cannot receive subsidies for tuition, fees, books.) Their approach to the caseworker should be honest and straightforward; knowledge of program benefits/limitations would be an asset.

5. No. Participants must attend classes regularly, make passing grades, and satisfy attendance requirements of the institution.

6. No. Participants in Project SUCCESS are advised of educational opportunities and types of financial assistance/aid during the assessment process. There are no planned discussions at this time with representatives of colleges/universities regarding single parent students.

7. The stated goal of this agency is, "to provide quality services, within available resources, which enable people to maximize their potential and to increase their abilities, preserve and enhance human dignity and worth, and prevent or reduce the need for services." We do recognize that the greater the educational level our clients can achieve, the more cost-effective it becomes for the state. No plans exist at this time to track single parent students.

8. As stated earlier, our policy is to assist all welfare recipients to attain their maximum potential, given their individual limitations, barriers, and the social setting in which they exist—and, of course, within available resources. When their employability goals indicate post secondary education, our welfare reform program—Project SUCCESS—is available to subsidize that training/education.

CALIFORNIA

1. Unknown. [in the thousands—author]
Although neither the Department of Social Services nor the colleges in California maintain statistics on the number of single parents attending college who utilize social service assistance, a recent survey of community colleges in California revealed that 25% of the students received some form of social services aid.

2. a. Yes, through the GAIN Program, for two years of college. Several community colleges have campus-based child care centers.
  b. No waiting list for mandatory GAIN participants.

3. Most services in California are geared toward those with the least skills; therefore, education and/or training is usually short-term and provided to help participants gain entry-level jobs. College is limited to two years for participants in the GAIN Program. 60-75% of GAIN participants involved in educational activities are receiving basic adult education. In addition, receiving a bachelor degree doesn't necessarily mean success.

4. California Social Services will currently only provide assistance for two years of a college program. New federal regulations for the JOBS Program may allow three years of school in the near future.

5. There is no work requirement while the single parent is in school. If a recipient works more than 15 hours a week, however, he or she is not required to be in the GAIN Program.

6. There has been some coordination between social services and financial aid offices. There are inconsistencies, though, in the way colleges and universities handle aid to students. In theory, all needs are met by social services and financial aid; however, in reality there is always some leftover need.

7. California has a strong prejudice to provide basic services to large numbers of people who need basic services. The goal is to raise the general educational level of many people, not to concentrate on those who are qualified to enter college. "Creaming," a term used to describe the provision of supportive services to those judged to have the least basic needs (people qualified for college study), is discouraged.

8. University of California campuses have alumni-supported programs that may assist single parent students. Programs also exist to assist teenage parents. In general, services through California Social Services are based on need, not marital status.

COLORADO

1. Our data systems do not collect this information. Any estimate would be meaningless.

2. a. Yes.
  b. Normally no—but this can vary with some counties due to numbers of participants.

3. Yes—for state budgeting reasons.

4. The key word here is "enter." The answer, then, is no—refer to question #3. Single parents with 24 months or less of schooling remaining to earn their BA/BS may be able to do so while receiving AFDC.

5. No.

6. No. Not at this time.

7. No. Our training is done through JOBS if the single parent student is a JOBS participant.

8. JOBS program staff at the local level work with educational facilities to obtain skills training in occupations which will supply a self-sufficiency wage and are available in the area.

CONNECTICUT

1. There are an average of 750 participants per month who are in the Job Connection program to receive their bachelors or associates degrees. (Aug. 1989–Feb. 1990 data.)

2. a. Participants in the Job Connection program are eligible to receive up to $75 per week per child for day care, or $100 per week per child (if handicapped).

   b. For Job Connection day care through the Department of Income Maintenance there is no waiting list. There may be waiting lists to get into specific day care centers.

3. Job Connection participants can receive support services for 36 consecutive months to get an associates degree and for 24 consecutive months to receive a bachelors degree, provided they are within 24 months of graduation.

4. The Job Connection program has what is called a self-initiated plan. So long as a participant goes through a self-sufficiency plan (an assessment and a Job Connection agreement) which is done by the recipient and the caseworker, the participant may use the self-initiated plan. The program still only offers its services for 24 and 36 consecutive months as mentioned earlier.

5. No, single parent college students aren't required to work in order to receive Aid to Families with Dependent Children (AFDC) benefits, as long as their self-sufficiency plan includes the schooling.

6. The discussion between social services personnel and university financial aid officers about the constraints on single parent students is ongoing.

7. Informal studies indicate much lower AFDC recidivism, suggesting that postsecondary education leads to greater opportunity for economic self sufficiency. Under JOBS (Job Opportunity Basic Skills Training Program) the state tracks monthly attendance in all educational and training activities by documenting 75% attendance on an on-line program status screen.

8. If a participant in Job Connection does the self sufficiency plan, assessment, and Job Connection agreement with their caseworker, he or she will qualify for the following if he or she decides to attend college: child care, transportation, equipment and material.

DELAWARE

1. 100-150.

2. a. Yes.
   b. No.

3. Recommendations are based on the individual client's needs and goals. In some cases clients prefer to enter the longer-term track.

4. Yes. Mandatory and non-mandatory clients are referred through the eligibility determination specialist to E&T case managers for services.

5. No. Working is based on individual needs and goals.

6. Currently no formal discussions; however, individual discussions do occur.

7. Yes, as long as it is in accordance with that individual's needs and goals.
   Yes.

8. Employment and Training Program (E&T). This program links with existing services geared toward single parents achieving a college education in institutions such as universities and community colleges. The First Step Program offers many employment and training choices to help clients obtain the skills needed to get and keep a job. Supportive services include child care, transportation, and eye care (free eye exam and glasses, if needed). Education is offered to help improve clients' reading, math, and verbal skills which may lead to a GED or high school diploma. If clients choose to continue education, they may be referred to a college level program.

DISTRICT OF COLUMBIA

1. We are unable to provide an estimate because persons attending colleges or universities are not captured as a select group in our master client file.

2. a. Yes.
   b. There is no waiting list.

3. No.

4. Yes. There are no special eligibility criteria a student receiving AFDC would have to meet. As long as s/he qualifies for the AFDC program, s/he has the flexibility to attend an institution of higher education.

5. No.

6. The D.C. City Council has passed legislation authorizing AFDC recipients to attend the state university at no cost.

7. Yes.
   We do not currently track parents engaged in this activity, nor do we plan to implement a tracking mechanism to do so in the future. In response to the second part of the question, please see response in number four.

8. Under the Welfare Reform program which became effective on October 1, 1990, an AFDC recipient could pursue a course of study in a post secondary insti-

tution if, during the assessment process, this is determined to be the best plan of self-sufficiency for the recipient.

FLORIDA

"All of our responses to your questions are given within the context of Florida's employment and training program for AFDC clients. We call this welfare-to-work program 'Project Independence.' This effort is part of the nationwide welfare reform initiative adopted by Congress through the Family Support Act of 1988."

1. We estimate 1,000 for the 1989-90 fiscal year.

2. a.   Yes. They are eligible for JOBS-funded child care and for child care funded by the Social Services Block Grant.

    b.   Yes. In January 1990, the statewide total on the waiting list was 1,800. The waiting lists in our 11 geographic service areas varied in length from 0 to 350 people. We have no statistics on waiting time.

3. Due to budget constraints, Florida limits college study to a maximum of two years.

4. No.

5. No. We encourage them to pursue their studies on a full-time basis in educational programs that lead directly to employment.

6. Yes. In Florida there is a long history of close collaboration between college financial aid officers and welfare staff.

7. Yes. In fact, the Florida legislature in 1989 granted our AFDC clients exemptions from instructional fees at public community colleges and public technical institutes for courses leading directly to employment. We currently are implementing an automated data system to track clients.

8. All of the responses to this survey are given within the context of Florida's Project Independence program—the welfare-to-work program under the Federal Family Support Act of 1988.

GEORGIA

1. Documented figures are not available for the state's general social services assistance population. However, in the 33 PEACH/JOBS counties in the state, there are 173 individuals enrolled in college and 622 individuals enrolled in vocational and technical school.

2. a.   Yes.

    b.   Yes. There is a waiting list to receive day care assistance. It is not known at this time the average length of time one must wait for assistance. This data has not previously been compiled, but there are plans to do so in the future.

3. Yes. Individuals are encouraged to enter short-term training programs rather than long-term programs to meet Federal guidelines. Our PEACH/ JOBS program will provide supportive services for a maximum of two years of college.

4. If an individual receives AFDC and Food Stamps, they may volunteer to participate in the PEACH/JOBS program. Once in the PEACH/JOBS program, an individual can work out an individualized program with his or her PEACH/JOBS case manager.

5. No. If an AFDC individual is attending school (post secondary), then he or she is mandatory PEACH/JOBS participant and must be referred to this program.

6. At this time, there has been no meaningful dialogue with educational institutions on the state or local level. There are currently no plans to initiate such a discussion. However, in the state's AFDC program, if an individual is receiving educational money, this money is totally disregarded for budgeting purposes.

7. Yes. Those individuals involved in the PEACH/JOBS program and who attend college are monitored by their PEACH/JOBS case managers. There is not a statewide monitoring mechanism in place at this time.

8. No comments provided.

HAWAII

"Responding to your questions was somewhat difficult since the state of Hawaii does not have a general policy with regard to AFDC families and post secondary education.

Since October 1987, the department has operated a state-funded voluntary workfare program, known as Project $uccess, for public assistance recipients. Recipients who volunteer to participate in the program are provided with career counseling, employability assessment, employability planning, skills or vocational training, basic education and an opportunity to pursue higher education, provided the career choice necessitates such an education, and there are jobs available upon graduation. In other words, the program will not approve higher education just for the sake of a degree. Participants can remain in the program for two years, or for six months after their eligibility for AFDC has terminated, whichever comes first.

Recipients whose employability plan includes post secondary education must apply for financial aid. The $uccess program will assist with initial costs such as books and fees, and with child care costs. Because of the two-year limitation, participants who are in higher education are helped to plan for the financing of their education after their time expires in the program.

Project $uccess will be phasing out on September 30, 1990 with the implementation of the Jobs Opportunity and Basic Skills (JOBS) Training Program on October 1, 1990. Our plan is to absorb Project $uccess participants into the new employment training program."

1. There is no departmental data base for this kind of information. Our state-funded voluntary work program does not keep this kind of information; however, a manual count indicates 117 recipients in the program are currently attending community colleges or the state university. All are receiving child care assistance through the program.

2. a. There is no state subsidy for day care for college students. The only students who receive day care assistance are those who are participating in the volun-

tary work program and whose plans for higher education are part of an employability plan.

    b. There is no waiting list for participants in the work program.

3. Recipients are not encouraged to go either way. Participating in an employment training program or in post-secondary education is determined by the employability assessment and the employability plan.

4. An AFDC recipient may volunteer to participate in the voluntary work program. Under the JOBS program which began in 10/90, an AFDC recipient who is exempt may volunteer to participate. At any rate, a determination of post-secondary education is based on the employability assessment and employability plan.

5. Recipients attending post secondary education are not required to do work study. They may do so if they are able to carry their academic load and work part time.

6. Colleges and university financial aid officers are aware of the impact of aid on an individual's financial assistance eligibility.

7. Yes, we are convinced that post secondary education is a way for recipients to become economically self sufficient. However, funding oftentimes does not always allow the department to pursue this end vigorously. The social services office does not have a tracking system to account for all recipients who are in post secondary education, to monitor progress, drop-out rate, or employment. There is no plan at this time to do this for all recipients except those who will be participating in the JOBS program.

8. No information is available in this area.

IDAHO

1. Unknown.

2. a. Yes.
    b. No, upon application.

3. Generally encouraged to obtain short-term training.

4. Yes—at the initial JOBS assessment.

5. No.

6. Yes.

7. We encourage clients to pursue reasonable plans.
No, we don't track but will soon.

8. No answer.

ILLINOIS

1. Based on the first quarter of JOBS, the estimated number of single parents attending a college or university who utilize social/supportive services is 2,333—average per month.

2. a.   Yes—all AFDC recipients are eligible for day care supportive services for undergraduate studies. The Department does not pay supportive services for graduate studies.

b.   There are no waiting lists for supportive services.

3. AFDC recipients are encouraged to enter training programs that will prepare them for employment with wages adequate to support a family. The duration of the training is not governed by state or federal budgetary constraints. The state's four-year college program is open to all recipients with the aptitude and interest level to succeed in a four-year college program.

4. Yes, the AFDC recipients and the Project Chance Specialist jointly develop an employability plan which outlines the steps necessary to achieve the employment goal. The AFDC recipient who is not participating in the Project Chance may do so by contacting the Income Maintenance Caseworker requesting a referral to the Project Chance Program, or by contacting the local Project Chance Office directly. After orientation, each participant is assessed and the employability plan is developed.

5. No. Project Chance participants are not required to work as a condition of eligibility for the receipt of social services while participating in education and training activities.

6. Project Chance personnel work closely with the state's education personnel. Project Chance provides supportive services to AFDC recipients attending four-year college in an effort to address the financial barriers.

7. The cost-effectiveness of the four-year college program has not yet been determined. The Project Chance Specialist monitors the progress of individuals in four-year college programs on a monthly basis.

8. Project Chance is a statewide program offering employment and training services to public assistance recipients, including single parents, between the ages of 16 and 64. Many teen parents in the state are provided employment and training assistance through two teen parent (under age 21) programs, Project Advance and The Young Parents Program. Project Chance, Project Advance, and The Young Parents Program all stress long-term self-sufficiency.

INDIANA

1. No answer given.

2. a.   Yes, to an even greater degree once the Title II of the Family Support Act is implemented.

b.   No.

3. Short term training, for both budget and Federal guidelines reasons.

4. Yes, on an individualized basis; however, they are generally encouraged to enter skilled training programs. Approach through normal channels or through employment and training staff.

5. No. Possibly, but not mandated. We can pay for child care, transportation, basic needs, plus they receive their regular grant.

6. Unsure; however, I would imagine so.

7. No. Not at this time. However, we are working on it. Our new system may permit it.

8. No comments provided.

IOWA

"Although other states have implemented JOBS programs that concentrate on job search and placement, Iowa's JOBS program heavily emphasizes post-secondary education as the best route to long-term self-sufficiency. Consequently, a large number of Iowa's JOBS participants are in two- or four-year vocational or educational post-secondary programs.

Also note that our answers are, for the most part, specific to Aid to Families with Dependent Children (AFDC) recipients, who are eligible for the state's JOBS program. Persons who are on Medicaid or Food Stamps only are not eligible for JOBS, and there are no other programs administered by the Iowa Department of Human Services that provide post-secondary educational services for non-AFDC recipients. However, these persons may be able to receive assistance through the state Child Care Assistance program, Vocational Rehabilitation, the Job Training Partnership Act (JTPA), or similar programs."

1. We cannot give a definite response to this question. At the moment, we have approximately 4,000 AFDC recipients who are attending two- or four-year institutions through the state's JOBS program. Given the size of the state's Food Stamp and Medicaid programs, I feel that it is safe to assume that there are at least an additional six thousand single parent undergraduate students in that population, for a total estimate of ten thousand.

2. a. The state is currently experiencing budget constraints in regard to subsidized child care. Low-income undergraduates who are not on AFDC may be able to receive assistance from subsidized child care. However, availability is affected by the amount of available funds for this program. Currently, there may be waiting lists for this type of assistance. If a person is eligible for AFDC, then the main source of child care assistance for that person is the state's JOBS program. However, we have already committed all of our state JOBS funding for the current fiscal year. Although we have not terminated any services to those persons who are already in the program, our ability to bring in new participants is limited, particularly in regard to post-secondary classroom training. As a result, clients have the choice of waiting until funding is available, or in going on their own without assistance. There are currently waiting lists in place for some of the components of the state's JOBS program. Waiting time can last anywhere from several months to a year.

   b. See above.

3. The mission statement for the state's JOBS program stresses long-term self-sufficiency. Therefore, we do not encourage one type of training over another. Our primary concern is that the training fulfill the participant's own goals and that it can be expected to result in long-term self-sufficiency. Although the majority of our JOBS participants are involved in short-term or two-year degree programs, we have a number of clients pursuing four-year programs. Our only limits are that we do

not subsidize the freshman year of a four-year program, and we do not subsidize post-baccalaureate degrees. We also limit the total calendar months of JOBS supportive services to 40, in order to ensure that the client completes schooling in a reasonable length of time and to control expenditures.

4. As explained in question 3, bachelor of arts or science degrees are allowable under the state's JOBS program for AFDC recipients. The client is referred to JOBS by the income maintenance case worker through the state's computer system. The client is then called in for assessment and interview by the JOBS worker. The income maintenance worker also has the ability to call or write the JOBS worker, to inform that worker that a client has requested priority service so that the client can be called in faster than by the normal processes. Once the participant has gone through orientation, the participant will meet with the JOBS worker to set up an Employability Plan. In most cases, a request for a post-secondary training plan will be approved, provided funding is available and the client appears to be capable of completing the training, and there is reasonable likelihood of the participant becoming self-sufficient at the end of the training program. Provided these conditions are met, the participant and the worker have considerable flexibility in designing a training plan specific to that particular client.

5. No, Iowa has no such requirement. In the state's view, gaining an education that will result in long-term self-sufficiency is preferable to a minimum-wage job that will reduce the grant currently but which really will not result in the family becoming self-sufficient.

6. In March 1987, Iowa Governor Terry Branstad implemented Iowa's own welfare reform program which is known as PROMISE. PROMISE stands for PROMoting Independence and Self-sufficiency through Employment. As a part of this effort, the Governor directed that a Welfare Reform Council be initiated. This council is made up of the heads of the following six state agencies: Human Services, Employment Services, Economic Development, Education, Human Rights, and Management. The Department of Education has been an integral part of PROMISE and representatives of that Department have been deeply involved in the issues involved in implementing the state's JOBS program.

Because of the involvement of the Department of Education, we have been able to communicate with the state's community colleges and with the state's universities and colleges, to a more limited extent. We also receive input from educational institutions on the local office level that have sometimes resulted in state-wide changes in the JOBS program. However, we have not been able to meet extensively with college and university officials to explain the JOBS program and to talk to them about problems with the program or the problems of single parents. We are planning on meeting with educational institution representatives in the course of the next 12 months to discuss mutual problems and to get their input on the program.

7. As stated above, the goal of the program is to help single parents and other AFDC recipients to achieve long-term self-sufficiency in the shortest length of time. We are convinced that education, rather than immediate placement in a low-paying job, is the most cost-effective method of achieving this result over the long-term. We have set up a component reporting data file for the JOBS program that allows

us to track each participant's progress through the program. We can accumulate information on satisfactory progress, successful completion, and can also obtain information on employment rates. We have recently received statistics on the first year of JOBS program operation and are in the process of reviewing this information. However, definite information on the topics that you mention has not yet been summarized. Once this is done, we will then look at whether we need to modify the items that we are tracking.

8.   As described above, the state has implemented the JOBS program and post secondary education is the most important component of that program. In regard to non-AFDC recipients, they may be able to receive assistance through state Child Care Assistance services but they are not specifically targeted by that program.

KANSAS

1.   A conservative estimate is 250 individuals in a given month. (Based upon a report of approved education and training plans.)

2.   a.   AFDC eligible individuals could be eligible for child care if the training plan is approved. AFDC individuals are limited to undergraduate studies. Low income individuals who do not receive AFDC may apply for Income Eligible Child Care.
      b.   Waiting lists are sometimes applicable to Income Eligible Child Care. Length of wait varies in different areas of the state.

3.   Single parents on assistance (cash or Food Stamps) are limited to training programs at the undergraduate level.

4.   Individuals who receive social services aid may be eligible to receive supportive services if the individual is attending college. Approval of training plans is limited to the undergraduate level. Job Preparation Programs (JPP) staff or designated staff in each area area assigned the responsibility of approving training plans. Supportive services include transportation and child care. Individuals are generally referred to the JPP or designated staff by the Income Maintenance Worker.

5.   There is no requirement at this time that a single parent college student must work at least part time while the individual is in school.

6.   Job Preparation Program staff are instructed to meet with local financial aid officers to discuss mutual areas of concern. Income Maintenance Food Stamp policy supervisor has met with state financial aid directors to discuss food stamp policy.

7.   Kansas allows for approval of plans for·individuals who attend college. At this time, there is no formal tracking system to monitor progress, drop-out rate, or post graduation employment status. We hope to monitor this in the future.

8.   There is a special single parents program at St. Mary's College, begun in 1988.

KENTUCKY

"Kentucky is committed to alleviating the barriers to long-term self sufficiency. Education is recognized as a necessary tool for low income families to achieve the goal of self-sufficiency. We, therefore, offer assistance to our program recipients for child care and transportation so they may earn a four-year college degree. Effective October 1, 1990, Kentucky implemented the JOBS Program, where AFDC recipients will receive more individualized case management and will be encouraged to become self-sufficient."

1. Of the 53,294 adults receiving AFDC, 2531 have attended school above the high school level. Currently, 47 recipients are receiving child care assistance while attending college.

2. a. Presently, students who receive AFDC are eligible for a child care payment under the Special Requirement Educational Allowance (SREA). Effective 10-1-90, Kentucky will implement the Jobs Opportunities and Basic Skills Program (JOBS) where AFDC recipients will be encouraged to enroll in educational programs. Child care payments will be paid to providers for those attending school.

    b. N/A

3. Under the SREA policy, AFDC recipients can receive child care payments for 50 months if they are enrolled in a college or university. This would allow for an individual to complete four-years of college or university study.

4. Presently, an individual who receives AFDC may indicate to her case worker that she is attending college. The case worker would authorize child care and transportation assistance. When JOBS is implemented, AFDC recipients, who are mandated or wish to volunteer to the JOBS program, will be assigned to a case manager. This case manager will work with the recipient in determining an employability plan. The Family Support Act of 1988, which mandates JOBS, offers states the option of allowing post-secondary education as a JOBS component. Kentucky has chosen to include post-secondary education as a component. Therefore, should the recipient and the case manager determine that a four-year degree is the best employability plan, the individual will be referred to a college/university and assisted in the enrollment and procurement of supportive services such as child care and transportation. In this situation, if a recipient does not qualify for financial assistance for tuition, the state will pay tuition, books, and fees. In the case that an individual is already enrolled in a college at the time the JOBS program begins, and a four-year program is determined to meet the employability goal, the JOBS program will provide assistance for child care, transportation, and other supportive services. In this "self-initiated" situation, assistance for tuition, books, and fees would not be provided.

5. No.

6. Presently, Kentucky is operating a WIN-Demo program, Jobs Through Education and Training (JET) in four counties and a food stamp program, Employment and Training (ET) program in 27 counties. When the JET Program was implemented in June 1989, letters were sent to the contracted Community Colleges advising them that financial aid, which exceeds amounts for tuition, books, and fees, would be considered as unearned income in the food stamp program and could decrease the amount of food stamps an individual would receive. The institutions were requested to consider this when awarding assistance.

7. Our administrative staff is convinced that providing assistance to our program recipients so they may obtain a post-secondary degree is cost effective. Our SREA

program has been designed to allow AFDC recipients to complete a four-year program. We will continue to provide assistance to a recipient who attends a four-year program under the JOBS program. Kentucky has demonstrated its commitment to post-secondary education for its recipients by choosing to allow post-secondary education as a component in JOBS. We are presently tracking progress, drop-out rates, and post-graduating employment status in JET and ET Programs.

8.   At this time, our SREA program facilitates single parents' long-term self sufficiency, in that child care and transportation assistance is offered for 50 months while an AFDC recipient attends a college or university. We will continue to offer child care and supportive services to AFDC recipients who attend a four-year college program, if this program meets the recipients' employability goals.

LOUISIANA

1.   Unknown.

2.   a.   The Job Opportunities and Basic Skills Training Program (JOBS) for AFDC recipients will be implemented initially in 10 selected parishes. This program will provide child care assistance in appropriate cases.
   b. N/A

3.   Not applicable at this time.

4.   This will be possible after the JOBS program is implemented.

5.   Food Stamps: Student eligibility criteria for "college" students allows students who are employed at least 20 hours per week to meet this eligibility factor.

   AFDC: No. However, if not otherwise exempt, these students must register with WIN or with Employment Security. WIN registrants may not refuse to participate in WIN or refuse to accept employment or reduce earnings without good cause. ES registrants may not fail or refuse to appear for an interview requested by LSES, refuse a job offer, terminate employment, or reduce earnings. The penalty is ineligibility for three months the first time, and six months each time thereafter.

6.   No.

7.   Tracking of all JOBS participants will be required.

8.   The JOBS program will allow certain flexibility in the pursuit of post secondary education in appropriate cases.

MAINE

   "We believe Maine has been and will continue to be innovative in our approach to assisting AFDC recipients obtain personal and economic self-sufficiency."

1.   Approximately 450 AFDC recipients are in four-year bachelor degree programs and 450 AFDC recipients are in two-year associate degree programs.

2.   a. Under our WIN DEMO, any AFDC participant can receive subsidies for child care. A participant is an AFDC recipient who has an approved Employability Development Plan (EDP).

b. There is a waiting list for enrollment into the WIN DEMO. Therefore, I assume recipients are waiting for child care assistance.

3. Each WIN DEMO participant is encouraged to fulfill their goal which may or may not be post-secondary education.

4. Yes, AFDC recipients are referred to the WIN DEMO program by their AFDC eligibility worker. During an assessment, the caseworker discusses with the participant goals, abilities, interests, personal situation, etc. Each participant has a plan which is individualized to achieve personal and economic self-sufficiency.

5. No.

6. Yes, we have ongoing discussions with financial aid officers at the state and local levels.

7. The WIN DEMO has developed a Management Information System (MIS) to track participants' progress, and we are continuing to refine this system.

8. Maine's WIN DEMO Additional Support for People in Retraining and Education (ASPIRE) has and will continue to assist appropriate AFDC recipients in post secondary education. Maine's Displaced Homemakers Program assists women to access post secondary educational institutions. Carl Perkins funding assists numerous programs to prepare single parents to access post-secondary institutions.

MARYLAND

1. Three hundred fifty-nine (359) Project Independence (PI) enrollees were attending college or other post-secondary education activities as of December 31, 1990. All PI enrollees are recipients of public assistance, in particular AFDC.

Currently there is no information available on total number of public assistance recipients attending post-secondary education activities other than PI enrollees.

2. a. Single parent students receiving AFDC are eligible for day-care subsidies.
   b. Currently there is no waiting list.

3. The state program JOBS/PI approved by HHS limits recipients to 6 months to 2-year training programs, or an AA degree, to meet federal guidelines.

4. Currently, JOBS/PI training is limited to an Associate of Arts degree program or any other two-year program which might result in a certificate, Associate of Science degree, or technical degree. JOBS/PI funding is also available for those participants who were enrolled in a four-year program leading to a Baccalaureate degree prior to April 1, 1990. Self-initiated educational opportunities are always encouraged, unfortunately not funded.

5. The State of Maryland has elected not to require single parent college students to work part time. Federal guidelines give the state discretion in this area.

6. There have been no discussions of this nature completed to date.

7. At the present time we do not have adequate information to determine if entering secondary degree programs are cost effective. It may be cost effective on an individual basis; however, this would be difficult to determine compared to other

training components. Project Independence enrollees are tracked while participating in training, and after terminating PI, to gather information to meet federal reporting requirements.

8.   In Baltimore, the Office of Employment Development with Morgan State University has supported the institution's four-year matriculation program—the Improved Opportunity for Parents program. This project provided AFDC recipients with the opportunity to obtain a Bachelor's degree from Morgan. Project Independence provides support in the form of child care, transportation, and counseling. The State's policy limiting post-secondary educational services to a two-year degree or certificate program has required a restructuring of Morgan's program. Enrollees entering Morgan's program after April 1990, work toward a two-year certificate program.

MASSACHUSETTS

1.   Because the Commonwealth tracks client participation in education programs and otherwise according to grant category, not marital status, the answers to your questionnaire refer to AFDC clients only. Thus, the numbers of clients participating in ET at the college level is higher than stated. Seven months into this fiscal year, there was AFDC participation as follows and with clients in all three categories of programming receiving day care and transportation costs if requested:
       a.   College Voucher program, which provides access to one course at a community college as an encouragment to the client to try this level of academic pursuit:

	214
b. Entered a community college as a full-time student:	2,286
c. Enrolled in other colleges:	1,048
Total:	3,548

The ET program provides the college voucher, but expects if the expense can be covered by the Pell Grant that the community college will reimburse the ET program. Otherwise the funding for the college level academic pursuits is supplied through the Pell, state scholarships, etc.

2.   a.   AFDC clients who are ET registered are eligible for day-care subsidy.
       b.   There is not a waiting list per se; however, there are almost as many again AFDC clients scheduled to attend college. They have yet to start for personal reasons by and large. It's our impression those AFDC clients who then decide to attend college do not wait long.

3.   No. As a Choices program, the ET client participates in that programming which meets the employment plan worked out between the AFDC individual and the ET specialist.

4.   Yes. That discussion should take place while developing the employment plan.

5.   No.

6.   Information-sharing is encouraged at all levels, so that clients and program managers can plan intelligently around the parameters of multiple state, federal, and local programs.

7.   Opinions vary. There is an equity issue if welfare parents can receive a cash subsidy through four years of college, while their non-welfare peers cannot (e.g.

women in low-income households who are just above welfare level, and women who are not parents but desire college.) An alternative for the welfare parent is a more modest job now, and college education later—a course of action followed by many non-welfare persons. Tracking is decentralized to the service provider level.

8. The Massachusetts Department of Public Welfare funds a college voucher program through the Board of Regents of Higher Education. An AFDC recipient is entitled to a "free" course at any two-year or four-year state college under this program.

MICHIGAN

1. 2,500

2. a. Yes. b. No.

3. If a single parent chooses to attend an institution of higher education, he/she is encouraged to secure some type of student financial assistance and to select the institution that he/she wishes to attend.

4. Yes. A single parent expressing a desire to attend college would state this to the caseworker. The caseworker will explain what the client has to do. The client needs to secure financial assistance, and needs to be accepted at the institution of higher learning. The educational goal needs to have an employment objective.

5. No.

6. Yes.

7. Yes, to both questions.

8. The community colleges offer specialized counseling to public assistance clients to help them to adapt to the demands of college training.

MINNESOTA

1. From July 1, 1989 to April 30, 1990, 6,388 single parents attended 1 or 2 year post high school level training (community college or vocational/technical schools). In the same time period, 783 attended a program over the 1-2 year training—mostly four-year degree programs.

2. a. Yes.

    b. Yes, the length of time varies as programs are administered locally—some areas may have a lengthy wait. This is changing as more child care funding was provided by the state in recently enacted legislation.

3. All training programs are based on an assessment by a case manager. The interests and abilities of the individual determine whether or not a program will be approved.

4. Yes. The individual should contact the local STRIDE program for case management assistance.

5. No.

6. Minnesota Departments of Jobs and Training and Human Services (financial and social services) jointly provide STRIDE programs. Policy and administrative issues are addressed by the departments as they occur.

7. STRIDE has a tracking system as required by federal regulations.

8. STRIDE—available for all levels of education and training.

MISSISSIPPI

1. No information given.

2. a. Yes.
   b. No, at present. Program was implemented April 1, 1990.

3. Yes, effective October 1990 via federal guidelines.

4. We do not offer any procedures for this situation. It is entirely the responsibility of the single parent. The caseworker is not involved in assisting the single parent with post-secondary education.

5. No.

6. No. No such discussions planned.

7. No. No plan.

8. No information given.

MISSOURI

1. No documented figures are available—no basis for an estimate.

2. a. AFDC recipients are eligible to receive day care if they are college students. Persons with incomes below the IE (income eligible) limits ($958.33/month for a family of two) can qualify to receive day care.
   b. AFDC day care had a 546 person waiting list as of 2-1-90. IE day care had a 1,002 person waiting list as of the same date.

3. No specific requirements are presently in effect in Missouri. In July, 1990, the federally-authorized JOBS program was implemented in parts of Missouri.

4. No.

5. No. Missouri currently has no required work programs for Income Maintenance (AFDC) recipients.

6. Not on a formal basis. Local social work staff may work with clients in their respective counties toward these ends, though.

7. No.

8. Missouri Social Services has no specific services, programs, or efforts directed toward single parents related to college attendance.

MONTANA

1. Unknown.

2. a. Yes, currently Title-IV A day-care, effective 7-1-90, only if enrolled in the JOBS program which will be operational in five (5) counties.
   b. No.

3. Yes, the purpose of WIN (no longer in existence) and the new JOBS program is to target recipients of assistance for training for employment.

4. Possible with the JOBS program effective 7-1-90 in five counties—other counties (remaining 51) will be phased in pursuant to the Federal guidelines and requirements of the Welfare Reform Act of 1988.

5. No.

6. Yes—current method of assessing students' grants and loans for AFDC and food stamps purposes does not affect their benefit amounts. However, there are non-financial considerations for food stamp applicants who are students.

7. Yes. No current tracking, but will have under the JOBS program.

8. None; JOBS is targeting short-term training programs and basic education (G.E.D.).

NEBRASKA

"In our Job Support Program, we encourage ADC recipients to become self-sufficient. Education is certainly a key element in attaining self-sufficiency."

1. Information not available.

2. a. Undergraduate—yes.
   b. No.

3. No.

4. If the single parent receives AFDC, s/he is required to participate in Nebraska's Job Support (JOBS) program unless s/he is exempt. The participant is expected to be involved in deciding the activities, or components, s/he will be assigned to. Applicants should tell their caseworker if they want to attend college.

5. For AFDC—not if school attendance is assigned Job Support activity. The requirement may be to participate in a work-training program, not necessarily to work part time. For Food Stamps—no.

6. Not that specific discussion for ADC. Food Stamps, yes. A Financial Assistance Form is used to share information between social services and financial aid offices. We also network with financial aid officers to assist with financial planning.

7. We think it is cost-effective. Tracking is planned for the future.

8. If college classes are an assigned activity under Job Support, child care, transportation costs, and other needed supportive services may be provided. Applicants meeting food stamp criteria may receive food stamps.

NEVADA

1. 108 during February 1990.

2. a. Yes. b. No.

3. No. However, Nevada only covers child care for AFDC recipients (JOBS

mandatory or volunteer) with a dependent child when such is required for employment or participation in an education/training activity if:

(1) It has been approved by the Nevada State Welfare Employment and Training (E&T) staff.

(2) The individual is making satisfactory progress.

(3) All other free resources have been exhausted.

ADC recipients in self-initiated education or training are evaluated on a case-by-case basis.

4. The single parent should see an E&T staff member in the welfare office. An evaluation would be done taking into consideration the amount of time and if the self-initiated activity will make them more employable in a demand occupation considering the current and anticipated needs of the labor market based upon input from the Private Industry Council and the Employment Security Department. Support services for ADC recipients in self-initiated higher education are only covered after funding all other required components/activities under JOBS. Priority is given to those already participating in a program and making satisfactory progress.

5. No.

6. No. No.

7. No. Nevada State Welfare E&T staff monitor progress only.

8. No specific state services, programs, or efforts other than those already covered in #3 and #4.

NEW HAMPSHIRE

"Our Office of Economic Services, Employment Support Service Unit, works closely with field staff to provide support services which include: child care for those in job search, training, education, or employment; books, fees, supplies, tools of the trade including clothing such as uniforms; and transportation and tuition assitance for AFDC recipients. Extended medical benefits are offered for up to 12 months after an individual is no longer eligible for money payment. An attempt to obtain child support is made at the initial eligibility interview.

Support is given by DHS staff social workers or individuals acting as case managers. The New Hampshire Division of Human Services is part of a network of social service agencies that work closely to assist applicants and recipients in referring them to appropriate agencies for services."

1. Statewide (as of 1/90) we have a total of 2,318 children in child care. We cannot differentiate those whose parents are receiving assistance due to participation in education or training; however, we would estimate 121 children are members of cases in which the single parent is on welfare and in college. We have 7,287 who are receiving AFDC financial and medical benefits, of whom we would estimate 93 while in college and receiving welfare and food stamps, and 4,302 receiving food stamps only not in conjunction with other programs, and 8,806 who are receiving food stamps in addition to other programs.

2. a. Yes. Single parent students who attend certificate or associate degree programs are eligible. We will also pay for child care if the individual is participating in

the 3rd or 4th year of a bachelors program. No child care assistance is paid to those in graduate programs nor four-year degree programs and we do not anticipate future assistance in this area.

    b. No.

3. Yes. Single parents are encouraged to enter short-term (two years or less) programs for a number of reasons, such as budgetary constraints, federal requirements, and to encourage those to seek employment as soon as possible. Those parents who are under 21 and lack a high school diploma are referred to ABE and GED programs by our social workers unless it is not in the individual's best interest to do so.

4. No. At initial application or at a later date, an individual (exempt from program participation) may volunteer to participate in the JOBS program. An initial appraisal is done to determine where an individual should be referred for an in-depth assessment of their employment and education history, interests, aptitudes, family circumstances, and barriers. This may be done by our own social workers or a Department of Employment Security, Vocational Rehabilitation, or Job Training Council. Parents who volunteer and who are exempt due to the age of their youngest child have more latitude than those who must participate and fulfill program requirements due to Federal mandates. Participation is limited to the last two years of a four-year degree program. Social service assistance (i.e., transportation, books, fees, tuition, and child care) is limited to a maximum of two years for those in training or educational programs, and excludes those in four-year degree programs. AFDC, medical, and food stamps may continue beyond the two years if the individual remains categorically and economically eligible. Parents may contact their caseworkers in person or by phone to receive help in pursuing employment, education and training pursuits.

5. Single parents in four-year programs may be requested to work or participate in another component while they attend school. Those in two-year education or training programs meeting program requirements are not required to work part time to either receive or continue to be eligible for AFDC benefits.

6. Our local office social workers may discuss this with the educational facilities they interface with, but no formal discussions are planned for the future.

7. We are currently in the process of developing an automated system to track client participation. Progress is monitored by field staff. It is felt that supporting efforts toward self-sufficiency are cost effective.

8. Currently, single AFDC parents may be eligible for assistance with child care, transportation, books, fees, supplies, and tools of the trade (including clothing required for participation in training), extended medical coverage, and tuition assistance. Those parents who are under 21 and lack a high school diploma are referred to ABE and GED programs by our social workers unless it is not in the individual's best interest to do so. They are served under New Hampshire's JOBS (Job Opportunities and Basic Skills) Program and referred to such programs as the Family Independence Program and Single Parents Assistance Programs. Unless their employability plan defines completion of a third and/or fourth year of a four-year bachelors program where the client already has two years of college, all college participation is limited to two-year associate degree programs and state technical college programs.

NEW JERSEY

1. Community Colleges: 681
    Four-Year Colleges: 242

2. a. AFDC recipients who are eligible under the REACH/JOBS Program receive child care allowances while attending college and for a year after they leave
AFDC (employed).

    b. Six- to twelve-month waiting lists exist for low-income single parents who
wish to receive subsidized day care through the Social Service Block Grant Programs.

3. AFDC recipients are encouraged to pursue the type of education and/or training that will enable them to obtain a job. Those programs are usually two years or
less. Four-year or longer programs are discouraged for state budgetary reasons.

4. If an AFDC recipient is already in a college program prior to requesting
REACH/JOBS services, they may, if the case manager agrees, continue that program. Currently, no AFDC recipient without college credits can enter a four-year
program and receive child care and transportation benefits.

5. There is no state and/or federal guidelines requirement.

6. Such discussions have occurred. The most critical service needed by single parents is child care. State regulations prohibit participants' benefits to be decreased if
financial aid or student loans is received and used for college expenses.

7. We have not evaluated the cost effectiveness of such a system. Participants enrolled through the REACH/JOBS Program are tracked and monitored.

8. The most significant program that is targeted to assisting single parents to become self-sufficient is the REACH/JOBS program. While it does not provide four-
year college programs, it does provide basic education, job training, and two-year
college programs, as well as the benefits of child care, transportation allowances,
and medicaid for AFDC recipients.

NEW MEXICO

1. Information not available.

2. a. Yes.   b. No.

3. Project Forward is the New Mexico Human Services Department's employment and training assistance program which provides services to recipients of Aid
to Families With Dependent Children and Food Stamps. The program is designed
to assist employable recipients in obtaining education, job skills, and work experience necessary to secure and maintain employment thereby reducing or eliminating
dependency on assistance benefits. Reimbursement will be made for day care costs
incurred in connection with attendance at a Project Forward orientation, or a
scheduled office visit for the purposes of assessment or employment planning, or in
connection with component activities designated in the employability plan. Hours
for which reimbursement may be allowed include a reasonable amount of time
while traveling to and from the day care facility and the activity site, as well as time
spent in the activity. Activity site hours will be allowed as follows:

Classroom programs: (Educational and Vocational Training)—Hours which will be allowed include class time, and reasonable intervals based on the class schedule, as well as time required for lab sessions or practice, and other required activities, as well as a reasonable amount of library time for programs which require library research. Reimbursement for study time at home will not be allowed. Reimbursement will be made for classroom activity only if the activity occurs in a program which is: (1) directly operated or supervised by one of the state's local public school districts, or a university, community college or post-secondary facility, or (2) directly operated by a tribe or by the Federal Bureau of Indian Affairs, or (3) directly operated by a private nonprofit or for profit organization, if the organization's program curriculum is certified and/or subject to supervision by the State of New Mexico.

4. The participant and counselor mutually develop a plan which identifies the long-term goal of unsubsidized employment. The employability plan details the employment goals and objectives of the participant, identifies needed education, support and child care services, identifies skills and prior work experience, and reviews family circumstances which result in barriers to employment. The employability plan is developed based upon information obtained from the Participation Needs Assessment, the literacy test, and the assessment interview. The employment goals are developed based on the counselor's knowledge of local labor market opportunities. The plan outlines a series of milestones and services necessary for accepting employment. The plan includes an anticipated completion date for each milestone.

5. Students participating in educational activities full time as defined by the institution are not required to work while attending school. However, students who receive grants such as Pell or SEOG may be eligible for work-study as a part of their financial aid. Students participating in educational activities part time may be required to conduct a job search as a part of their employability plan.

6. Coordination between program development staff and State Department of Education and Vocational Education have occurred. Local project staff coordinate with staff from individual institutions within the community.

7. Program development staff are committed to assist AFDC single parents in attaining education needed to secure employment. Tracking of Project Forward participants is monitored by project staff via the project automated system in order to monitor program, compliance, employment, and reimbursement of supportive services.

8. See response to #3.

NEW YORK

1. Current college enrollment in PACE (see #8) is 1,030 students. We do not know how many recipients attend college outside of PACE.

2. a. Single parent AFDC recipients enrolled in college programs of up to two years duration approved by their local social services department are eligible for day care subsidies up to the local market rate. There are significant variations in subsidy amount from district to district.

b. As a general rule, there is no waiting list for this assistance, though there may be in those counties funding child care with Title XX funds (vs. IV-A funds).

3. Under the Federal AFDC program, college training of more than two years' duration could not be approved, that is, cash benefits and training related expenses (child care, transportation, etc.) could not be paid beyond the two years. Under federal welfare reform, to be implemented in New York State in October 1990, the provisions for post-secondary education may change somewhat, depending upon agreements reached in discussions currently going on in the New York State Legislature.

4. No. See #3. Such an individual could attend college for two years while receiving AFDC, but would have to finance the last two years independently.

5. No. However, they must maintain good academic standing as defined by the institution they attend, and must be making satisfactory progress.

6. In connection with the operation of the PACE program (see #8), the parties involved have jointly explored all facets of student financial aid and how it affects benefits. Efforts are made to arrange for the disbursement of financial aid, and to document expenses, so as to minimize any reductions in benefits.

7. The PACE program, described below, has been operating on a significant scale for only two years. Therefore, data as to its cost-effectiveness are inconclusive at present.

8. NYSDSS, in cooperation with selected community colleges and their local social services departments, operates the Public Assistance Comprehensive Employment (PACE) program. This program provides extensive counseling and support services to AFDC caretaker parents while they complete one-year certificate or two-year degree programs. An individual's participation in PACE must be approved by the local social services departments.

NORTH CAROLINA

". . . North Carolina is in the middle of its planning process for the implementation of the JOBS (Job Opportunities and Basic Skills) program in October 1990.

"North Carolina is different from many other states in that we have a county-administered system of social services. This system accommodates the wide variations of our population and resources. There is much diversity among the counties in the composition of services provided based on identified need and local resources.

"The information provided to you is based on present data and anticipated program expansion under JOBS. As you are no doubt aware, the JOBS program places a strong emphasis on education in assisting AFDC recipients with their plans for self-sufficiency through career employment. North Carolina is pleased with the direction the federal government is taking through these changes in the Family Support Act."

1. No information available.

2. a. Yes. However, when North Carolina implements its JOBS program, these resources will be expanded significantly.

b. Yes. There is a waiting list in some counties. Length of time varies with available resources on a county-to-county basis.

3. No. In 40 out of 100 counties, based on an extensive employability planning process with a trained social worker, clients are encouraged to identify employment goals and establish a comprehensive plan toward achievement of those goals. Short-term is included in this plan as it relates to the identified employment goal.

4. Yes. The client need only indicate her/his interest in pursuing a bachelor's degree. The caseworker will then work with the cleint for referral to an appropriate educational institution. While some JOBS funding will be available to support education, it will be essential that recipients receive financial support from scholarships and grants.

5. No.

6. In our county-monitored system, this linkage varies from county to county. In many counties, the financial constraints of AFDC parents have been discussed at length with college and university financial aid officials. In other counties, this linkage is not well established. However, under JOBS these linkages will be established solidly in all counties.

7. Yes. The State Plan for the N.C. JOBS program will include post-secondary education as a component for JOBS participation. Following a thorough educational assessment to determine the appropriateness of this pursuit as directly related to the participant's employment goal, funding opportunities will be explored including scholarships and grants. Limited funding to support post-secondary education will be available.

8. Under JOBS, post-secondary education shall be an approved activity for AFDC recipients participating in the JOBS program. The Welfare Reform Task Force recommended this option which reflects a firm commitment among a broad range of policy makers statewide and Division staff to this academic pursuit as a valuable course for AFDC recipients in progressing toward self-sufficiency. While funds for post-secondary education will be limited at the outset of the JOBS program, we believe the inclusion of this activity in the State's Jobs Plan demonstrates a recognition of its importance.

NORTH DAKOTA

1. I can speak only for the AFDC Program in North Dakota since that is the only program I have figures on. During the month of December 1989, we had 5239 eligible caretakers on AFDC. Except for a small number of cases involving incapacity or disability of the second parent, our caseload consists almost entirely of single parent households. In December we had 1244 eligible caretakers involved in training or education either full or part time. This represents about 23.75% of our AFDC caretakers. I feel we would also find a fairly larger number of adults in the Food Stamps and Medical Assistance households who are in training or education. We also have a large percentage of the eligible caretakers who are employed either full or part time. Of the 5239 eligible AFDC caretakers in December, we find that 1204 were employed, which represents 23%.

2.   a.   There are no Federal or state-supported day care programs available in the state of North Dakota, and we do not see any such program becoming available in the future. In AFDC, we provide training-related child care to those in education

or training, and we allow the child care as an income disregard for recipients who are employed. Food Stamps and Medical Assistance allow work and training-related child care in the calculation of benefits or recipient liability.

b. There is no waiting list for this service. It is provided as part of the eligibility determination process. I would estimate that the average time from the date of application until the grant is authorized would be 10 to 15 days.

3. We have had only a few counties involved in the WIN Program for the past few years due to the drastic funding cuts by the federal government. The goal of WIN, by Federal directive, was to place the individual in a job with a minimum of cost or involvement. Consequently, the goal of WIN was reduced to minimal training or education. Wherever possible, they tried to limit involvement to two-year programs or to the last year or two of a four-year program. They were criticized for this, but I think they did the best they could do with the rules and the money they were given. Most of the long-term students are involved with educational loans/grants which we totally exempt in all programs except Food Stamps, which must follow the Federal Food Stamp law. As a department, we do not become involved in the recipient's plan. There does come a point in some recipients' lives that one must become involved, such as the one who seems to be in school forever, who changes majors every so often, who begins to take on the character of a professional student. That, I personally believe, is going a little far when the public is being asked to provide AFDC, Food Stamps, and medical care.

4. There is no specific effort put forth by the eligibility specialist to encourage the recipients to enter work or training. It is just part of their effort in doing a good job every day in what they do. Our clients are also highly motivated to help themselves, as evidenced by the fact that almost 50% of them are in work or training activity. Other states, as we understand it, have less than 5% of the clients in training and less than 8% employed. Regardless of who is responsible for the achievement of our clients, we are very pleased with the results. By the way, our AFDC error rate for the period of 10-01-88 to 9-30-89 was .843%, and we are very proud of that, also. That reflects cooperation by both clients and agency staff.

5. There is currently no provision in AFDC or Medical Assistance that the client must also work at least part-time while they are in school. The Food Stamp program, I believe, is required by federal law to have such a provision.

6. The financial aid officers are fully aware of the impact of loans and grants on Food Stamps. They also know that the receipt of AFDC affects the amount of their educational loans and grants. I'm sure they have talked to congress persons and federal program administrators about this the same as we have. No one seems willing to change the law.

7. Any effort on the part of clients to enter the world of education or work is viewed as a very positive move on their part. You must also realize that job opportunities in North Dakota are very poor for both high school graduates and college graduates, and that the primary job opportunities are out-of-state. This adds the trauma of a move to the scenario. We have done no tracking of clients, and, at present, have no plan to follow up on their success.

8. I have nothing more to report on this item other than our relationship with Job Service has always been excellent. Their goals and attitudes toward clients and work/training have always been quite similar to ours and there has never been a need or desire to have to protect anyone's "turf" to get the job done.

OHIO

"We have responded to these questions from the perspective of the Job Opportunities and Basic Skills (JOBS) Training program which our department implemented in July 1989. For your information, Ohio has been in the forefront for education and training programs beginning in 1983. At the current time, the JOBS program is available for AFDC recipients in 42 of our counties. It is our intent to expand the JOBS program statewide by January 1, 1991."

1. This information is not available. Our current Job Opportunities and Basic Skills (JOBS) Training reporting system is being reviewed for various reporting factors that may be needed.

2. a. Yes. AFDC recipients are eligible through JOBS funding for day care but they must be in a course of study for an undergraduate degree.

    b. There may be a waiting list which would vary from county to county for the length of the wait. We have 88 counties in Ohio.

3. The Family Support Act of 1988 does not encourage long-term training. Under that act, shorter term education and training is more appropriate. On a case-by-case basis, some individuals may be allowed to pursue a four-year program to accomplish the goals of an employability plan developed by the county department of human services and the individual.

4. A JOBS caseworker, in conjunction with the recipient, will develop an employability plan which outlines steps to be taken to achieve perceived goals. As part of the employability plan, the individual may provide records of aptitude, test results, or other information. The county department of human services may schedule the individual for tests if otherwise not available. The individual who is interested in higher education would express an interest to the JOBS caseworker.

5. If you mean by "work" to be in a paid position, the answer is no.

6. This varies from county to county. Ohio has Ohio Instructional Grants, OIG, which the JOBS caseworkers utilize to assist individuals to pursue higher education.

7. No. We are, however, convinced of the necessity of higher or further education/training which is determined on an individualized basis. (See responses to questions 3 and 4.) At this time, we do not have the means to track designated individuals which you have identified. Please see our response to question 1.

8. Through the Family Support Act of 1988, there is a great deal of emphasis on education and training. As previously stated, this is determined on an individualized basis. Those individuals with potential for education and training are encouraged to pursue these activities. JOBS caseworkers do promote the use of federal and state grants for E&T.

OKLAHOMA

1. 2,487 (approximate).

2. a. Undergraduate students can receive day care assistance to complete their education. Oklahoma DHS does not provide day care assistance for post-baccalaureate degrees.

   b. No.

3. No. Post-secondary education is appropriate if necessary to obtain employment in a recognized occupation.

4. Yes. An Employability Plan is made by the client and worker. If the plan specifies college attendance, the worker assists the client in applying for grants, scholarships, etc. The worker can also assist the client in locating the educational program that will meet the client's employability plan. Clients receive assessment at time of application, certification or recertification.

5. No, although work study programs are available. If a client does work, it could possibly reduce the amount of the grant or food stamps.

6. Oklahoma DHS has job developers who act as liaisons between the Agency and colleges/universities throughout the state. Job Developers work with all aspects of the educational facilities to assure proper financial aid needs are met.

7. Yes, to all.

8. Oklahoma has a Family Enhancement Program, developed and implemented by the Oklahoma Department of Human Services, the Eastern Private Industry Council, and Oklahoma State University Technical Branch at Okmulgee. These organizations are cooperating in a pilot program, called Project ESTEEM: Encouraging Special Talents and Enriching Esteem and Morale.

   Project ESTEEM is a five-tiered skill enhancement program for DHS and PITC clients. This program provides students with the skills necessary to earn their GED and thus broaden their employment options. Project ESTEEM is held at TJC Northeast Campus, providing a community college environment that will encourage the students to see themselves as successful and integral parts of post-secondary education. Then, the Family Enhancement Program is directed toward participants obtaining the Associate in Applied Science Degree at OSU Tech. OSU Tech can provide needed support services which enable clients to successfully earn their associates degrees, and can assist with job placement.

OREGON

1. The state of Oregon has limited numbers of single parents attending colleges or universities and also utilizing some form of social service assistance. At seven sites in the state, we are running a demonstration project to allow some day care for single parents to attend training; some of the training is at the college level but for only up to two years. For the last six months of 1989, about 20% of the single parents were in classroom training; this includes those in college. This number represents less than 10% of the caseload for the total state.

2. a. Generally single parent students, both undergraduate or graduate with low incomes or receiving AFDC, are not eligible for state day care subsidies. The exceptions are: at the seven sites in the state running demonstration projects. At these sites some day care is given for single parents to attend training. Some of the training is at the college level and can be for up to two years. Low income students engaged in paid work-study can receive day care, from state funds.

b. Because of the limited nature of the assistance, there is no waiting list for the day care help.

3. Single parents on assistance are encouraged and required to become self supporting. In other than the seven demonstration sites, single parents are only allowed to be in training plans for up to 92 days. In the demonstration sites, the help cannot be for over two years, and only if this is the best means for the single parent to become self-supporting. This is done to meet federal guidelines and for budgetary considerations.

4. It is possible for a single parent who has dependent children of any age to work out an individualized program to attend college, but only in the demonstration sites, and then only for up to two years. A single parent needs to only request help from the caseworker. If a single parent is exempt from the work requirement because the youngest child is under three years of age, and the training program can be completed before the child is over three, they can receive AFDC while the parent attends school.

5. It depends on the program whether single parent college students need to work in order to receive help while they are in school. If they receive food stamps only and have a child under 6, they can receive food stamps while going to school. If they have a child over 6, they need to be working over 20 hours per week, or be involved in work-study. To get state day care help, they must work or be in work-study. Otherwise, they come under the guidelines explained above.

6. Yes, especially in relationship to the food stamp and ADC programs. State staff was recently invited to the meeting of financial aid officers for the state. At this meeting ways were discussed to work out problems to mutually help single parents who are in school.

7. Since the availability of opportunities for a single parent to enter college and get a college degree is still limited because of the availability of funding, the state of Oregon is still evaluating the results of our demonstration sites. The cost-effectiveness for the state has not been shown yet. The results are being monitored both internally and externally to determine the final results. New federal legislation, the Family Support Act (FSA), does not allow a single parent to attend college for over two years.

(Author's note: The last sentence is not correct; states determine [according to their resources, budgets, and spending priorities] just how long low-income single parents will be provided with social services support through college. Since other states have chosen to provide support through a four-year college program, it is very possible under federal guidelines. This has been a point of confusion, though, for some states.)

8. There is a program called Project Independence. It is located in Portland, Oregon. By using funding from the Oregon Department of Education, the program helps single parents who receive AFDC and have multiple barriers. It gives help while the single parent takes a five-week life skills course for nine credit hours. Portland Community College in Portland, Oregon, does the testing and orientation for this program.

PENNSYLVANIA

1. Our best estimate is that 750 single parents are participating in a post-secondary activity and receive additional services such as case management and other supportive services. This is based on available statistics from March 1990.

2. a. Undergraduate students receiving AFDC may qualify for payments for day care if their education is part of the AFDC agency's approved training program. Low income students could be eligible for Title XX day care subsidies. However, slots are limited.

    b. There is usually a waiting list for Title XX. The length of wait varies from one area of the state to another. Persons who need child care for employment purposes are given priority over persons in training/education programs.

3. Based on the results of the individual's assessment that determines such factors as the person's educational background, past employment, skills, aptitudes, and preferences, an Employment Development Plan is completed. The plan is developed jointly with the client and takes into account his/her preferences and needs. Each case is handled on an individual basis.

4. Yes. At each application or reapplication for public assistance and/or food stamps, employment and training services are discussed with the individual. The client is also given a pamphlet describing the training, education, and employment opportunities and the supportive services that may be granted. Eligible individuals are encouraged or required to enroll in the New Directions for Employment Program. Volunteers are given priority for available services. Any individual indicating interest is referred to a specialized Employment and Training worker for in-depth assessment and the completion of an Employment Development Plan. If the individual is not interested at the time of application or reapplication, there is a section on the pamphlet that can be mailed to the local office if the recipient wants services at a later date.

5. There are no state guidelines which require employment during college attendance. The only Federal guideline related to this issue is the food stamp requirement at 7 CFR 273.5(b). This requirement specifies that a student attending an institution of higher education at least half-time cannot receive food stamps unless he/she works 20 hours/week, participates in a work-study program, is responsible for the care of a dependent household member under age six, is responsible for the care of a household member between the ages of 6 to 12 if adequate child care is not available, is placed in the program by JTPA, or receives AFDC.

6. Our local county assistance offices are in regular contact with colleges and universities throughout the state in order to obtain the amount of school expenses and educational assistance for AFDC and food stamp recipients who attend these facili-

ties. College officials are aware that we need to evaluate the type and amount of financial aid received by recipients.

7.   Responding to an individual's education, training, or employment needs is the foremost concern. When it is determined that college best suits the individual's needs, the plan is approved. The local office provides case management services and monitors their progress. At this time, we do not have the ability to track the dropout rate or post-graduation employment status routinely. The ability to track this is desirable and we would like to do so in the future. However, there are more urgent data collection requirements to be met requiring systems modification at this time.

8.   Our program services eligible clients regardless of whether or not the individual is a single parent. We recognize that single parents have more difficult barriers to overcome to achieve economic self sufficiency. We provide case management, education, training, and employment services, as well as supportive services, based on individual needs and preferences.

RHODE ISLAND

1.   Approximately 1,900 (1,700 post-secondary, 200 proprietary schools).

2.   a.   Yes.
     b.   No waiting list as of April 1, 1991. This may change as the fiscal year draws to a close.

3.   The Department of Human Services provides supportive services for up to 24 months (not necessarily consecutive months) or an equivalent period of time of full-time college work. Support could be provided for up to four years or more for half-time college study.

4.   Yes. State regulations allow the Department of Human Services to provide supportive services for any two out of four years of full-time college study. Our state is working toward the goal of providing supportive services through four years of full-time college study.

5.   No.

6.   Yes. Tremendous efforts have gone into working towards minimizing problems regarding the interaction of different forms of aid. The Pathways Advisory Council has advocated for clients with post-secondary personnel. The Office of Higher Education has also been involved in these efforts.

7.   In the Pathways Program, about 46% of clients are involved in post-secondary educational activities. The remainder are involved in basic education, and a small percentage are involved in short-term skills training or job search. This large percentage of clients involved in post-secondary education points to Rhode Island's philosophy and commitment in enabling clients to become better educated and self sufficient. The Department is convinced that investing in post-secondary education for clients will result in a long-term better yield of benefits to both clients and their communities. Rhode Island plans to track clients more closely in the future. Some efforts in follow-up have already been made.

8.   The Educational Opportunity Center (EOC), a federally-funded service, pro-

vides career counseling and assessment for AFDC recipients. Special programs encourage post-secondary education. EOC coordinates with the Pathways Program to help clients become better educated and obtain higher-paying careers. The TRIO Program works with first generation, low-income (mostly AFDC) students, many of whom are teen parents, to provide special support in entering and succeeding in post-secondary education. Tracking is done through EOC regarding retention in post-secondary education and follow-up. The SPEAR Program, funded by the Carl Perkins Act, provides counseling and support services that is tied in with community college programs. The majority of clients are in Community Colleges of Rhode Island.

SOUTH CAROLINA

1.   93 participants (total).

2.   a.   Yes, if they meet eligibility requirements for Work Support Programs (JOBS) and are self-initiated with no more than 2 years to graduate, and meet the participant's Individual Employment Plan (IEP) and State Plan requirements. Any participant whose IEP indicates potential success in a four-year college program are also eligible for service.

   b.   Unknown; however, child care is in short supply regardless of income levels, specifically infant care services.

3.   South Carolina has implemented the Family Support Act of 1988 in 26 of our 46 counties. If these students are "self-initiated" and are required to participate in JOBS, they may be able to continue their post-secondary education for up to two years if resources are available. Also, any student whose career goal must include a college degree will be assisted in obtaining necessary scholarships/loans, and support services will be provided if available.

4.   The Work Support Services Program may allow participation in a four-year BA or BS [bachelor of arts or sciences degree] if their IEP so indicates. If an individual enters the Work Support Program and is a self-initiated AFDC client who has less than two years to complete their college degree and it fits their individual employment plan, then they could continue their education subject to available resources. All AFDC clients, unless exempt, are referred to the South Carolina Work Support Program for assessment and evaluation to develop a plan for them to reach their goal of economic self sufficiency. Any AFDC client may volunteer to participate in the Work Support Program.

5.   No.

6.   Staff has resolved the problem of decreased food stamps because of student loans with the technical colleges. The individual colleges and universities will be contacted as Work Support participants begin to matriculate.

7.   The public assistance grants are very low in South Carolina. Staff has not determined the cost-effectiveness of obtaining a post-secondary degree; however, we feel that it can only be beneficial. We do track Work Support participants for one year upon leaving the welfare rolls due to employment.

8. Services available to Work Support Services participants will be available to those enrolled in college/universities. There are limited funds for child care, so in-home relative care will be used if available.

SOUTH DAKOTA

1. There are about 400 ADC cases with caretakers in some sort of self-initiated post-secondary training, and about 1,600 food stamp cases. The counts are duplicated.

2. a. Yes, if they are in "approved training" and have child care needs. Child care may be provided under Part 255 of the Family Support Act revisions.
   b. No.

3. No, the length of any training program is determined individually and is dependent on additional factors including those that are most likely to help the individual become self-sufficient. Of course, the sooner this can be achieved, the better.

4. Yes, this would be part of the state's JOBS program and the individual would need to be appraised/tested and accepted into a training program that is consistent with their employability plan.

5. No.

6. Yes.

7. Yes, in some situations. We will be monitoring/tracking these students more in the future than we did in the past.

8. None at the present time.

TENNESSEE

1. 750, which includes vocational/technical schools and community colleges.

2. a. Day care subsidies are available through the Job Opportunities and Basic Skills (JOBS) program. DHS has contracted with JTPA to complete assessments, employability plans, and enroll the JOBS participants into whatever educational/ training resource provides them the best opportunity to reach their potential and become self-sufficient. A limited number of these will go into post-secondary education, including vocational/technical schools and community colleges. JOBS day care funds will be available to pay for child care when needed to allow the participants to participate in this educational activity.
   b. No answer.

3. Some consideration would have to be given to budgetary restraints, but generally decisions such as this are made more on the circumstances and abilities of the participants. Most of our AFDC clients prefer short-time training in JTPA classes, vocational/technical schools, community colleges, etc.

4. A single parent with dependent children would need to volunteer for the JOBS program at the local Tennessee Department of Human Services (DHS) office. This parent would then be referred to the JTPA counselor (in some counties the JTPA counselors are co-located in the DHS office) who would work with the parent in deciding on an individualized program, if feasible.

5. There are no guidelines which require an AFDC recipient to work in order to receive or continue to receive aid.

6. Staff from the Tennessee DHS and the State Board of Regents have worked together in the past to eliminate barriers to our AFDC and Food Stamp clients having access to post-secondary education. Also in preparation for the JOBS program, District Family Support councils and a State JOBS Advisory Council were created. Key individuals from every level of education are members of these councils, and the problems facing our AFDC clients in regard to higher education as well as other educational activities have been discussed in detail during the council meetings.

7. It has been well documented that the higher the education level, the less likely a single parent will have to rely on welfare for their subsistence. The amount of welfare savings over the years make receiving a degree a cost-effective endeavor. In the past, there has been no way of tracking single parent students to monitor their progress, drop-out rate, or post-graduation employment status. The Howards State Management and Policy Center (The City University of New York), in cooperation with the Ford Foundation, has awarded Dr. Anne Cook, Chairman, Department of Home Economics, U.T. Martin, an agreement to conduct a study of AFDC graduates in the state of Tennessee who graduated between 1980 and 1990. This study should be helpful in updating information regarding AFDC clients who attended college in the 1980s and, hopefully, in the future better tracking of these individuals can be accomplished through the JOBS program.

8. There is an educational program in higher education being conducted at the University of Tennessee at Martin for AFDC clients, called "Project Success." The program ended up with nine students for the first year. Three of these students made the Dean's list—one with a 3.8 average was on the National Dean's list. Information about this program spread throughout the West Tennessee area and a great deal of interest in this program was shown by AFDC recipients. Beginning the second year, 17 AFDC clients are enrolled in this Project and everyone connected with "Project Success" is excited not only about the initial success of the program but about the potential it has for the future.

TEXAS

"The responses to your questions represent the policies and procedures of our agency and do not address services offered by other agencies in our state."

1. Presently, our current data gathering system does not capture whether single parents attend a college or a university.

2. a. Yes, they are eligible until they have completed two years of post-secondary education, 65 credit hours, or the equivalent A.A. degree [Associates degree]. AFDC recipients are categorically eligible. Families must have income at or below 150% of the federal poverty guidelines.

   b. Yes, the number of clients on the waiting list and the length of wait varies dramatically across the state. AFDC clients have a higher priority and thus have greater access to care than income eligible parents.

3. Single parents with children 6 years of age or older are required to register for

employment or training services. An individual plan for AFDC recipients is developed for employment, training, or educational needs. The goal is for the client to become employed. A college plan can be included in the employability plan if it meets the following criteria: (1) the client is enrolled in a two-year program from an accredited institution; (2) the client pursues a degree, diploma, or certificate in a field for which there will be a demand in the labor market.

4. A college plan can be included in the employment plan that was mentioned in question 3. The client may be enrolled in a program that must be completed in two years. The institution in which the client is enrolled must be an accredited institution. The client must pursue a degree, diploma, or certificate in a field for which there will be a demand in the labor market.

5. AFDC and Medicaid recipients are required to participate in employment services. Participation in employment services is delayed if a recipient is a student who is attending an institution of higher education at least half-time. Food stamp recipients ages 16 through 59 must register for employment services. A recipient enrolled in an institution of higher education must be enrolled in a work/study program during the school year or employed for pay at least 20 hours a week in order to continue to receive food stamp benefits.

6. No formal discussions with college and university financial aid officers have taken place at the state or the regional level. Caseworkers in the local offices across the state will provide information of the financial aid options available to the recipients. There are no plans for discussion of this issue in the future.

7. While obtaining a post-secondary degree is an alternative to a cost-effective employment plan for a recipient, so is a good training program. We are presently focusing on training programs that will allow recipients to pursue a degree, diploma, or certificate in a field for which there will be a demand in the labor market. Our goal is for the recipient to be employed.

8. As previously mentioned, our agency is focusing on training programs that will allow recipients to pursue a degree, diploma, or certificate in a field for which there will be a demand in the labor market. We have no plans to implement specific programs for the single parent trying to achieve a college education.

UTAH

1. Estimate 730. Does not include any single parents using food stamps only and attending college, etc. No way to obtain that information.

2. a. Yes.
    b. No.

3. Single parents on AFDC develop individual self sufficiency plans with worker assistance. Post-secondary education is one of the options a participant may choose. They are neither encouraged nor discouraged from choosing this option.

4. Refer to #3. A single parent on AFDC is required to participate in the Utah Self Sufficiency Program unless he/she is exempt. Others may volunteer.

5. No.

6. In developing the state JOBS program, called the Self Sufficiency Program in Utah, state specialists met with representatives of universities and colleges throughout the state.

7. Generally the answer is no. The state does have a way of tracking and monitoring the progress of such students, but at present no data on drop-out rate, or post graduation employment status. We are in the process of developing data which will evaluate the effectiveness of each "component" offered in the Utah Self-Sufficiency Program.

8. There are no Department of Social Services programs specifically directed toward single parents relative to college education.

VERMONT

"Vermont's welfare to work program is called Reach Up. The Reach Up Program offers single parents an array of activities including post-secondary education. Some colleges in Vermont have started special programs to encourage participation of single parents. They are listed in the survey. The Vermont Student Assistance Corporation has tailored financial aid for low-income people.

Governor Madeline Kunin has frequently expressed her support of Reach Up and single parents in college courses."

1. 389 AFDC single parents active in a post-secondary activity 1/30/90.

2. a. Low-income and AFDC parents are eligible for state funded day care based on a sliding scale.
   b. No.

3. There is no set formula for length of time in education, training, work experience, or job search activity. Each parent is evaluated individually to determine the right combination of program activities best suited to helping him/her become independent from welfare.

4. Yes. The single parent and the caseworker must agree that the parent is capable of successfully completing the area of study; the area of study must have a specific occupational objective shown in the Employability Plan, jobs for the occupation must be available in the labor market area, and the job must pay a wage sufficient for the parent to become independent from welfare. The AFDC participant should contact the Reach Up Program for further information.

5. In some cases, work experience has been judged a requirement for participation in post-secondary education.

6. Yes. Goddard College, Champlain College, and Trinity College have special programs for AFDC single parents attending school. The Reach Up Program works very closely with schools in the area of financial aid.

7. Each AFDC client entering the Reach Up Program is given a needs assessment to determine the best avenue to welfare independence. College is not the best track for everyone. Each parent's situation is evaluated and, when appropriate, the parent may enter a degree program. Each parent in Reach Up is assigned a case manager who monitors the participant's progress.

8. As stated in #6, some schools in Vermont have specialized programs for single parents. The key effort is to coordinate needed support services with the academic program. The primary support services offered by the Reach Up Program are day care and transportation.

VIRGINIA

1. As of 3-3-90, 350 ADC recipients were attending college. Hence, the various forms of social services were also available.

2. a. Virginia has always supported AFDC recipients with child day-care needs while in education or training activities. Virginia has several child day-care options for ADC and non-ADC families enrolled in post-secondary education or working:

(1) A state child day care program, known as Fee System, is available on a sliding scale to low-income parents who are employed or in training. There is no time limit for this service.

(2) Through Welfare Reform efforts (Family Support Act of 1988) child care is available for some single parents receiving AFDC if the parent is in education or training activities.

b. With AFDC recipients, there is no waiting list because we consider this a mandated service. With Fee System, however, there is a waiting list in some areas of the state. The average length of waiting time may vary according to available funding, providers, and enrollment dates of community college programs. In Virginia, community colleges are on a semester system.

3. As Virginia nears implementation of the Jobs Opportunities and Basic Skills (JOBS) Program as of 10-1-90, as a part of Welfare Reform, a 2-year limitation has been established for payment of education. Recipients who elect/need to attend school beyond 2 years may continue to be eligible for Supportive Services for the duration of their education. Low-income non-recipients may be eligible for the Child Day Care Fee System for an indefinite time based on their income and the availability of funding.

4. The availability of a case manager to assist recipients with their post-secondary educational goals is based on the service(s) they receive from the department. The Employment Services Worker/Case Manager is charged with helping program recipients develop a viable Employability Plan towards achieving self-sufficiency:

(1) ADC recipients must be enrolled in the Employment Services Program (ESP) to receive educational assistance and supportive services. Although Virginia's ESP limits payment for education to 2 years, the availability of various forms of financial help (e.g., Pell Grants and GSL) are discussed with participants for the completion of post-secondary education.

(2) Food stamp recipients are subject to the same participation requirements as ADC recipients, but generally are not offered educational assistance because of their generally brief duration on food stamps. This group of recipients is also eligible for various forms of financial aid.

(3) Recipients of Medicaid only are not eligible for education/training/employment program assistance. However, like other recipients, Medicaid recipients may qualify for financial aid.

5.   In Virginia, employment is not a prerequisite for public assistance recipients to attend post-secondary education.

6.   Preliminary discussions have taken place with Virginia's community college system, but not with most of the four-year institutions. The low incidence and statewide spread of ADC recipients enrolled in post-secondary institutions has not warranted meeting with the four-year institutions.

7.   Virginia's state office of the Department of Social Services has always encouraged recipients to seek their educational potential. However, funding constraints have always limited long-term enrollment in the ESP. Therefore, the case manager assists clients with accessing other service providers when time runs out in ESP.

8.   Again, the implementation of JOBS will allow for greater provision of educational services not exceeding two years. Therefore, ADC recipients and low-income parents who have initiated post-secondary education may receive more assistance with their educational goals.

WASHINGTON

1.   Documented figures are not available at this time. An estimate is that 2,250 attend colleges and universities and receive financial assistance. We do not keep data on students receiving food stamps or medical assistance.

2.   a.   Single parents receiving AFDC are eligible for state day care subsidies, as long as the individual recipient's course of study is approved by a departmental social worker. There is no day care funding from this agency for non-AFDC families attending college or university.

Washington State also has a demonstration project called the Family Independence Program (FIP) that covers day care costs for students of higher education receiving financial assistance. This program has been in effect since July 1988, and is currently scheduled to run through June 1993.

b.   There is no waiting list for students receiving AFDC for help with day care costs. There is, however, a lid to the overall monies available for the state day care subsidies.

3.   The State of Washington does not require single parents receiving AFDC to limit education/training for budgetary reasons or to meet Federal guidelines as long as the educational program is approved by a departmental social worker.

4.   It is possible for an AFDC or FIP recipient to attend a school of higher education and continue to receive financial assistance. If already involved in the AFDC or FIP work program, he or she need only discuss the educational program with the social worker. If not already involved in the work program, a referral to a departmental social worker from a Financial Services Specialist is necessary. The recipient's educational plan must be reasonable and be approved by the social worker. If not approved and the recipient continues with the plan, the student's needs are removed from the grant and assistance is only provided for the remaining household members.

5.   No, student AFDC recipients are not required to work part time while in school as a condition of receiving the assistance.

6. College and university financial aid officials participated in the development of FIP specifically so these issues would be addressed. Additionally, DSHS has a short-term contract with Helping Ourselves Means Education (H.O.M.E.), a nonprofit organization which offers supportive services to single parents attending college. H.O.M.E. regularly sponsors financial aid workshops with financial aid counselors in attendance.

7. The State of Washington currently has a demonstration project called the Family Independence Program, whose goal is to break the cycle of dependence on public assistance by encouraging self-sufficiency. Educational goals are suppported in FIP. Because the project has been in operation a relatively short period of time, we do not have information on the cost-effectiveness. FIP keeps track only of clients who have left the program and subsequently reapply for regular AFDC or for FIP benefits. Further tracking is not currently planned.

8. AFDC clients who attend college or university are enrolled in the OPPORTU-NITIES Program and receive services from DSHS social workers and the Employment Security Department's (ESD) local job counselors. Social workers arrange for supportive services such as day care and assist the client in eliminating other barriers to self-sufficiency. Clients living in encatchment areas that offer FIP work primarily with local ESD job counselors to develop an approvable educational plan, to arrange for day care and transportation payments, and for general support services. Some money is available for tuition payments, as well, through ESD.

WEST VIRGINIA

1. Six hundred seventy (670) individuals are enrolled in college and are also enrolled in the Jobs Opportunity and Basic Skills Program (JOBS).

2. a. Yes. They are eligible for Title XX funded day care or JOBS day care if they are enrolled in JOBS.

b. For public assistance there would not be a waiting period. There might be a waiting period for Title XX day care assistance if an approved provider must be found or if a new provider must be approved.

3. We do not discourage single parents from entering four-year college programs which will lead to employment such as teaching degrees, accounting, etc. If employment is available at a decent wage rate, individuals are encouraged to enter shorter term programs.

4. One of the state's Jobs Opportunities and Basic Skills Training Program (JOBS) activities is college. Only AFDC recipients are eligible to enroll in JOBS. Any JOBS enrollee who can meet admittance requirements and obtain the funds for tuition, books, fees, etc., can attend college. The JOBS program will provide the supportive payments for child care and transportation, if needed.

5. No, JOBS participants are not required to work to continue to receive public assistance.

6. Yes, Income Maintenance policy personnel have made college and university financial aid officers aware of this problem. The financial aid officers do try to make sure low income students' (AFDC and food stamp recipients) benefits are affected as little as possible.

7. We do not yet collect the data described above. Data for each individual is in the JOBS data file. Our current priority is to meet federal JOBS reporting requirements. Local staff do monitor progress while JOBS participants are in college. Employment entries are part of each individual's data file. It would not be difficult to extract this data if it is necessary.

8. The state's Jobs Opportunities and Basic Skills Training (JOBS) Program recipients of Aid to Families with Dependent Children (AFDC) are able to attend college as a program activity. JOBS provides supportive services for child care and transportation to attend, and one-time expenses. These one-time supportive services include tools up to $150.00, special clothing up to $150.00, drivers license, relocation for exmployment, and professional license up to $100.00.

WISCONSIN

1. At this point, we would estimate that between 200-400 single parents statewide attend four-year colleges and receive some form of social service assistance (as you define it).

2. a. At this point, single parent students not on AFDC who meet certain income eligibility standards could qualify for Community Aids (old Title XX) day care. Single parents who are AFDC recipients may be eligible for day care support under the JOBS category of self-initiated education, as long as they meet certain criteria.

   b. There have, historically, been waiting lists (in certain areas of the state) for Community Aids child care, especially because it is used to provide services to the "working poor." This still might be the case in certain places. Our experience with JOBS self-initiated day care is very new—however, there should not be a waiting list problem.

3. The state's policy, currently in final approval stages, would limit JOBS-funded education to two-year training in vocational, technical, and related subjects (i.e., at our post-secondary Vocational, Technical, and Adult Education system). While AFDC recipients may qualify for self-initiated status and attend four-year college, they are not eligible to receive JOBS funds for books, fees, or tuition. This is consistent with the provisions of Federal law.

4. All single parents participating in the JOBS program work out an individualized approach with their JOBS case manager. An Employment Development Plan is developed which includes an employment goal and intervention strategies, that may combine options of work experience, education, or training. For individuals who have not begun a four-year degree program prior to entering the JOBS program, beginning a bachelor degree is not an option.

5. At this point, individuals who are in school full time and making progress will not be required to work. During summer, if the individual is not attending school, a w   expectation could be imposed.

6. There have been discussions at the state and local levels between JOBS/AFDC personnel and financial aid experts. More work needs to be done in this area and more coordination needs to occur. At the local, operational level there is strong interaction between the two sectors.

7. At this point the subject is open to debate and unresolved. There are plans to track recipients in four-year college programs and more coordination is needed with the University system on this issue.

8. Nothing really significant.

WYOMING

1. Approximately 500 recipients are in some kind of educational or training program.

2. a. Yes, Wyoming pays on a sliding fee scale according to family income. Students are given time as documented in their class schedules and up to three hours per day during breaks in the class schedule.
    b. Wyoming does not have any waiting lists.

3. Wyoming does not discourage long-term educational programs.

4. Currently WIN handles the planning for this in two counties; Wyoming Opportunities for Work (1115 project) in five counties, and the rest are self-initiated. Individuals would contact the WIN worker, the WOW case manager, or the Economic Assistance Specialist, as appropriate.

5. No. In the WIN counties, they could be required to be available to accept employment depending on the WIN plan.

6. Wyoming's university and community colleges have excellent programs to inform students on financial aid issues.

7. Yes.
    Not currently. We will do this when we implement welfare reform.

8. Wyoming takes a lenient interpretation of AFDC policy and totally disregards monies identified for "educational" purposes.

Appendix B: Child Care Resource and Referral Agencies

National Directory of Child Care Resource and Referral Agencies

Note: These organizations frequently change addresses and phone numbers, or (when funds run out) can disappear entirely. If you have no luck with these listings in your area, contact the National Association of Child Care Resource and Referral Agencies for more information. They have up-to-date information on child care resources in your area. You may write to them or call:

National Association of Child Care
Resource and Referral Agencies
2116 Campus Drive, S.E.
Rochester, Minnesota 55904
(507) 287-2220

ALABAMA
Childcare Resources
309 23rd Street North
Birmingham, AL 35203
(205) 252-1991

Jefferson County Child Development
  Council-Child Care Connections
1608 13th Avenue South, Suite 221
Birmingham, AL 35205
(205) 933-1095

Family Guidance Center
925 Forest Avenue
Montgomery, AL 36106-1098
(205) 262-6669

ALASKA
Child Care Connection
825 L Street
Anchorage, AK 99510
(907) 279-5024

Department of Community and Regional Affairs
949 East 36th, Suite 400
Anchorage, AK 99508
(907) 563-1955

ARIZONA
Association for Supportive Child Care
2218 South Priest, Suite 119
Tempe, AZ 85282
(602) 829-0500

Parent Child Care Resource Network
Tucson Association for Child Care, Inc.
1030 N. Alvernon Way
Tucson, AZ 85711
(602) 881-8940

ARKANSAS
None listed (call your local social services
  or family services office)

CALIFORNIA (by county)

Alameda County
Community Child Care Coordinating
  Councilof Alameda County
22430 Foothill Boulevard
Hayward, CA 94541
(415) 582-2182

Resources for Family Development
1520 Catalina Court ˉ
Livermore, CA 94550
(415) 455-5111

Bananas
6501 Telegraph Avenue
Oakland, CA 94609
(415) 658-7101

Alpine County
Choices for Children
Woodfords House
P.O. Box 47
Markleeville, CA 96120
(916) 694-2129

Amador County
Mountain Family Services Agency
1001 Broadway, Suite 103
Jackson, CA 95642
(209) 754-1028

Butte County
Valley Oak Children's Service, Inc.
1024 The Esplanade
Chico, CA 95926
(916) 895-1845

Calaveras County
Mountain Family Services Agency
P.O. Box 919
San Andreas, CA 95249
(209) 754-1028

Colusa County
Child Care Resource and Referral
Colusa County Superintendent of
   Schools
741 Main Street
Colusa, CA 95932
(916) 458-7711

Contra Costa County
Contra Costa Children's Council
3020 Grant Street
Concord, CA 94520
(415) 676-5442

Del Norte County
Del Norte Child Care Council
P.O. Box 1350
Crescent City, CA 95531
(707) 464-8311

El Dorado County
Choices for Children
3441 Spruce
P.O. Box 413
South Lake Tahoe, CA 95705
(916) 541-5848

Fresno County
Central Valley Children's Services
   Network
841 North Fulton Avenue
Fresno, CA 93728
(209) 264-0200

Glenn County
Valley Oak Children's Services
629 First Street
Orland, CA 95965
(916) 625-5625

Humboldt County
Humboldt Child Care Council
805 Seventh Street
Eureka, CA 95501
(707) 444-8293

Imperial County
Imperial County Office of Education
Child Development Service
1398 Sperber Road
El Centro, CA 92243
(619) 339-6431

Inyo County
Community Connection for Child Care
407 West Line #6
Bishop, CA 93514
(619) 873-5123

Kern County
Community Connection for Child Care
420 18th Street
Bakersfield, CA 93301
(805) 322-7633

Kings County
King's County Community Action
   Organization
Resource and Referral
122 West Lacey Boulevard
Hanford, CA 93230
(209) 582-4386

Lake County
Rural Communities Child Care
2559 Lakeshore Boulevard
Lakeport, CA 95453
(707) 263-4688

Lassen County
Lassen Child Care Resource and Referral
1850 Main Street
Susanville, CA 96130
(916) 257-9781

Los Angeles County
Equipoise Endeavor Children's Services
216 East Bennett
Compton, CA 90220
(213) 537-9016

Crystal Stairs, Inc.
101 N. La Brea Avenue, Suite #100
Inglewood, CA 90301
(213) 673-3355

Children's Home Society of California
920 Atlantic Avenue, Suite D
Long Beach, CA 90813
(213) 436-3201

Child, Youth, and Family Services
1741 Silverlake Boulevard
Los Angeles, CA 90026
(213) 664-2937

Mexican American Opportunity
  Foundation
664 Monterey Pass Road
Monterey Park, CA 91754
(818) 289-0286

Child Care Information Service
330 South Oak Knoll Avenue, Room 240
Pasadena, CA 91101
(818) 796-4346

Pomona Unified School District
Pomona Child Care Information Service
153 East Pasadena Street
Pomona, CA 91767
(714) 629-5011

Options: A Child Care and Human
  Services Agency
1046 South San Gabriel Boulevard
San Gabriel, CA 91776
(818) 309-9117

Connections for Children
1539 Euclid Street
Santa Monica, CA 90404
(213) 393-5422

Child Care Resource Center of the San
  Fernando Valley
14410 Sylvan Street, Suite 116
Van Nuys, CA 91401
(818) 781-7099

Madera County
Madera County Resource and Referral
  Child Care
110 North D Street, Suite 102
Madera, CA 93638
(209) 673-2284

Marin County
Project Care for Children
828 Mission Avenue
San Rafael, CA 94901
(415) 454-7959

Mariposa County
Mariposa Child Care Resource and
  Referral
5131 Highway 140 #4
P.O. Box 1898
Mariposa, CA 95338
(209) 966-4474

Mendocino County
Rural Communities Child Care
413A North State Street
Ukiah, CA 95482
(707) 462-1954

Merced County
Children's Services Network of Merced
  County
616 West Main Street
Merced, CA 95430
(209) 722-3804

Modoc County
Modoc Child Care Resource and Referral
839 North Main Street
P.O. Box 1011
Alturas, CA 96107
(916) 233-5437

Mono County
Community Connection for Child Care
P.O. Box 8571
Mammoth Lakes, CA 93546
(619) 934-3343

Monterey County
Mexican American Opportunity
  Foundation
1021 Montana
Salinas, CA 93905
(408) 757-0775

Napa County
Rainbow Child Care Council
1801 Oak Street
Napa, CA 94558
(707) 253-0366

Nevada County
Community Services Council
P.O. Box 718
Grass Valley, CA 95945
(916) 272-5970

Orange County
Children's Home Society of California
1823 East 17th Street, Suite 123
Santa Ana, CA 92701
(714) 835-8252

Placer County
Motherlode Child Care Assistance
    Network
1098 Melody Lane #102
Roseville, CA 95678
(916) 624-5436

Plumas County
Plumas Rural Services, Inc.
P.O. Box 1079
Quincy, CA 95971
(916) 283-4453

Riverside County
Coordinated Child Care R&R
Riverside County Schools
P.O. Box 868
Riverside, CA 92502
(714) 788-6610

Sacramento County
Child Action, Inc.
2103 Stockton Boulevard #B
Sacramento, CA 95817
(916) 453-1110

San Benito County
Growth and Opportunity, Inc.
Resource and Referral
16430 Monterey Road
Morgan Hill, CA 95037
(408) 637-9205

San Bernardino County
San Bernardino County Superintendent
    of Schools
Child Development Services
601 North E. Street
San Bernardino, CA 92410
(714) 387-3114

San Diego County
YMCA Childcare Resource Service
1033 Cudahy Place
San Diego, CA 92110
(619) 275-4800

San Francisco County
Children's Council/Child Care
    Switchboard
1435 Market Street
San Francisco, CA 94103
(415) 647-0778

Wu Yee Resource and Referral Center
777 Stockton Street, Suite 202
San Francisco, CA 94108
(415) 391-8993

San Joaquin County
Family Resource and Referral Center
1149 N. El Dorado Street, Suite C
Stockton, CA 95202
(800) 526-1555

San Luis Obispo County
EOC - Child Care Resource Center
880 Industrial Way
San Luis Obispo, CA 94301
(805) 544-4355

San Mateo County
Child Care Coordinating Council of San
    Mateo County, Inc.
1838 El Camino Real, Suite 214
Burlingame, CA 94010
(415) 692-6647

Santa Barbara County
Children's Resource Center
1124 Castillo Street
Santa Barbara, CA 93102
(805) 963-6632

Santa Clara County
Growth and Opportunity, Inc.
Resource and Referral
16430 Monterey Road
Morgan Hill, CA 95037
(408) 779-9343

Palo Alto Community Child Care
3990 Ventura Court
Palo Alto, CA 94306
(415) 493-2361

Community Coordinated Child
 Development Council of Santa Clara
 County, Inc.
160 E. Virginia Street
San Jose, CA 95112
(408) 947-0900

Child Care Resource Center
Administration Building
859 Escondido Road
Stanford, CA 94305
(415) 723-2660

Santa Cruz County
Child Development Resource Center
809 H Bay Avenue
Capitola, CA 95010
(408) 476-7140 Ext. 282

Shasta County
Shasta County Office of Education
Child Care Referral and Education
1644 Magnolia Avenue
Redding, CA 96001
(916) 244-4600 Ext. 213

Sierra County
Community Services Council
P.O. Box 805
Loyalton, CA 96118
(916) 993-4878

Siskiyou County
Siskiyou Child Care Council
P.O. Box 500
Weed, CA 96094
(916) 938-2748.

Solano County
Solano Family and Children's Council
746 N. Texas Street, Suite G
Fairfield, CA 94533
(707) 642-5148 or (707) 422-2882

Sonoma County
River Child Care
16315 First Street
Guerneville, CA 95446
(707) 887-1809

Community Child Care Council of
 Sonoma County
1212 College Avenue
Santa Rosa, CA 95404
(707) 544-3170

Stanislaus County
Child Care Resource and Referral
Stanislaus County Department of
 Education
801 County Center III Court
Modesto, CA 95355
(209) 571-5049

Tehama County
Tehama County Child Care Referral and
 Education
1156 N. Jackson Street
Red Bluff, CA 96080
(916) 529-3131

Trinity County
Child Care Project
P.O. Box 1746
Weaverville, CA 96093
(916) 623-2542 or (916) 628-4565

Tulare County
Resource and Referral Services
Tulare County Child Care Educational
 Program
7000 Doe Street
Visalia, CA 93291
(209) 651-3026

Tuolumne County
Infant/Child Enrichment Services
14326 Tuolumne Road
Sonora, CA 95370
(209) 533-0377

Ventura County
Child Development Resources
Resource and Referral Center
P.O. Box 6009
Oxnard, CA 93031
(805) 487-4931 or (805) 659-1413

Yolo County
City of Davis—Child Care Services
23 Russell Boulevard
Davis, CA 95616
(916) 756-3747

Child Action, Inc.
500 First Street
Woodland, CA 95695
(916) 666-5082

Yuba County
Children's Home Society of California
760 Joy Way #C
Yuba City, CA 95991
(800) 552-0400

COLORADO
Boulder Child Care Support Center
P.O. Box 791
Boulder, CO 80306
(303) 441-3564

Work and Family Consortium
999 18th Street, Suite 1615
Denver, CO 80202
(303) 293-2444

Mile High United Way
2505 18th Street
Denver, CO 80211-3907
(303) 433-8900

YWCA of Metropolitan Denver
1038 Bannock Street
Denver, CO 80204
(303) 825-8141

The Women's Center
649 Remington Street
Fort Collins, CO 80524
(303) 484-1902

Child Care Clearinghouse
1129 Colorado Avenue
Grand Junction, CO 81501
(303) 242-4453

Children's Resource Network of Weld
  County
P.O. Box 369
LaSalle, CO 80645
(303) 284-5535

The Loveland Resource Center
320 E. Third Street
Loveland, CO 80537
(303) 663-2288

CONNECTICUT
Child Care Resource and Referral Service
117 Osborne Street
Dansbury, CT 06810
(203) 794-1180

Information Line, North Central
900 Asylum Avenue
Hartford, CT 06105
(203) 249-6850

Child Care Info Line
7 Academy Street
Norwalk, CT 06850
(203) 853-9109

Help Unlimited, Inc.
285 Main Street
Onkville, CT 06779
(203) 274-7511

Child Care Council of Westport-Weston,
  Inc.
245 Post Road East
Westport, CT 06880
(203) 226-7007

Working Parent Solutions, Inc.
40 Lennox Avenue
Windsor, CT 06095
(203) 688-8442

DELAWARE
Child Care Connection
213 Greenhill Avenue
Wilmington, DE 19805
(302) 428-3993

DISTRICT OF COLUMBIA
Washington Child Development Council
2121 Decatur Place N.W.
Washington, D.C. 20008
(202) 387-0002

FLORIDA
Child Care Resource and Referral
551 S.E. 8th, Suite 500
Del Ray, FL 33483
(407) 265-2423

Child Care Connection of Broward
County/Early Childhood Development Association
4740 N. State Road 7, Bldg. C, Suite
200
Fort Lauderdale, FL 33319
(305) 486-3900

Alachua County Coordinated Child
Care, Inc.
P.O. Box 12334
Gainesville, FL 32604
(904) 373-8426

Latchkey, Inc.
1712 E. Bay Drive, Suite H
Largo, FL 34641
(813) 581-7134

Metro-Dade Division of Child Development Services
111 NW First Street, Suite 2210
Miami, FL 33128-1985
(305) 375-4670

Community Coordinated Child Care for
Central Florida, Inc.
1612 E. Colonial Drive
Orlando, FL 32803
(407) 894-8393

Pinellas County License Board for
Children's Centers and Family Day
Care Homes
4140 49th Street North
St. Petersburg, FL 33709
(813) 521-1850 or (813) 521-1853

GEORGIA
Save the Children/Child Care Solutions
1340 Spring Street, NW, Suite 200
Atlanta, GA 30309
(404) 885-1578

Save the Children Information and
Referral
4 Harris Street
Carrollton, GA 30117
(404) 834-7879

HAWAII
Child Care Information and Referral
Service
Hawaii YWCA
145 Ululani Street
Hilo, HI 96720
(808) 935-7141

PATCH (People Attentive to Children)
419 Waiakamilo Road, #203A
Honolulu, HI 96817
(808) 842-3097

IDAHO
Child Care Connections
P.O. Box 6756
Boise, ID 83707
(208) 343-5437

South East Idaho Community Action
Agency
P.O. Box 940
Pocatello, ID 83204
(208) 232-1114

ILLINOIS
Day Care Action Council of Illinois
4753 North Broadway, Suite 726
Chicago, IL 60640
(312) 561-7900

JAC/FIRST (Jane Addams Hull House)
3212 North Broadway
Chicago, IL 60657
(312) 549-1631

DeKalb County Coordinated Child Care
145 Fisk Avenue
Dekalb, IL 60155
(815) 758-8149

Evanston Committee for Community
Coordinated Child Care
518 Davis Street
Evanston, IL 60201
(312) 475-2661

YMCA—DuPage Child Care Resources
1880 Glen Ellyn Road
Glendale Heights, IL 60139
(312) 858-4863

Illinois Child Care Bureau
512 Burlington #104
La Grange, IL 60525
(312) 579-9880

Association for Child Development
P.O. Box 1370
La Grange Park, IL 60525
(312) 354-0450

Day Care Resources Information and Referral Services
320 East Jackson
Morton, IL 61550
(309) 263-8287

BASICS
P.O. Box 604
Park Forest, IL 60466-0604
(312) 754-0983 or (312) 748-2378

Child Care Resource Service—University of Illinois
1105 West Nevada
Urbana, IL 61801
(217) 333-3869

Child Care Information and Referral Services
YWCA of Lake County
445 North Genesee Street
Waukegan, IL 60085
(312) 662-4248

INDIANA
YWCA
2000 Wells Street
Fort Wayne, IN 46808
(219) 424-4908

YWCA
4460 Guion Road
Indianapolis, IN 46254
(317) 299-2750

Tippecanoe County Child Care, Inc.
P.O. Box 749
Lafayette, IN 47902
(317) 742-4033

4-C for the Wabash Valley
619 Washington Avenue
Terra Haute, IN 47802
(812) 232-3952

IOWA
Polk County Child Care Resource Center
1200 University, Suite F
Des Moines, IA 50314
(515) 286-2004

Marshall County Child Care Services
P.O. Box 833
Marshalltown, IA 50158
(515) 753-9332

Child Care Coordination and Referral Services, Exceptional Persons, Inc.
2530 University Avenue
Waterloo, IA 50701
(319) 232-6671

KANSAS
Reno County Child Care Association
103 South Walnut
Hutchinson, KS 67501
(316) 669-0291

Family and Children's Service, Inc.
5424 State Avenue
Kansas City, KS 66102
(913) 287-1300

Johnson County Child Care Assocation
5311 Johnson Drive
Mission, KS 66205
(913) 262-2273

The Day Care Connection
8931 West 75th Street
Overland Park, KS 66204
(913) 648-0424

Every Woman's Resource Center
Pozez Education Center, 2nd Floor
1505 South West 8th Street
Topeka, KS 66606
(913) 357-5171

Child Care Assocation of Wichita/
Sedgwick County
1069 Parklane Office Park
Wichita, KS 67218
(316) 682-1853

KENTUCKY
Child Care Council of Kentucky
880 Sparta Court, Suite 104
Lexington, KY 40504
(606) 254-9176

Community Coordinated Child Care
1355 South Third Street
Louisville, KY 40214
(502) 636-1358

LOUISIANA
Kinderhaus, Inc.
5201 West Napoleon Avenue
Metairie, LA 70001
(504) 454-2424

St. Mark's Community Center
1130 North Rampart Street
New Orleans, LA 70116
(504) 529-1681

MAINE
Penquis Child Care Services
161 Davis Road
Bangor, ME 04401
(207) 947-4100

Diocesan Human Relations Services, Inc.
87 High Street
Portland, ME 04101
(207) 871-7449

Finders/Seekers
P.O. Box 278
South Paris, ME 04281
(800) 543-7008

MARYLAND
LOCATE Child Care
Maryland Committee for Children
608 Water Street
Baltimore, MD 21202
(301) 752-7588

Babysitting Referrals/Choice Nanny
P.O. Box 991
Columbia, MD 21044
(301) 465-9659

Child Care Connection, Inc.
332 West Edmonston Drive
Rockville, MD 20852
(301) 279-1276

MASSACHUSETTS
Child Care Resource Center
552 Massachusetts Avenue
Cambridge, MA 02139
(617) 547-1063

Pre-School Enrichment Team, Inc.
276 High Street
Holyoke, MA 01040
(413) 536-3900

Child Care Circuit
190 Hampshire Street
Lawrence, MA 01840
(617) 686-4288 or (617) 592-8440

Child Care Search
11 Kearney Square
Lowell, MA 01852
(617) 452-6445

PACE, Inc., Child Care Resource
  Exchange
4 Park Place
P.O. Box D 626
New Bedford, MA 02740
(508) 999-9930

Resources for Child Care
311 North Street
Pittsfield, MA 01201
(413) 499-7983

Community Care for Kids
1509 Hancock Street
Quincy, MA 02164
(617) 479-8181

Child Care Resource Connection
17 Tremont Street
Taunton, MA 02780
(508) 823-9118

PHPCC/CCR and RC
200 Fifth Avenue
Waltham, MA 02154
(617) 890-8781

Child Care Connection
United Way of Central Massachusetts
484 Main Street, #300
Worcester, MA 01608
(617) 757-5631

MICHIGAN
Gratiot County Child Advocacy 4C
503 North State Street
Alma, MI 48801
(517) 463-1422

Child Care Coordinating and Referral
  Service/Washtenaw 4-C
408 North First Street
Ann Arbor, MI 48103
(313) 662-1135

4-C's of Detroit/Wayne County
5031 Grandy
Detroit, MI 48211
(313) 579-2777

Flint Genesee County 4-C Association
202 East Boulevard Drive, Suite 220
Flint, MI 48503
(313) 232-0145

Community Coordinated Child Care of
the Upper Penninsula
P.O. Box 388
Gladstone, MI 49837
(906) 428-1919

Kent County Coordinated Child Care
1432 Wealthy Street, SE
Grand Rapids, MI 49506
(616) 451-8281

Ottawa County 4-C/SCAN
533 Michigan Avenue
Holland, MI 49423
(616) 396-8151

Child Care Resource and Referral of
Kalamazoo
Nazareth College
3333 Gull Road
Kalamazoo, MI 49001
(616) 349-3296

Office for Young Children/Ingham
County 4-C
P.O. Box 30161
Lansing, MI 48909
(517) 887-6996

Community Coordinated Child Care
(4-C), Oakland
P.O. Box 98
Pontiac, MI 48056
(313) 858-5140
Child Care Council

Northwestern Michigan College
P.E. 102
Traverse City, MI 49864
(619) 922-1115

MINNESOTA
Child Care Information Network
1006 West Lake Street
Minneapolis, MN 55408
(612) 823-7243

Child Care Resource Center and Library
3602 Fourth Avenue South
Minneapolis, MN 55409
(612) 823-5261

Child Care Resource and Referral, Inc.
2116 S.E. Campus Drive
Rochester, MN 55904
(507) 287-2020

Resources for Child Caring, Inc.
906 North Dale Street
St. Paul, MN 55103
(612) 488-7284

MISSISSIPPI
No listed agencies (contact your local
social services office)

MISSOURI
Young Women's Christian Association of
Kansas City
1000 Charlotte
Kansas City, MO 64106
(816) 842-7538

Child Day Care Association (CDCA)
915 Olive Street, Suite 913
St. Louis, MO 63101
(314) 241-3161

MONTANA
Family Resource, Inc.
1610 Floweree
Helena, MT 59601
(406) 443-6309

Child Care Resources
Worden and Phillips
P.O. Box 7038
Missoula, MT 59807
(406) 728-6446

NEBRASKA
Omaha Child Care Referral, Inc.
5015 Dodge
Omaha, NE 68132
(402) 551-2379

NEVADA
Bureau of Services for Child Care
505 East King Street, Room 606
Carson City, NV 89710
(702) 885-5911

United Way of North Nevada
P.O. Box 2730
Reno, NV 89905
(702) 329-4630

NEW HAMPSHIRE
UNH Child Care Resource and Referral
O'Kane House
Durham, NH 03824
(603) 862-2895

Child Care Project
302 Parkhurst Hall
Hanover, NH 03755
(603) 646-3233

Greater Nashua Child Care Center
2 Shattuck Street
Nashua, NH 03060
(603) 883-4431

NEW JERSEY
Camden County Department of
    Children's Services
County of Camden Administration
    Building, Lower Level
600 Market Street
Camden, NJ 08102
(609) 757-4424

Community Coordinated Child Care
60 Prince Street
Elizabeth, NJ 07208
(201) 353-1621

Bergen County Office for Children
355 Main Street
Hackensack, NJ 07601
(201) 646-3694

The Child Care Connection, Inc.
P.O. Box 6325
Lawrenceville, NJ 08648
(201) 896-2171

Children's Services of Morris County
1 West Hanover Avenue
P.O. Box 173
Mt. Freedom, NJ 07970
(201) 895-2703

Child Care Clearinghouse of Middlesex
    County
Davison Hall, Room 10, Nichol Avenue
New Brunswick, NJ 08225
(609) 646-1180

Passaic County Child Care Coordinating
    Agency, Inc.
262 Main Street, 5th Floor
Paterson, NJ 07505
(201) 684-1904

E.I.R.C. Southern Regional Child Care
    Resource Center
P.O. Box 209
Sewell, NJ 08080
(609) 228-6000 Ext. 235

Apple Pie
P.O. Box 43162
Upper Montclair, NJ 07043
(201) 746-7813

Programs for Parents, Inc.
56 Grove Avenue
Verona, NJ 07044
(201) 857-5177

NEW MEXICO
Carino Child Care Resource and Referral
    of the YWCA of Albuquerque
P.O. Box 27748
Albuquerque, NM 87125
(505) 266-9922

Roswell Child Care Resource and
    Referral, Inc.
P.O. Box 3038
Roswell, NM 87125
(505) 623-9438

NEW YORK
Capitol District Child Care Coordinating
    Council, Inc.
88 North Lake Avenue
Albany, NY 12206
(518) 434-5214

Steuben Day Care Project
117 East Steuben Street
Bath, NY 14810
(607) 776-2125

Broome County Child Development
Council
29 Fayette Street
Binghamton, NY 13901
(607) 723-8313

Child Development Support
Corporation
677 Lafayette Avenue
Brooklyn, NY 11216
(718) 782-5888

Child Care Resource and Referral Center
of the Niagara Frontier
YWCA of Buffalo
190 Franklin Street
Buffalo, NY 14202
(716) 852-6124

Day Care Council of Nassau County
54 Washington Street
Hempstead, NY 11550
(516) 538-1362

Child Care Council of Suffolk, Inc.
145 Pidgeon Hill Road
Huntington Station, NY 11746
(516) 427-1206

Day Care and Child Development
Council of Tompkins County, Inc.
306 North Aurora Street
Ithaca, NY 14850
(607) 257-2950

Child Care, Inc.
275 Seventh Avenue
New York, NY 10001
(212) 929-7604

Family Resource Center
137 East Second Street
New York, NY 10009
(212) 677-6602

Dutchess County Child Development
Council, Inc.
53 Academy Street
Poughkeepsie, NY 12601
(914) 473-4141

Western New York Child Care Council,
Inc.
1257 University Avenue, #201
Rochester, NY 14607
(716) 244-2960

Rockland Council for Young Children,
Inc.
185 North Main Street
Spring Valley, NY 10977
(914) 425-0572

Onandaga County Child Care Council
215 Bassett Street
Syracuse, NY 13210
(315) 472-6919

Child Care Council of Weschester, Inc.
470 Mamaroneck Avenue
White Plains, NY 10605
(914) 761-3456

NORTH CAROLINA
Buncombe County Child Development
50 South French Broad Avenue
Asheville, NC 28801
(704) 255-5725

Child Care Networks
Carr Mill Mall, Suite 222
Carrboro, NC 27510
(919) 942-0186

Child Care Resources, Inc.
700 Kenilorth Avenue
Charlotte, NC 28204
(704) 376-6697

Durham Day Care Council
119 Orange Street
Durham, NC 27701
(919) 688-8661

Child Care Information Program of
United Day Care Services
1200 Arlington Street
Greensboro, NC 27406
(919) 273-9451

Child Care Resource and Referral
Agency of High Point
P.O. Box 5461
High Point, NC 27260
(919) 887-3714

Davidson County Community College
Child Development Center
P.O. Box 1287
Lexington, NC 27292
(919) 475-7181

Wake Up for Children
Wake County CCR and R
103 Enterprise Street, Suite 208
Raleigh, NC 27607
(919) 821-0482

First Line (Forsyth Information and
  Referral Service Telephone Line)
660 West Fifth Street
Winston-Salem, NC 27106
(919) 727-8100

NORTH DAKOTA
None listed (contact your local social
  services office)

OHIO
Comprehensive Community Child Care
240 Reading Road, #109
Cincinnati, OH 45202
(513) 621-8585

Center for Human Services Child Care
  Resource Center
1240 Huron Road, 5th Floor
Cleveland, OH 44115
(216) 241-6400

Action for Children
92 Jefferson Avenue
Columbus, OH 43215
(614) 224-0222

Child Care Clearinghouse
414 Valley Street
Dayton, OH 45404
(513) 461-0600

OKLAHOMA
Child Care Connection
3014 Paseo
Oklahoma City, OK 73103
(405) 525-8782

Child Care Resource Center
1430 South Boulder
Tulsa, OK 74119
(918) 585-5551

OREGON
West Tuality Child Care Services
2813 Pacific Avenue, Suite C
Forest Grove, OR 97116
(503) 648-0838

A.M.A. Family Day and Night Care
P.O. Box 11243
Portland, OR 97211
(503) 285-0493

Child Care Information Service
325 13th Street, NE
Salem, OR 97301
(503) 585-2789

PENNSYLVANIA
Lehigh Valley Child Care, Inc.
1600 Hanover Avenue
Allentown, PA 18103
(215) 820-5333

Community Services for Children, Inc.
431 East Locust Street
Bethlehem, PA 18018
(215) 691-1819

Child Care Systems, Inc.
840 West Main Street, 3rd Floor
Lansdale, PA 19446
(215) 362-5070

PROBE
PSU/Capital College
Middletown, PA 17057
(717) 948-6313

CHOICE—Child Care Choices
125 South Ninth Street, Suite 603
Philadelphia, PA 19107
(215) 592-7644

Community Services for Children
431 East Locust Street
Philadelphia, PA 18018
(215) 691-1819

Child Care Network
200 Ross Street
Pittsburgh, PA 15219
(412) 392-3131 or (800) 392-3131

Child Care Consultants
1427 East Market Street
York, PA 17403
(714) 854-2273

RHODE ISLAND
Options for Working Parents
30 Exchange Terrace
Providence, RI 02903
(401) 272-7510

SOUTH CAROLINA
Yes, Inc.
2129 Santee Avenue
Columbia, SC 29205
(803) 252-4216

Greenville's Child
P.O. Box 8821
Greenville, SC 29604
(803) 242-8320

SOUTH DAKOTA
None listed (contact your local social
  services office)

TENNESSEE
None listed (contact your local social
  services office)

TEXAS
Austin Families, Inc.
3305 Northland Drive, Suite 410
Austin, TX 78731
(512) 454-4732

Child Care Answers
1499 Regal Row, Suite 400
Dallas, TX 75247
(214) 630-7911

Child Care Resource and Referral
Houston Committee for Private Sector
  Initiatives
1233 West Loop South, #1325
Houston, TX 77027
(713) 840-1255

City of San Antonio Child Abuse
  Prevention Program
P.O. Box 9066
San Antonio, TX 78285
(512) 299-7137

UTAH
Child Care Connection
576 East South Temple
Salt Lake City, UT 84102
(801) 355-7444

VERMONT
Child Care Resource and Referral Center
179 South Winoosky Avenue
Burlington, VT 05401
(802) 863-3367

Child Care Information Service
Vermont College
Montpelier, VT 05602
(802) 223-8771

VIRGINIA
City of Alexandria—Child Care Office
2525 Mt. Vernon Avenue, Unit 2
Alexandria, VA 22301
(703) 838-0750

CVCDA Office for Children and Youth
310 East Market Street
P.O. Box 424
Charlotteville, VA 22903
(804) 977-4260

Fairfax County Office for Children
Child Care Information System
11212 Waples Mill Road
Fairfax, VA 22030
(703) 691-3175

Concepts in Child Care
9127 Euclid Avenue
Manassas, VA 22110
(703) 369-8647

The Planning Council
First Virginia Bank
130 West Plume Street
Norfolk, VA 23510
(804) 622-9268

Council of Community Services
920 South Jefferson
P.O. Box 496
Roanoke, VA 24003
(703) 985-0131

Council for Children's Services
P.O. Box 895
Williamsburg, VA 23187
(804) 229-7940

WASHINGTON
Child Care Resource and Referral Service
9224 Holly Drive
Everett, WA 98204
(209) 347-6661 or (800) KID-LINE

Washington State CCR and R
Common, Room 103
Pullman, WA 99164
(509) 335-7265

Crisis Clinic—Day Care Referral Service
1515 Dexter Avenue, North #300
Seattle, WA 98109
(206) 461-3213

WEST VIRGINIA
Central Child Care of West Virginia
P.O. Box 5340
Charleston, WV 25361-0340
(304) 340-3667

WISCONSIN
Wisconsin Child Care Improvement Project
P.O. Box 369
Hayward, WI 54843
(715) 634-3905

Community Coordinated Child Care
(4-C)
3200 Monroe Street
Madison, WI 53711
(608) 238-7338

Community Coordinated Child Care
(4-Cs of Milwaukee County)
2014 West McKinley Avenue
Milwaukee, WI 53205
(414) 933-9324

WYOMING
None listed (contact your local social services office)

Appendix C: Consortium for Single Parent Scholarship

Third National Conference
New Perspectives: Single Parents and Self-Sufficiency
June 13–15, 1991
University of Kentucky
Conference Agenda

The following is the agenda of the third national conference on education and training for single parent self-sufficiency. Days and times have been omitted; session titles and speakers are given. This agenda will give you an idea of the depth and breadth of concern and action that professionals across the country are exhibiting in this field.

Day One: Opening session and panel discussions.
Keynote speaker: Mark Greenberg, Senior Attorney
Center for Law and Social Policy
"Implementation of the JOBS Program: Challenges, Questions, Concerns"

Roundtables

A. What are the most crucial characteristics of an effective program designed to help single parents achieve self-sufficiency?

B. What is the relationship between children at risk and single parents on welfare?

C. What are some of the strengths of one-parent families?

D. How can colleges adapt their procedures and policies to facilitate educational opportunities for single parents?

E. What have been the strengths and weaknesses of the JOBS program?

F. Are special interventions necessary for children of one-parent families?

G. What questions should researchers be addressing?

H. What counseling strategies are most effective?

I. What are the prosepcts for achieving self-sufficiency without a college education?

Day Two: Keynote speaker: Valora Washington, W.K. Kellogg Foundation
"Making Program Evaluation Meaningful: Some Guidelines and Examples"

General Session

"A Multiple Method Approach to Positive Public Welfare Reform"
Co-presenters: Ronald Feinstein, STEP-UP, Philadelphia Community College; William Stroup, Philadelphia County Assistance Office
Moderator: Mark Greenberg, Center for Law and Social Policy

Luncheon Session
"Kentucky's Education Reform: Implications for Single Parents"
Ronnie Dunn, Kentucky Family Resource and Youth Service Centers

Afternoon Sessions
"Adaptations made by educational institutions to facilitate
educational opportunities for single parents"
Moderator: Desiree Ham-Ying, Andrews University

"Parent education for single mothers: Is it needed? Is it wanted?"
Nancy S. Dickinson and Dorothea J. Cudaback, University
of California-Berkeley

"Success and survival: Implications for retention of single parents and
homemakers in training and employment"
Joanne F. Coté-Bonanno and Joan D. Bernstein, Montclair State
College

"From dependency to self-sufficiency"
Moderator: Betty Gabehart, University of Kentucky

"Reformulating the work disincentive effect of welfare"
Karen Falconer and John Paul Jones, University of Kentucky, and
Janet E. Kodras, Florida State University

"Adolescent African-American single parents: Barriers to
self-sufficiency"
Loretta Pinkard Prater, University of Tennessee at Chattanooga

"Preparing AFDC single parents for nontraditional occupations in
areas of trade"
Moderator: Susan Moore, Oklahoma Department of Human Services

"Impacts of a self-sufficiency program for single parents on AFDC"
Richard A. Chase, Wilder Research Center, St. Paul, Minnesota

"History and follow-up study of Virginia Place: Pilot program for
one-parent family self-sufficiency"
Claudia J. Peck and Peggy S. Meszaros, University of Kentucky

Day Three: Morning Sessions
"What works? What doesn't? Factors contributing to the success of
single-parent programs"
Moderators: Gina Bertolini, Sandra Krajewski, and Elizabeth Reedy,
University of Wisconsin-LaCrosse

"A new look at single parent families—the weaknesses and strengths"
Troy Daniels and Vera S. Maass, Living Skills Institutes, Indianapolis,
Indiana

"Developing integrated and collaborative systems to meet the needs of single parents"
Moderator: Joanne Truesdell, Portland Community College

"The Family Support Act: An idea whose time has come or a reinvention of the wheel?"
Anthony P. Halter, University of Illinois

"When college is not college: Poor women, short-term job training, and the community college system"
Colleen O'Connell, Community Women's Education Project, Philadelphia, Philadelphia

"Parent education as a means of reducing children's risk status"
Moderator: Sharon Campbell, Wayne State University

"Toward self-sufficiency: Report on the Single Parent Family Project"
William Conway, Health and Welfare Planning Association, Pittsburgh, Pennsylvania

"Nurturing single parents: Family/community interdependence"
Sharon J. Alexander, California State University, Sacramento, California

General Session
"Designing two-generation programs: Meeting the needs of children and families in welfare-to-work programs"
Sheila Smith, Foundation for Child Development, New York

For information about future national conferences on *Single Parents and Self-Sufficiency,* or to receive the newsletter, contact:

Bruce Spector, Director
Community Service Scholars Program
Mercy Hall
Trinity College
208 Colchester Avenue
Burlington, Vermont 05401
(802) 658-0337, ext. 331

or

Doug North, President
Prescott College
220 Grove Avenue
Prescott, Arizona 86301
(602) 778-2090

Bibliography

(References to Help You Along Your Way Or That Are Just Plain Interesting)

Abarbanel, K., and Siegel, G.M. 1975. *Woman's Work Book*. New York: Praeger.

Abramovitz, M. 1988. Why Welfare Reform is a Sham. *The Nation*, September 26.

Abramson, J. 1975. *The Invisible Woman: Discrimination in the Academic Profession*. San Francisco: Jossey-Bass.

Ackell, E.F. 1982. Adapting the University to Adult Students: A Developmental Perspective. *Continuum*, 46(2) 30–35.

Anderson, J.W. 1983. *Teen is a Four-Letter Word*. Crozet, VA: Betterway Publications, Inc.

Ashery, R. and Basen, M. 1983. *The Parents With Careers Workbook*. Washington, D.C.: Acropolis Books.

Barrass, R. 1984. *Study: A Guide to Effective Study, Revision and Examination Techniques*. New York: Chapman and Hall.

Basta, N. 1989. *Top Professions: The 100 Most Popular, Dynamic, and Profitable Careers in America Today*. Princeton, NJ: Peterson's Guides.

Bayard, R. and Bayard, J. 1981. *How To Deal With Your Acting-Up Teenager*. New York: M. Evans and Co.

Bell, B.C. 1984. *Tools in the Learning Trade: A Guide to Eight Indispensable Tools for College Students*. Metuchen, NJ: Scarecrow Press.

Bell, R. and Wildflower, L.Z. 1983. *Talking With Your Teenager: A Book for Parents*. New York: Random House.

Bell, R. 1980. *Changing Bodies, Changing Lives: A Book for Teens on Sex and Relationships*. New York: Random House.

Benavot, A. 1989. Education, Gender, and Economic Development: A Cross-National Study. *Sociology of Education*, 62: 14–32.

Berezin, J. 1991. *The Complete Guide to Choosing Child Care*. New York: Random House.

Berg, A.G. 1985. *Your Kids, Your Money*. NJ: Prentice-Hall.

Bergmann, B.R. 1987. A Fresh Start in Welfare Reform. *Challenge*, November/December.

Bernstein, A. 1988. Where the Jobs Are Is Where the Skills Aren't. *Business Week*, 3070: 104–105, 108 (September 19).

Bernstein, A. 1988. So You Think You've Come a Long Way, Baby? *Business Week*, 48–50 (February 29).

Bitters, B. 1988. Teen parents: Achieving Gender Equity. *Wisconsin Vocational Educator*, 12(2): 6, 17 (Spring).

Bodenhamer, G. 1983. *Back in Control*. Englewood Cliffs: Prentice-Hall. (Child discipline)

Bolles, R.N. 1988. *The 1988 What Color is Your Parachute?* Berkeley: Ten Speed Press. (Careers)

Bolles, R.N. 1978. *The Three Boxes of Life and How to Get Out of Them: An Introduction to Life/Work Planning*. Berkeley: Ten Speed Press.

The Boston Women's Health Book Collective. 1978. *Ourselves and Our Children: A Book By and For Parents*. New York: Random House.

Briggs, D.C. 1975. *Your Child's Self Esteem*. Garden City: Dolphin Books.

Buntman, P., and Saris, E. 1979. *How to Live With Your Teenager: A Survivor's Handbook for Parents*. Pasadena: The Birch Tree Press.

Burge, P. 1987. Career Development of Single Parents. Information series no. 324. Columbus: ERIC Clearinghouse on Adult, Career, and Vocational Education.

Calvert, R., Jr. 1973. *Career Patterns of Liberal Arts Graduates*. Cranston, RI: The Carroll Press.

Campbell, D. P. 1974. *If You Don't Know Where You're Going, You'll Probably End Up Somewhere Else.* Niles, Illinois: Argus Communications. (Career planning)

Canter, L., with Canter, M. 1982. *Assertive Discipline for Parents.* Los Angeles: Canter and Associates, Inc.

The Career Guide. 1989. Parsippany, NJ: Dun's Employment Opportunities Directory.

Cargill, G.H. 1977. Child Care on Campus. *Young Children,* 20. (January).

Carothers, J., and Gasten, R. 1978. *Helping Children to Like Themselves: Activities for Building Self Esteem.* Livermore: R J Associates.

Career Information Center. 1987. 3rd edition. Mission Hills, CA: *Child Support: Methods of Collecting Everything You're Entitled To.* Available for $7.00 from: Resources, P.O. Box 5019-B, 155 East "C" Street, Upland, California 91786.

Chapman, E.N. 1990. *The College Experience: Your First Thirty Days on Campus.* Los Altos, CA: Crisp Publishing.

Cheek, E.H. 1985. *Strategies for Reading Success.* Columbus, OH: C.E. Merrill.

Cherry, R. and Goldberg, G. 1988. Fresh Start or False Start? (welfare reform) *Challenge,* May/June.

Christoffel, P. 1985. *Working Your Way Through College: A New Look at an Old Idea.* Washington, D.C.: The College Board.

Churgin, J.R. 1978. *The New Woman and the Old Academe: Sexism and Higher Education.* Roslyn Heights, NY: Libra.

Clarke, C. and Bean 1980. *How to Raise Teenagers' Self-Esteem.* San Jose: Enrich, Division of OHAUS.

Cohen, W.A. 1987. *The Student's Guide to Finding a Superior Job.* San Diego: Slawson Communication.

Coker, V. and Hammock, B.G. 1978. Campus Child Care: A Service for Low Income Students. *Children Today,* September/October.

Cole, J.R. 1981. Fair Science: Women in the Scientific Community and Women in Science. *Scientific American,* 385–391, July-August.

The College Scholarship Service. 1990–1991. *The College Cost Book.* New York: The College Board.

Community Solutions for Child Care. 1979. Women's Bureau, U.S. Department of Labor, August.

Conable, C.W. 1977. *Women at Cornell: The Myth of Equal Education.* Ithaca, NY: Cornell University Press.

Consolloy, P. (Ed.) 1981. *After Scholarships, What? Creative Ways to Lessen Your College Costs—and the Colleges that Offer Them.* Princeton, NJ: Peterson's Guides.

Cox, C. 1971. *How to Beat the High Cost of College.* New York: Dial Press.

Creange, R. *Campus Child Care: A Challenge for the 80's.* Project on the Status and Education of Women.

Crocker, P.L. 1982. *Sexual Harassment in Higher Education: An Annotated Bibliography.* NOW Legal Defense and Education Fund.

Corss, K.P. 1981. *Adults as Learners.* San Francisco: Jossey-Bass.

Crystal, J.C. and Bolles, R.N. 1974. *Where Do I Go From Here With My Life?* New York: Seabury Press.

Darkenwald, G.G. and Merriam, S.B. *Adult Education: Foundations of Practice.* New York: Harper and Row.

Davis, K. and Taylor, T. 1979. *Kids and Cash: Solving a Parent's Dilemma.*

Dennis, M.J. 1986. *Mortgaged Futures: How To Graduate From School Without Going Broke.* Washington, D.C.: Hope Press.

Dictionary of Occupational Titles, latest Edition. Published by the U.S. Department of Labor, Employment and Training Adminstration. (Careers)

Dinkmeyer, D., and McKay, G. 1983. *The Parent's Guide: Systematic Training Effective Parenting of Teens.* Circle Pines: American Guidance Service.

Dinkmeyer, D., and McKay, G. 1982. *The Parents Handbook: Systematic Training For Effective Parenting.* Circle Pines: American Guidance Service.

Dobson, J. 1978. *The Strong-Willed Child.* Wheaton, IL: Tyndale House.

Dobson, J. 1970. *Dare to Discipline.* Wheaton, IL: Tyndale House Publishing.

Dodson, F. 1987. *How to Single Parent.* NY: Harper & Row.

Dodson, F. 1978. *How to Discipline with Love.* New York: Signet Books.

Dodson, F. 1975. *How to Father.* New York: New American Library.

Dreikurs, R., and Gray, L. 1970. *A Parent's Guide to Child Discipline.* New York: E.P. Dutton.

Dreikurs, R., and Gray, L. 1968. *A New Approach to Discipline: Logical Consequences.* New York: E.P. Dutton.

Duncan, B. 1984. *The Single Mother's Survival Manual.* Saratoga: R and E Publishers.

Dundle, M.C. *Financial Aid: Helping Re-entry Women Pay College Costs.* Project on the Status and Education of Women.

Eble, K.E. 1983. *The Aims of College Teaching.* San Francisco: Jossey-Bass.

Eckert, R.E., et al. 1971. Academic Women, In: *The Professional Woman.* Schenkman Publishing Co.

Einstein, B.W. 1967. *Guide to Success in College.* New York: Grosset and Dunlap.

Ekstrom, R.B., Harris, A.M., and Lockheed, M.E. 1977. *How to Get College Credit for What You Have Learned as a Homemaker and Volunteer.* Princeton, NJ: Educational Testing Service.

Eliot, Dr. R.S. and Breo, D. 1984. *Is It Worth Dying For? A Self-Assessment Program to Make Stress Work for You, Not Against You.* New York: Bantam Books.

Encyclopedia of Careers and Vocational Guidance. 1975. Chicago, IL: J.G. Ferguson.

Every Woman's Guide to Colleges and Universities. 1982. New York: Feminist Press.

Eyre, L., and Eyre, R. 1984. *Teaching Children Responsibility.* Salt Lake City, UT: Deseret Book Co.

Falvey, J. 1986. *After College: The Business of Getting Jobs.* Chartotte, VT: Williamson Publishing.

Farley, J. 1981. *Coordinating a Women's Conference: Finding Help for Women on Campus.* Write author at: 112 ILR Extension, Cornell University, Ithaca, New York, 14853.

Farnsworth, M.W. 1974. *The Young Woman's Guide to an Academic Career.* Richards Rosen Press.

Farquhar, W.W. 1960. *Learning to Study.* New York: Ronald Press.

Ferber, M.A., et al. Summer 1979. Women's Expected Earnings and Their Investment in Higher Education. *Journal of Human Resources,* 14 (3): 405–420. (Summer).

Fiske, E.B. 1985. *The Best Buys in College Education.* New York: Times Books.

Flesch, R., et al. 1957. *How You Can Be a Better Student.* New York: Sterling Publishing Co.

Ford Foundation. 1980. *Women in the World: A Ford Foundation Position Paper.* New York: Ford Foundation.

The Forgotten Half: Pathways to Success for America's Youth and Young Families. 1988. Washington, D.C.: Youth and America's Future: The William T. Grant Commission on Work, Family, and Citizenship.

Fortune, M. 1988. In Face of Labor Shortage, Congress Reforms Welfare. *Black Enterprise,* 15, September.

Franklin, P., et al. 1981. *Sexual and Gender Harrassment in the Academy: A Guide for Faculty, Students, and Administrators.* New York: Modern Language Association of America.

Freudenberger, H. 1980. *Burn-Out: How to Beat the High Cost of Success.* New York: Bantam Books.

Friedman, J.T. 1982. *The Divorce Handbook.* New York: Random House.

Gale, B., and Gale, L. 1982. *Discover What You're Best At: The National Career Aptitude System and Career Directory.* New York: Simon and Schuster.

Gappa, J.M., et al. 1979. *Women in Academe: Steps to Greater Equality.* Washington, D.C.: ERIC Clearinghouse on Higher Education, George Washington University.

Galper, M. 1980. *Joint Custody and Co-Parenting: Sharing Your Child Equally.* Philadelphia: Running Press.

Gardner, R. 1983. *The Boys and Girls Book About One Parent Families.* New York: Bantam Books.

Gardner, J. and Jewler, A. J. 1985. *College is Only the Beginning.* Belmont, CA: Wadsworth Publishing Co.

Garfinkle, I., and McLanahan, S.S. 1986. *Single Mothers and Their Children: A New American Dilemma.* Washington, D.C.: The Urban Institute Press.

Gideonse, S.K., and Meyers, W.R. 1989. Why the Family Support Act Will Fail. *Challenge,* September/October.

Ginn, R. J. 1981. *The College Graduate's Career Guide.* New York: Scribner.

Gittell, M., Schehl, M., and Fareri, C. 1990. *From Welfare to Independence: The College Option.* A Report to the Ford Foundation. Howard Samuels State Management and Policy Center, The Graduate School and University Center of The City University of New York, 25 West 43rd Street, Suite 1512, New York, NY, 10036.

Goldberg, G.S., and Kremen, E. 1987. The Feminization of Poverty: Only in America? *Social Policy,* Spring.

Gordon, S. 1981. *The Teenage Survival Book.* New York: Times Books.

Gordon, T. 1976. *P.E.T. in Action.* New York: Bantam Books. (Parent Effectiveness Training)

Gordon, T. 1970. *Parent Effectiveness Training.* New York: Peter H. Wyden, Inc.

Graham, P.A. 1970. Women in Academe. *Science,* 169(3952): 1284–1290 (September 25).

Greene, E. 1985. Colleges Hard Pressed to Meet Demands for Child Care: Funds Called Inadequate. *The Chronicle of Higher Education,* September 23,.

Greene, L.J. 1985. *Getting Smarter: Simple Strategies for Better Grades.* Belmont, CA: David S. Lake Publishing.

Greywolf, E.S. 1984. *The Single Mother's Handbook.* New York: Morrow and Co.

Grossman, B.D., and Keyes, C. 1977. Child Care on the Campus. *Children Today,* 34 (May-June).

Hagen, R., et al. 1975. Discrimination against competent women. *Journal of Applied Social Psychology,* 5(4): 362–376 (October-December).

Hall, R.M., and Gleaves, F.D. *Re-entry Women: Special Programs for Special Populations.* Project on the Status and Education of Women.

Hansen, J.S. 1986. Alternatives to Borrowing: How Colleges Are Helping Students Avoid Debt. *Change,* 20–26 (May/June).

Hawes, G.R. 1984. *The College Money Book: How to Get a High-Quality Education at the Lowest Possible Cost.* New York: Macmillan.

Hecht, M., and Traub, L. *Alternatives to College.* New York: Macmillan.

Hirschoff, P. 1988. *Wider Opportunities: Combining Literacy and Employment Training for Women: A Program Model.* Washington, D.C.: Wider Opportunities for Women, Inc.

Hodges, M.H. 1987. Children in the Wilderness. *Social Policy,* Spring.

Hodgkinson, H.L. 1985. The Changing Face of Tomorrow's Student. *Change,* 38–39 (May/June).

Holland, J.L. 1973. *Making Vocational Choices: A Theory of Careers.* Englewood Cliffs, New Jersey: Prentice-Hall, Inc.

Hooper, J.O., and March, G.B. 1980. The Female Single Parent in the University. *Journal of College Student Personnel,* March.

Hope, K., and Young, N., editors. 1976. *MOMMA: The Sourcebook for Single Mothers.* New York: New American Library.

Hopke, W.E., editor. 1987. *Encyclopedia of Careers and Vocational Guidance.* Volume I: Reviewing Career Fields. Chicago, IL: J.G. Ferguson Publishing Co.

Howe, F., editor. 1982. *Everywoman's Guide to Colleges and Universities.* Old Westbury, NY: Feminist Press.

Irish, R.K. 1973. *Go Hire Yourself an Employer.* Garden City, NY: Anchor Press/Doubleday.

Jackson, T., and Mayleas, D. 1976. *The Hidden Job Market: A System to Beat the System.* New York: Quadrangle/The New York Times Book Company.

Jaffe, D.T., and Scott, C.D. 1984. *From Burnout to Balance: A Workbook for Personal Self-Renewal.* New York: McGraw-Hill.

Janson, J.L. 1985. More Minorities and Women Attend Urban Colleges, Study Says. *Higher Education Daily,* August 8.

Johnston, W.B., and Packer, A.H. 1987. *Workforce 2000: Work and Workers for the 21st Century.* Indianapolis: Hudson Institute.

Kahn, S. 1974. *Effective Studying and Learning: Hints to Students and Teachers.* New York: Philosophical Library.

Kamerman, S.B., and Kahn, A.J. 1987. *A Workplace for People: Employers and a Changing Labor Force.* New York: Columbia University Press.

Kaplan, S. 1987. AASCU's Clarion Call to State Colleges and Universities. *Change,* 19(2): March/April.

Kehoe, M., et al. 1981. *Handbook for Women Scholars: Strategies for Success.* San Francisco: Center for Women Scholars.

Kerka, S. 1988. *Single parents: Career-related Issues and Needs.* Digest no. 75. Columbus: ERIC Clearinghouse on Adult, Career, and Vocational Education.

Kessler, O., editor. *Financial Aids for Higher Education.* Dubuque, IA: Wm. C. Brown Company, updated biennially.

Kiley, D. 1982. *Keeping Parents Out of Trouble.* New York: Warner Books.

Kiley, D. 1978. *Keeping Kids Out of Trouble.* New York: Warner Books.

Klein, C. 1978. *The Single Parent Experience.* New York: Avon Books.

Knight, B.M. 1980. *Enjoying Single Parenthood.* New York: Van Nostrand Reinhold Ltd.

Kramer, M.A., and Van Dusen, W.D. 1986. Living on Credit. *Change,* 10–19 (May/June).

Lakein, A. 1973. *How to Get Control of Your Time and Life.* Texas: Success Motivation Cassettes. (Time management)

Lathrop, R. 19776. *Who's Hiring Who.* Berkeley, CA: Ten Speed Press.

Leape, M.P. 1983. *The Harvard Guide to Careers.* Cambridg, MA: Harvard University Press.

Lees, D. 1985. *Successful Parenting for Stressful Times.* Saratoga, CA: R&E Publishers.

Lefkowitz, R., and Withorn, A., editors. 1986. *For Crying Out Loud: Women and Poverty in the United States.* New York: The Pilgrim Press.

Leider, R. 1985. *Lovejoy's Guide to Financial Aid.* New York: Monarch Press.

Leider, R. 1982. *Don't Miss Out: The Ambitious Student's Guide to Scholarships and Loans.* Virginia: Octameron.

Lenz, E., and Shaevits, M.H. 1977. *So You Want To Go Back To School.* New York: McGraw-Hill.

Leona, F. C. 1990. *Getting Into College: A Guide for Students and Parents.* New York: Hill and Wang.

Lerman, S. 1980. *Parent Awareness Training: Positive Parenting for the 1980's.* New York: A & W Publishing, Inc.

Leslie, C. 1988. The Graying of the Campus. *Newsweek*, June 6.

Levine, J. 1976. *Who Will Raise the Children?* New York: Bantam Books.

Lewis, A.B. 1985. *Better Resumes for College Graduates*. NY: Barron's Educational Series.

Lloyd, C.B., editor. 1975. *Sex, Discrimination, and the Division of Labor*. New York: Columbia University Press.

Long, L., and Long, T. 1983. *The Handbook for Latchkey Children and Their Parents*. New York: Arbor House Publishing Company.

Ludeman, K. 1989. *The Worth Ethic: Eight Strategies for Leading the New Work Force*. New York: Dutton.

Madara, E.J., and Meese, A. (1988) *The Self-Help Sourcebook: Finding and Forming Mutual Aid Self-Help Groups*. Self Help Clearinghouse, Saint Clares-Riverside Medical Center, Denville, New Jersey, 07834.

Malnig, L.R., and Morrow, S.L. 1975. *What Can I Do With a Career In . . . ?* New Jersey: Saint Peter's College Press.

Mayle, P. 1975. *What's Happening to Me?* Secaucus, NJ: Lyle Stuart. (Puberty changes—for kids)

McCoy, K., and Wibblesman, C. 1984. *The Teenage Body Book*. New York: Wallaby Books.

McCoy, K. 1982. *Coping With Teenage Depression: A Parent's Guide*. New York: New American Library.

McCrea, J.M. 1979. The New Student Body: Women Returning to College. *Journal of the National Association of Women Deans, Administrators and Counselors*, 31(1): 13 (Fall).

McDaniels, C. 1978. *Developing a Professional Vita or Resume*. Garrett Park Press.

Mead, L.M. 1988. The New Welfare Debate. *Commentary*, March.

Medley, H.A. 1978. *Sweaty Palms: The Neglected Art of Being Interviewed*. Belmont, CA: Lifetime Learning Publications. (Job interviews)

Mendelsohn, Pam. 1980. *Happier by Degrees: The Most Complete Sourcebook for Women Who Are Considering Going Back to School*. New York: E. P. Dutton.

Meyer, T.J. 1985. Revamp Policies to Recognize 'Non Traditional' Students, Congress Urged. *The Chronicle of Higher Education*, July 17.

Minard, S., and Berka, P. 1976. *Eat Alone With Your Children and Like It*. Portola Valley, CA: Mynabird Publishing Company.

Mitchell, J.S. 1990. *The College Board Guide to Jobs and Career Planning*. New York: College Entrance Examination Board.

Mitchell, J.S. 1986. *College to Career: The Guide to Job Opportunities*. New York: College Entrance Examination Board.

Mitchell, J.S. 1975. *I Can Be Anything: Careers and Colleges for Young Women*. New York: College Entrance Examination Board.

Mudrick, N.R. 1980. *The Interaction of Public Assistance and Financial Aid*. The Washington Office of the College Board, September.

Munschauer, J.L. 1986. *Jobs for English Majors and Other Smart People*. Princeton, NJ: Peterson's Guides.

Murdock, C.V. 1980. *Single Parents Are People, Too!* New York: Butterick Publishing.

Murdock, E.E. 1970. *Self-Management: A Guide to More Effective Study*. San Rafael, CA: Independent Learning Systems, Inc.

Murphy, J.S. 1989. College-Going Must Be a Realistic Option for the Four Million Americans on Welfare. *The Chronicle of Higher Education*, February 8.

Nadler, B.J. 1989. *Liberal Arts Jobs: What They Are and How to Get Them*. Princeton, NJ: Peterson's Guides.

Nason, L.J. 1973. *Removing the Roadblocks to Learning*. New York: Associated Press.

The National Association of Student Employment Administrators. *Education at Work: Productivity Through Student Employment.* P.O. Box 1428, Princeton, New Jersey, 08542.

The New Our Bodies Ourselves. 1984. The Boston Women's Health Book Collective.

The 1991 College Money Handbook. Princeton, NJ: Peterson's Guides.

Norris, G., and Miller, J. A. 1984. *The Working Mother's Complete Handbook.* New York: New American Library.

North, Douglas M. 1989. Widening Horizons by Degrees. *Public Welfare,* Fall.

North, Douglas M. 1987. AFDC Goes to College. *Public Welfare,* Fall.

Norton, A.J., and Glick, P.C. 1986. One Parent Families: A Social and Economic Profile. *Family Relations,* 35(1): 9–17.

Novak, J.D. 1984. *Learning How to Learn.* New York: Cambridge University Press.

Occupational Outlook Handbook. 1988-1989. U.S. Department of Labor, Bureau of Labor Statistics, Bulletin 2300.

O'Connor, K. 1980. Why don't women publish more journal articles? *Chronicle of Higher Education,* 21(11) 25 (November 3).

O'Keefe, M. 1986. College Costs: Have They Gone Too High Too Fast? *Change,* 6–8 (May/June).

On Campus With Women. (Quarterly) Project on the Status and Education of Women, Association of American Colleges, 1818 "R" Street NW, Washington, D.C., 20009.

O'Neill, J.P. 1984. *Corporate Tuition Aid Programs.* NJ: Conference University Press.

Paine, R.W. 1975. *We Never Had Any Trouble Before: First Aid for Parents of Teenagers.* Briarcliff Manor: Stein and Day.

Palmer, R. 1984. *Brain Train: Studying for Success.* New York: E and F Spon.

Pappas, J.P., and Loring, R.K. 1985. Returning Learners. In *Increasing Student Retention.* Edited by L. Noel, R. Levitz, and D. Saluri. San Francisco: Jossey-Bass.

Parish, R. 1988. Messages from a Welfare Mom. *Newsweek,* May 23.

Pauk, W. 1974. *How to Study in College.* Boston, MA: Houghton Mifflin.

Pendergrass, V.E., editor. 1979. *Women Winning: A Handbook for Action Against Sex Discrimination.* Chicago, IL: Nelson-Hall.

Phipps, R. 1983. *The Successful Student's Handbook: A Step-By-Step Guide to Study, Reading, and Thinking Skills.* Seattle, WA: University of Washington Press.

Powell, C.R. 1978. *Career Planning and Placement Today.* Dubuque, IA: Kendall/Hunt.

Pressman, S. 1988. Feminization of Poverty: Causes and Remedies. *Challenge,* March/April.

Procaccini, J., and Kiefaber, M. 1983. *Parent Burnout.* New York: Signet Books.

Project on Equal Education Rights. 1980. Summary of the Title IX Regulation. Washington, D.C.: Project on Equal Education Rights, 1112 13th Street NW, Washington, D.C., 20005.

Purves, A.C. 1984. *How to Write Well in College.* San Diego, CA: Harcourt, Brace, Jovanovich.

Ramaley, J.A., editor. 1978. *Covert Discrimination and Women in the Academic Profession.* Boulder, Co: Westview Press.

Reinhard, ___. 1985. Experts Call for New Programs to Assist Non-Traditional Students. *Higher Education Daily,* July 10.

Reskin, B.F. 1978. Scientific Productivity, Sex, and Location in the Institution of Science. *American Journal of Sociology,* 83(5): 1235–1243 (March).

Reskin, B.F. 1978. Sex Differentiation and the Social Organization of Science. *Sociological Inquiry,* 48(3–4): 6–37.

Rhatigan, J.J., and Noel, M. 1979. Financing Pre-Schools in Higher Education. *Journal of the National Association of Women Deans, Administrators and Counselors,* 31(1): 21 (Fall).

Ricci, I. 1980. *Mom's House, Dad's House: Making Shared Custody Work.* New York: Macmillan.

Richards, A., and Willis, I. 1977. *How To Get It Together When Your Parents Are Coming Apart.* New York: Bantam Books. (For kids in divorce)

Riessman, F. 1986. Women: Vanguard of the 90's? *Social Policy,* 17(2): Fall.

Riessman, F. 1987. The New Welfare Fraud, *Social Policy,* Spring.

Riley, R.T. 1978. *How to Manage Your Time Successfully.*

Robson, B. 1980. *My Parents are Divorced, Too: Teenagers Talk About Their Experiences and How They Cope.* New York: Dodd, Mead and Company.

Rogers, F. 1979. *Parenting the Difficult Child.* Radnor, PA: Chilton Book Co.

Rogers, H.R., Jr. 1986. *Poor Women, Poor Families: The Economic Plight of America's Female-Headed Households.* Armonk, NY: M.E. Sharpe, Inc.

Rosenbaum, J., and Rosenbaum, V. 1980. *Living with Teenagers.* Briarcliff Manor, NY: Stein and Day.

Rossiter, M.W. 1978. Sexual Segregation in the Sciences: Some Data and a Model. *Signs: Journal of Women in Culture and Society.* 4(1): 146–151 (Autumn).

Rowe, M.P. 1981. Dealing with Sexual Harrassment. *Harvard Business Review,* 59(3): 42–46 (May-June).

Ruetten, M.K. 1986. *Comprehending Academic Lectures.* New York: Macmillan.

Salk, L. 1978. *What Every Child Would Like His Parents to Know About Divorce.* New York: Warner Books.

Salzman, M. L. 1987. *Wanted, Liberal Arts Graduates.* New York: Doubleday.

Samtur, S.J., with Tuleja, T. 1979. *Cashing in at the Checkout.* (Saving money)

Sawhill, I.V. 1988. What About America's Underclass? *Challenge,* May/June.

Schlachter, G.A. 1987. *How to Find Out About Financial Aid: A Guide to Over 700 Directories Listing Scholarships, Fellowships, Loans, Grants, Awards, and Internships.* San Carlos, CA: Reference Service Press.

Schlossberg, N.K., Lynch, A.Q., and Chickering, A.W. 1989. *Improving Higher Education Environments for Adults.* San Francisco: Jossey-Bass.

Shank, S.E. 1988. Women and the Labor Market: The Link Grows Stronger. *Monthly Labor Review,* 111(3): 3–8.

Shechtman, S., and Singer, W.G. 1983. *Real Men Enjoy Their Kids: How to Spend Quality Time With the Children in Your Life.* Nashville, TN: Abingdon Press.

Sher, B. 1983. *Wishcraft: How to Get What You Really Want.* New York: Ballantine Books.

Schorr, L.B., and Schorr, D. 1988. *Within Our Reach: Breaking the Cycle of Disadvantage.* New York: Doubleday.

Siegel-Gorelick, B. 1983. *The Working Parents' Guide to Child Care.* Boston: Little, Brown.

Sidel, R. 1986. *Women and Children Last: The Plight of Poor Women in America.* New York: Viking.

Singleton, J., and Bao, R. 1977. *College to Career: Finding Yourself in the Job Market.* McGraw-Hill, Inc.

Smith, R.E., editor. 1979. *The Subtle Revolution: Women at Work.* Washington, D.C.: The Urban Institute.

Solomon, B.M. 1985. *In the Company of Educated Women, A History of Women and Higher Education in America.* New Haven, CT: Yale University Press.

Speizer, J.J. 1981. Role models, mentors, and sponsors: The elusive concepts. *Signs: Journal of Women in Culture and Society,* 6(4): 692–712 (Summer).

Steltenpohl, E., and Shipton, J. 1986. Facilitating a successful transition to college for adults. *Journal of Higher Education,* 57(6): November/ December.

Sticht, T. G. and McDonald, B. A. 1990. Teach the Mother and Reach the Child: Literacy Across Generations. *Literary Lessons for International Literacy Year*, UNESCO, 1990.

Sticht, T.G., and McDonald, B.A. 1989. *Making the Nation Smarter: The Intergenerational Transfer of Cognitive Ability*. San Diego: Applied Behavioral and Cognitive Sciences, Inc.

Terkel, S. 1974. *Working*. New York: Avon Books.

Tifft, S. 1988. The Over-25 Set Moves In: Adults are Fast Becoming the Majority on College Campuses. *Time*, October 24.

Tinto, V. 1987. *Leaving College*. Chicago: University of Chicago Press.

Tobias, S. 1978. *Overcoming Math Anxiety*. New York: Norton.

Toropon, B., editor. 1987. *1988 National Job Bank*. 4th Edition. Boston: Bob Adams, Inc.

Tullock, G. 1983. *Welfare for the Well-To-Do*. Dallas, TX: The Fisher Institute.

U.S. Department of Labor. 1990. *Occupational Outlook Handbook*. 1990-91 Edition. Washington, D.C.: Department of Labor.

U.S. Department of Labor. 1977. *Dictionary of Occupational Titles*. 4th edition. Washington, D.C.: U.S. Employment Service.

Voeks, V. 1964. *On Becoming an Educated Person*. Philadelphia, PA: Saunders.

Walterscheid, E. 1988. All the Wrong Moves: Sexual Harassment in the Office. *Women in Business*, March/April.

Walterscheid, E. 1988. The Dilemma of the Single Working Mother. *Women in Business*, May/June.

Watkins, K.P. 1987. *Day Care: A Source Book*. New York: Garden Publishing.

Watson, J. 1989. *Women, Work, and the Future: Workforce 2000*. Washington, D.C.: National Commission on Working Women.

Weidman, J.C., and White, R.N. 1985. Postsecondary "High Tech" Training for Women on Welfare. *Journal of Higher Education*, 56(5): September/October.

Weisstein, N. 1977. How Can a Little Girl Like You Teach a Great Big Class of Men? In: *Working It Out: 23 Women Writers, Artists, Scientists, and Scholars Talk About Their Lives and Work*. Edited by Ruddick and Daniels. New York: Pantheon.

Women's Action Alliance. 1981. *Women Helping Women: A State-by-State Directory of Services*. New York: Neal-Schuman Publishers, Inc.

Wood, N.V. 1978. *College Reading and Study Skills*. New York: Holt, Rinehart, and Winston.

Wood, P., and Schwartz, B. 1977. *How to Get Your Children to Do What You Want Them to Do*. Englewood Cliffs, NJ: Prentice-Hall.

Woolever, E. 1989. *Selecting Day Care: Birth–12 Years*. Des Moines, IA: Meredith.

Wright, J.W. 1987. *The American Almanac of Jobs and Salaries*. 3rd Edition. New York: Avon Books.

INDEX